ANOTHER CAMINO STORY

ANOTHER CAMINO STORY

Learning to walk my own Camino through life
on 500 miles to Santiago de Compostela, Spain

John Seegers

Self-*Published by John Seegers*

For information, please contact:
John Seegers
14336 Flo Rd
Orlando, FL 32832
www.johnseegers.com

Ordering information:
For details contact jfseegers@gmail.com

First Edition

ISBN: 979-8-9870151-0-0

Photo credits: the author, unless otherwise identified.
Author Photo © Frederick E Boyd
Illustrations © Gene Russell, GRussell Creations

Disclaimer: *Statements in this manuscript are not intended to substitute for legal or medical advice, treatment, or diagnosis. The author is not an attorney, medical or health professional, nutritionist, or dietitian.*

Some names have been changed to protect the identity of certain individuals and to protect their privacy. Otherwise, every reasonable effort has been made to ensure that the information contained in this book is accurate. However, no guarantee is made regarding its accuracy or completeness. Reader assumes responsibility and liability for all actions in relation to using the provided information, including if actions result in injury, death, loss or damage of personal property or other complications.

I dedicate this book to my four brothers, George, Ronald, David and Thomas. May George and Ron have a Buen Camino in heaven.

This book is also dedicated to all those special volunteers along the Camino Frances that provide the hospitality and the services required for pilgrims to complete their journey to Santiago de Compostela.

Acknowledgments

A special thank you to Rick Boyd for introducing me to the concept of walking the Camino de Santiago, the motivation to keep training, and allowing me to join him on the Camino.

David Schuster, the first member of my Camino family, for becoming my new friend and for putting up with me on our walk.

Thanks to Joe Stinson for being a great friend and for keeping everything going on at the home front while I was gone.

I would like to thank Steve Tricarico for an early look at my manuscript and feedback on the direction it should take.

My niece, Sarah Seegers Karlo, for her support and for giving me her treadmill with an incline feature to help with my training and, more importantly, for reviewing of my manuscript.

Another special thank you to Linda Wiman for copy-editing my work. She found so many mistakes that I had missed.

Barbara Ann (Bonny) Cox. A friend that inspired and encouraged me to write and offered to edit the manuscript for this memoir. Unfortunately, Bonny passed way in May 2022. She was a wonderful woman and may she rest in peace.

Thank you to Gene Russell, a very talented friend, at GRussell Creations for the illustration of the triple bells at the Monasterio de San Juan de Ortega and the lighthouse at Finisterra.

For all the volunteers at the refugios. They deserve a special place in heaven for all the kindness they give to pilgrims.

For all the support from my family and friends.

To my Camino friends:

Les, who showed the meaning and purpose of the Camino by "Walking for Isla."

Phil and Muriel, their obvious love for each other is inspiring. and inspired me.

Barry, for motivation about writing and publishing.

Marta Marciano, for her enthusiasm and for the songs she sang at a communal dinner and breakfast.

Matthew Krause, a deep thinker and videographer.

Laura, especially for Laura, for touching my heart. Thank you for being you.

Introduction

Thank you for considering *Another Camino Story* for your reading pleasure. There are dozens, if not hundreds, of titles about the Camino de Santiago. I am honored you have selected this one.

This is my story about a journey through a part of my life. A story about my decision to retire. My decision to lose weight, get healthy and, eventually, my decision to walk the Camino de Santiago, a 500-mile pilgrimage through Spain. It's a story about "the walk."

The walk actually began over a year before the planned travel dates with research about the Camino de Santiago. Beginning with Internet searches, then watching movies and short videos online, and reading books and guides, I learned as much as I could about the Camino de Santiago, also known as the Way of Saint James.

As my research moved along, I became enamored with the idea of joining my neighbor when he walks the Camino. Naturally, I would bring my camera to record the trip with some fantastic photographs of medieval rural Spain. Then it dawned on me that I could write about my adventure, as well, combining two of my favorite hobbies. I found myself headed towards a lifelong dream of successfully publishing a story that others may enjoy.

At this point, I began thinking about how to put together a draft manuscript. I decided to separate the project into several parts. The first part about my quest to lose weight is short, included mostly to show people what can be achieved if you put your mind to it. The second part is some history of the Camino de Santiago found through my research. Finally, the third part is my take on the actual journey including stories about the people I met and historical information about the shrines, cathedrals, villages, and cities visited along "the way."

Even though this book contains information about Spain and the Camino de Santiago gathered during my research and, subsequently, my Camino, this is not meant to be a guide. There are guide books and apps that will serve you better. This is a story about the journey, the journey of my life along the Camino, representing all our life journeys. Maybe some of my experiences and observations will help you along your journey in life.

I hope you find this story informative and enjoyable entertainment.

Remember, in life, to Walk Your Own Camino. The time to walk is now.

Buen Camino!

PART ONE

LOSING THE WEIGHT

CHAPTER ONE

Retirement

For most of my adult life, I worked in the hospitality industry, starting in 1975 when I moved to Florida from New Jersey at age 20 to work at Walt Disney World. After about three years, the pixie dust fell off and I tried several other professions, such as delivering potato chips to supermarkets and convenience stores, selling life insurance, and a construction job doing sheet metal duct work. None of these really suited me. So I kept looking for something I could enjoy. Eventually, in 1980, I ended up as a convention services manager at one of the hotels on Walt Disney World property. For most of the next 35 years, I served the hotel industry as a catering convention services manager coordinating group events at the hotel or as a group sales manager responsible for booking group accommodations for different markets. Bookings included government and association meetings, youth tour groups or sports groups, religious meetings and so on. My marketing and sales efforts would vary based on the hotel.

Over the years I worked for several different hotels, except for a short stint trying to own and operate a farm supply and feed store. The farm and feed business didn't work out as expected, ending in bankruptcy in about a year and a half. I returned to the hotel industry as a group sales manager until 2016 when the current hotel owner sold the property. Experience told me new owners will hire their own team.

Turning 62 in August and not in the mood for job hunting, I decided to retire. I had put in my time. My house was paid for. My truck was paid for. The only bills I had were for normal monthly expenses, such as electric, telephone and Internet service. I could live off my social security benefits without having to dig into the small sum I saved for retirement. I could do it. It was time to retire.

CHAPTER TWO

How easy the weight goes on

For the most part, I really enjoyed working in the hospitality industry. Over the years, I met many wonderful people and made good friends with many industry associates and clients. Even after retirement, I managed to keep up with a few of them, mostly through social media apps like Facebook.

Along with great people, the industry is also noted for great food and beverages. As a catering manager I worked closely with clients and the hotel chef to create menus for their catered events. As a sales manager, I often entertained clients to discuss their events over a meal in the hotel restaurant. Other responsibilities included travel around the country for sales calls, conventions and trade shows. With an expense account and a meal per diem, I ate in restaurants regularly while out of town. Most conventions I attended included scheduled meals and receptions, as well as refreshments during meeting breaks. All offered in abundance to impress attendees or showcase the convention facility.

Although, I traveled a bit, most of my sales efforts were by telephone with follow up in the early years by regular postal mail and later by email. All this means is I spent most of my time sitting at a desk giving me ample opportunity to pack on the pounds, which I did successfully.

When I moved to Florida in 1975 at the age of 20, I was about 175 pounds. This grew over the years until I reached well over 300 pounds by the time I retired in 2016. The markings on the scale at the Publix Supermarket went up to 300. When I stepped on, it flew past the 300 and back past the zero again. I estimated my weight at 320. At a weigh-in at the doctor's office in August 2017 for an annual exam, I weighed in at 307, already down a few pounds, but hardly enough to be healthy. I was obese.

Now retired, I could not use time as an excuse for not exercising. I had all the time in the world. The fifty to sixty hours each week, not including travel time, given to my employer was now mine to use as I wished.

My plans for retirement never included sitting around watching television all day. I knew I had to stay busy. With that in mind, I did a lot of yard work, replaced the siding on my house and other happy homeowner chores. All this activity away from the desk did help me lose a few pounds, but not so many to be noticeable. More needed to be done.

CHAPTER THREE

One Step at a Time

I reside in a rural neighborhood surrounding Lake Mary Jane in southeast Orlando. Originally plotted in the mid-1950s, the wooded lots were sold off to individual buyers to build their homes. Unlike current land development, the Isle of Pines is not a cookie cutter community with clear cut lots and every fifth house looking the same. A quiet, quaint, and eclectic community, it features individually built homes reflecting the owner's personality. Most homeowners left the pine trees and live oaks, keeping the rural atmosphere intact. The Isle of Pines became a pleasant community with friendly neighbors appreciating the special nature of our neighborhood. Because it's a limited access neighborhood backed up to a protected wildlife corridor and preserve, there is only one way in and out. A great neighborhood to walk around since traffic is limited. Fellow neighbors walk or ride the streets on bicycles or golf carts every day.

Although I have the privilege of living in such a great neighborhood for walking, it took the example of my neighbor Rick across the street to wake me up to this wonderful activity. You see Rick, like me, had packed on quite a few pounds, approaching three hundred pounds himself. However, he had blown out a knee and needed to go in for a second knee replacement. Learning from the first operation, Rick knew recovery would be much easier if he lost weight.

He began his daily walks and invited me to join him.

For a while I came up with a variety of excuses to avoid walking. It took too much time. I had other things to do. It was too hot. My arthritic knee couldn't take the pounding. Eventually, I succumbed to his suggestion when I saw him successfully shedding pounds.

When I started walking, I started slowly. At first, I only walked a block or two and on my own. Rick walked much too fast and I couldn't keep up. Eventually, over time, I could keep up and extended the distance walked to seven to ten miles each day. Walking helped me lose over 100 pounds.

As we walked together, among other things, Rick discussed his plans for walking the Camino de Santiago in Spain, a 500 mile journey to Santiago de Compostela, staying in a hostel or an albergue along the way and sleeping in bunkbeds with up to fifty people in a room. He told me the walk took about 30 to 35 days. He began referring to his daily walks around the neighborhood as training. Good for him, I thought, but no way would I be joining him. I spent my career in the hotel business and learned to enjoy the luxury of hotel accommodations with comfortable beds, restaurants and room service. Staying in a hostel and sharing a dormitory room with many strangers did not sound exciting to me. But, as I lost weight and the walking became easier, I considered the idea of walking the Camino de Santiago as feasible.

The COVID-19 pandemic delayed Rick's trip. Originally, he planned to take "The Walk" in May/June 2020, but then the Corona Virus showed up in December 2019 in China and quickly became a world wide pandemic by March 2020. To stem the pandemic, throughout the world, borders closed, all but essential businesses closed, and curfews and stay at home orders implemented. Mask and social distancing soon became a new normal. All in an effort to curb this virus infecting millions and taking thousands of lives.

With all this going on and the borders of Spain closed, it was unhealthy, unwise and nearly impossible to take the pilgrimage walk. It looked like May/June 2021, or possibly September 2021, would be the earliest we could go.

It wasn't until June 2021 that the European Union started opening borders, first among themselves, then for Americans. Even with the borders open, there were still hoops to jump through such as presenting a negative covid test or proof of vaccine. Spain had a form that needed to be completed. A QR code provided by the Spanish Department of Health allowed access to transportation if vaccinated. Eventually, all this is worked out and we went on our way.

When I finally decided to do "The Walk," I knew I needed to train for the journey.

The need to train for this walk brings me to the topic of setting goals. I believe it is important to have a goal in order to measure and achieve success. If you don't have a concrete or precise goal, you should still set some type of goal, even if it is vague. Once this is done, start taking steps to reach your goal. As you take those steps, the goal becomes more concrete and you will learn what you are seeking. Then, you move on.

It is important to take the first step. When I started walking, I needed to take that first step. Once I took the first step, a second followed, then a third and a fourth. I guess by now well over a million. All this walking eventually led me to the 500 mile Camino de Santiago pilgrimage across northern Spain. A few years ago, I would have considered walking 500 miles insane. Now, with my mind made up, I had a goal and took the first step. There is a great deal of satisfaction in working towards and achieving one's goals.

For the first step of my journey, I learned about the Camino de Santiago, its history and traditions. The more I learned, the more excited I became about this adventure. Although delayed a few years by the covid pandemic which caused border closures and local lockdowns where you could hardly leave your house, I did get to my goal. To keep motivated on daily walks I imagined walking the old cobblestone Roman roads of the Camino de Santiago. My walks took me through imagined farmlands, vineyards and small hamlets of Spain. I climbed the Pyrenees and crossed the expanse of the Meseta. I knew these imaginary walks around the neighborhood would lead to the real walk in Spain.

One thing I learned from 30 years in the hotel business, is the importance of goals. Now, I did moan and groan many times about unrealistic goals. Goals, I believe, should be tough but achievable. Goals are a target, something to shoot for.

When you set your goals, think about a target. For sales it may be a certain amount of revenue or bookings per month, per year. Break it down into small sections: a week, a month, a year. My walking goal started with a block, then two blocks, then three and eventually 500 miles on the Camino de Santiago. What a trip.

Along with my goal to walk the Camino de Santiago, I made a step towards a childhood goal, the goal to write and publish my story.

At 10 or 11 years old, I wrote my first short story about dinosaurs, mimicking the Japanese monster movies of the day. Unfortunately, those pages are long gone. Since then I have been looking for my story.

Throughout the years, I attempted to write something worth publishing, something people would read. I completed a couple novels but did not publish. They weren't good and not worth publishing. The stories weren't good because they lacked the passion and the heart needed to be worth reading. Writing this book became a calling when I decided to walk the Camino de Santiago. I felt this story would interest an audience and somehow serve a purpose for some people. If nothing else, I leave a story for my family and friends.

With the writing and publishing of this journal, I achieved another goal from my childhood, the dream of being a published and successful author. We will see how the success part goes by the sales of this book. Nonetheless, I do consider the completion of this book as a success in itself.

I worked on the draft manuscript regularly and, eventually, finished. I hope this is the book people read and learn from.

So, my point is that personal goals should be real. You should have your heart in it. If you don't believe in reaching your goal, you're probably not going to get your goal. You have to want it. Not just want it as an "as if" or a "maybe." You have to believe it. You have to see yourself there. I saw myself walking 10 miles a day, 15 miles a day and as interest grew, I saw myself walking the Camino without any issues. I looked at it and said, hey, I can do that. Losing weight, the same thing, I can do that. I lost the weight. I went from over 300 pounds to under 200. Now, it's maintaining, so I walk everyday. Writing this book, the same thing. I saw the completed book in my head, on people's ebook readers and bookshelves.

Now, with the pilgrimage over, I learned the journey getting to your destination is as important as the goal. The steps you take are as important as the goal itself. The goals of losing weight, walking the Camino de Santiago, writing and publishing the memoir, and a happy life are all about making the journey, taking the steps. The journey is about what I achieve, what I experience, the people I meet along the way, the life I live as I walk my own Camino.

Use the guidebooks, but don't set a strict itinerary, walk at your own pace. Stop worrying. Live in the moment and focus on the present.

We all walk the same road but come at it in our own way.

Walking the Camino should be as stress free as possible, which means you will want to leave your worries behind. "The Camino provides" is a common belief along the pilgrimage trail. Somehow you will manage. The things you truly need will be there and you will learn to live without the things you don't need. As many people do, I brought too much with me and shed some of this extra baggage after just a few days. I mailed home the many items I didn't need.

In a scene in the movie *The Ten Commandments* the Hebrews wake to find mounds of leaven. Moses warns not to store the leaven, but to believe God will provide.

Live your life believing that God will provide. Take worry from your life and believe that what should be will be.

PART TWO

A HISTORY OF CAMINO DE SANTIAGO

CHAPTER FOUR

History Camino de Santiago

The Camino de Santiago is all about Saint James. It is also known as "The Way of Saint James." The Way is a pilgrimage to the Cathedral of Santiago de Compostela containing the remains of Saint James. Medieval Pilgrims, called peregrinos, made the Way of Saint James seeking penance, healing, or answers to their prayers. Christians visited the site for plenary redemption to reduce time spent in purgatory before their entrance into heaven. Some were sentenced by the judiciary to make the pilgrimage as part of their punishment. Should their pilgrimage take place during a Compostelan Holy Year, the years in which the feast of the Apostle Santiago, July 25, falls on a Sunday, all sins may be forgiven. Passing through the Holy Door of a Catholic Church grants the sinner a plenary indulgence provided they confess their sins, attend Mass, receive Holy Communion and proper prayer. If this is done, all sins are forgiven and they can skip purgatory and go directly to heaven.

On the New Year's Eve preceding the Holy Year or *Año Xacobeo* (Jacobean Year), a ceremony is performed and the doors are unlocked for the pilgrims to enter. The doors are locked again at the following New Year's Eve.

The concept of a Holy Year started in 1122 when Pope Calixtus II allowed the Compostela to grant plenary indulgences during years the Saint's day fell on a Sunday.

The Camino de Santiago is not a single pilgrim's route to Santiago de Compostela but a network of routes ending at the Cathedral de Santiago de Compostela. Each pilgrim's Camino route actually starts when leaving home.

The following are the best know Camino routes:[i]

Camino Frances: The French Way is the most popular Camino route. The traditional starting point for the Camino Frances is Saint Jean Pied de Port. This route takes pilgrims over the Pyrenees, through northern Spain and La Rioja wine region.

Camino Portuguese: The Portuguese Way usually starts in the city of Lisbon and follows the northern coast of Portugal heading inland at Porto to Spain.

Camino Portuguese Coastal: This is the same route as the Camino Portugues until Porto when pilgrims decide to stay along the Atlantic coast before moving inland.

Camino del Norte: The Northern Way runs along Spain's northern coast to join the Camino Primitivo Route in Oviedo. Pilgrims get to enjoy the breathtaking scenery along the coast.

Camino Primitivo: The Original Way, believed to be the first pilgrimage route begins in Oviedo and proceeds through Galicia to Santiago de Compostela. The first reported pilgrim was Alfonso II of Asturias (c. 760-842) known as the Chaste.[ii]

Via de la Plata: The Silver Way or Camino Mozarabe begins in Seville and up the western peninsula.

Le Puy Camino: this section of the Camino starts in Le Puy, France and joins the Camino Frances at Saint Jean Pied de Port.

Camino Finisterre: Muxia Way, a walk from Santiago to Cape Finisterre, considered by pilgrims to be the end of the world, is on the Atlantic Ocean in the northwestern part of Galicia.

Camino Ingles: The English Way is a route taken by pilgrims arriving by sea from Northern Europe to ports on the coast of Galicia.

Codex Calixtinus

The Codex Calixtinus, written about 900 years ago, is one of the most import documents of Christian history and is kept at the Santiago Cathedral. It is considered to be one of the first pilgrim guides. The manuscript is composed of over 200 parchments and divided into 5 books with two appendices. It is believed to be written in the mid 1100s. However, no one knows the real author of the Codex.

Book I: Book of the Liturgies, a collection of liturgical text to honor Saint James in Masses, sermons, etc.

Book II: Book of Miracles, recounts 22 of the miracles of Saint James.

Book III: Transfer of the body to Santiago, recounts the voyage of Santiago's remains from Jerusalem to Galicia.

Book IV: The History of Charlemagne and Roland, recounts Charlemagne's battles against Muslims, including stories of Roland.

Book V: A Guide for the Traveller, believed to be one of the first guides for the pilgrimage including information about towns, churches, and places to stay along the way.

Musical Appendix: Contains the Polyphonic Corpus, pieces representing European polyphony.[iii]

CHAPTER FIVE

Saint James

Saint James[iv] is one of the 12 apostles chosen by Jesus. When James, his father Zebedee and his brother John were fishing, unsuccessfully, in the Sea of Galilee, Jesus, walking along the shore, called out to them and told the men to dip their nets once again whereupon they found the nets full. Their boat nearly sinks from the weight when they empty the net into the boat.

Saint James was referred to as "the greater" because he was taller than James, the Lesser, another apostle.

Following the death of Jesus, the apostles went their separate ways to spread the word of God. James went to Iberia in Northern Spain, now Galicia, to convert the pagans to Christianity. He experienced limited success. Upon his return to Jerusalem, James was arrested and beheaded by King Herrod Agrippa. James was the first of the apostles martyred due to his faith.[v] Following his death, Saint James ashes, accompanied by two of his disciples, Theodore and Athanasius[vi], were set adrift on a rudderless boat that landed in the northwest corner of Spain in Galicia where they buried the remains. Queen Lupa provided a marble tomb for the saint and the two disciples.

The burial site of Saint James was forgotten until the 9th century when the hermit Pelagius had a vision of a star that led him to an ancient tomb with three bodies. He reported the find to Theodomir, the local bishop, who deemed the remains to be of Saint James and his two disciples. Theodomir reported the find to Alphonso II, the King of Asturias who made Saint James the patron saint of the area which would eventually become Spain.

Throughout Spain, Saint James is depicted as a pilgrim with staff, gourd and scallop shell. At other times, he is depicted as a warrior, Saint James the Moor-slayer or Saint James Matamoros

According to the myth, Saint James appeared at a battle at Clavijo in 844 C.E., charging into the battlefield on a white horse attacking the Moors with his sword resulting in a victory for Christian forces. It is believed over 5000 Moors were killed in this battle. He earned the title *Matamoros* or "Moor-slayer."[vii]

While walking the Camino, scallop shells and yellow arrows are used to mark the way, but why a scallop shell?

It is believed that Saint James used the scallop shell during his pilgrimage to beg for food and water. Since the shell was small, even the poorest could provide a little help. The scallop shell is abundant along the coast of Spain and early pilgrims used the shell for food and water. Followers of Saint James began wearing the scallop shell and it became the symbol of the pilgrimage, the journey a Christian makes through life. Life's journey for Christians begins at baptism with the baptismal font often shaped like a scallop shell. A scallop shaped saucer is often used to pour water over the heads of the person being baptized.

Metaphorically, the lines of a scallop shell represent all the paths leading to the tomb of Saint James at Santiago de Compostela with all lines on the shell leading to one point.

Today, pilgrims still wear the shell around their necks or on their backpacks to identify themselves as pilgrims.

CHAPTER SIX

Order of the Templar

The beginnings of the Knights Templar[viii] started with the Crusades when several religious military orders were created to fight a war between Christians and Muslims for Jerusalem and surrounding areas. In 1118 Hugues de Payens, a French knight, and Godofredo de Saint-Adhemar, a Flemish knight, created a military order called the Poor Knights of the Temple of King Solomon or the Order of the Poor Soldiers of Christ. They became more commonly known as the Knights Templar.

The order started with ten or less friends and family of Hugues de Payens with a vow of poverty, chastity, and a pledge to protect pilgrims traveling to Jerusalem and later to Santiago de Compostela. King Baldwin II of Jerusalem allowed the knights to live at the Temple on Mount Moriah which led to their common name of Knights Templar.

Members of the Knights Templar donated their wealth and lands to the order. Many nobles and kings also donated to the order, eventually the order became very wealthy which led to the Knights Templar banking activities, including loans to monarchs to support the cost of their wars. Interest charged on these loans further increased their wealth.

Since many pilgrims were robbed of their possessions during their pilgrimage, The Templar allowed them to use a credit system during their travels with the first use of "letters of credit."

Also, to protect the pilgrims, the Templars built or took over missionaries or buildings, such as the Knights Templar Castle in Ponferrada. Pilgrims were provided food, a place to rest and medical assistance.

King Philip IV of France dissolved the Knights Templar in 1307 due to his distrust of the organization and his great financial debt to the order. Their growing wealth became a threat to Catholic monarchs and to the Papacy. On Friday October 13, 1307 joint forces of Pope Clement V and King Philip of France arrested, tortured and eventually put to death most of the members of the Knights Templar, including their Grand Master Jacques de Molay. The massacre of the Knights Templar on this day may have lead to the belief that Friday the 13th is unlucky.

Jacques de Molay, the 23rd and last Grand Master of the Knights Templar,[ix] was born in 1243 in Bourgogne, France. He died on March 18, 1314. After seven years of torture in prison he was burned at the stake by order of King Philip. From the flames was heard the curse of Jacques de Molay against King Phillip and his family, Pope Clement, and anyone else that supported his execution. He called on God to prove the Order's innocence and pass judgement on the accusers. Within a year of Jacques de Molay's death, both Pope Clement and King Phillip died. Over the next fourteen years, the sons and grandsons of the King also died and the Capetian dynasty came to an end.

Following the disbanding of the Knights Templar, the Knights Hospitallers of Saint John[x], who already had an active presence along the Camino became responsible for protecting and providing for the pilgrims. Originally, the Knights Hospitallers began their order following the First Crusade in 1100 AD setting up a hospital in Jerusalem for sick pilgrims. As with the Knights Templar, the knights and monks of the Knights Hospitallers took a vow of poverty, chastity and a pledge to protect pilgrims.

Today the Way of Saint James is maintained by the Associations of Friends of the Way of Saint James[xi] which began on July 25, 1950 in Paris as the Society of Friends of Santiago de Compostela with the dual purpose of studying and maintaining the art, history and literature of the Camino and to assist current pilgrims, including setting up hostels and sign posting. In 1962 an affiliate association was founded in Spain, then throughout Europe and eventually throughout the world.

CHAPTER SEVEN

Medieval Architecture

Along the Jacobean Route, another name for the Way of Saint James, we will encounter castles, cathedrals, and Roman remains as we walk through the mountains, plains and hills of Spain.

Much of the architecture along the Camino de Santiago was built in the Medieval Period or Middle Ages which began with the fall of the Western Roman Empire in the 5th century and lasted into the 15th century. Historians divide the Middle Ages in three periods.

- The Early Middle Ages (475 to 1000)

- The High Middle Ages (1001 to 1300)

- The Late Middle Ages (1301-1500)[xii]

Each of these periods had their own architectural style.

Most of the architecture of the Early Middle Ages is considered Romanesque, holding onto some of the elements of the Roman Empire, such as vaults and arches. Builders used stone as the primary building material.

During the High Middle Ages, the Gothic style gradually replaced the Romanesque. The architecture included buttresses, arches, and vaults but with stylistic differences from the older designs. Religious influence grew during this period and had a big influence on structures signifying a shift in power from the politicians to the Church.

Over centuries, architectural styles changed along the Camino de Santiago depending on the people in charge. Through the centuries, the Basque, Franks, Romans, and Moors controlled areas of the Camino de Santiago. Since cathedrals took decades or hundred years to build, cathedrals often exhibit several styles of architecture.

Romanesque

Apse is a semicircular recess in a church with an arch or domed roof containing the alter. It can also be used as a niche to hold a stature. This style of architecture was used in pre-christian Roman temples.

Gothic

https://www.architecturecourses.org/origins

Key features of Gothic architecture are the Pointed Arch, Ribbed Vaulting and Flying Buttress and large open vertical spaces with expansive windows to increase interior lighting. Carvings and paintings with intricate detail, often of biblical stories. The facades were large and embellished to emphasize extravagance.

Baroque

The Baroque style of architecture originated in Italy in the late 16th century. It took basic elements of Renaissance architecture making them grander, more decorated and more dramatic with an emphasis on excess to arouse emotions

PART THREE

THE WALK

CHAPTER EIGHT

Why The Walk

The Camino de Santiago, like your journey through life, is filled with joy and sadness, freedom and constriction, frustration and satisfaction, elation and pain.

Before I started this whole thing, The Walk looked like a spiritual journey. I can see why. Walking alone, silently, for many hours will make you introspective. It makes you look into yourself. When I walked around my neighborhood in preparation for a 15-25 km daily hike on the Camino, I became introspective when walking alone. Even when walking with Rick, we ran out of things to talk about and walked stretches in silence. My introspection often centered on mundane daily life. Things I needed to do, like mowing the lawn, laundry, grocery shopping and on and on. Sometimes I anguished over how bad my knee hurt or the heat of the day. When walking for several hours your mind will wander in many directions. Walking allows you to reflect on many things and come up with ideas, some ordinary and unimaginative, some surprisingly eloquent or profound. Walking allows you to be one with yourself, to be one with nature, to be one with God.

When I realized I was on the anguishing side of this introspection, I would do something to change the direction of my thoughts. Look up and around instead of down at the pavement. I start to look outward instead of inward. Change my pace, quicken the tempo or slow down to look around, maybe take a picture of a flower or a sunrise with my cell phone. I thought about the wonders to see on the Camino to keep me going.

I didn't have a particularly spiritual reason for doing the Camino, but thought maybe I better get one for I understood this to be a requirement to get the certificate of completion, the Compostela, when you arrive in Santiago. They ask for the purpose of your pilgrimage.

Two activities in life make me feel creative and good about myself, writing and photography. These were my thoughts when I decided to take this journey. Do the pilgrimage, take photographs and write a memoir about my journey with the hope others may enjoy the fruits of my effort. If lucky, somehow I may motivate or otherwise help someone get through their journey in life.

A year or so before leaving, I started my research for this manuscript and put together an outline based on anticipated stops for each day. I looked up things to see at each stop. I tried to learn the history of each hamlet, village or city along the way. My interest grew as I did this and I found myself wishing we could somehow leave at an earlier date.

Although raised a Catholic, I haven't practiced in years, decades. Disillusioned by the Catholic Church and churches in general, my relationship with God became more private. So, for me, the walk was not about being Catholic. Yet, to immerse myself into this adventure, I felt a need to do some research on Saint James and the history around the pilgrimage. My research only enticed me more.

CHAPTER NINE

Preparation for the Journey

During my research for this trip, I encountered many books, web sites and videos suggesting to travel light. A 30 liter backpack is all you need. It took me a while to comprehend if this would be large enough for me. I planned on bringing my digital SLR camera with an additional long lens and my MacBook to store the photos and to work on this manuscript. To reduce weight, I decided not to bring the MacBook. I also didn't want to lose it. Too much of my life was on the computer. I bought a 512GB Scan Disk card for the camera, hopefully enough to hold my photos. If not, I supposed I could buy another one in Spain. After a couple days of walking, I did end up sending my camera and lens home to reduce the weight I carried. My iPhone was sufficient. I actually bought the iPhone just a few weeks before I left to get quality photos my old Android phone didn't provide. I took over five thousand photos using it. There were times that the long lens of the SLR would have been nice, but you work with what you have.

Many books and web sites suggested leaving all electronics behind, including cell phones, but I wasn't about to lose an opportunity to share my wonderful experience with others through photographs. Besides, I also found it ironic that most books and web sites suggesting this included photographs of the Camino.

I ended up buying a 55 liter backpack by Teton to ensure I had enough space. Empty space doesn't weigh anything, so I wasn't worried about any unnecessary weight. I only needed to be careful about picking up additional weight along the way.

Another thing I did when considering taking this walk was to watch a few films and then read a few books. These are listed in the bibliography.

A good Hollywood film version about the Camino is *"The Walk"* starring Martin Sheen. This is a story about a father (Martin Sheen) whose son (Emilio Estevez) gets lost and dies while walking the Camino. After retrieving his son's ashes and belongings, he decides to walk the Camino himself distributing his son's ashes along the way. He joins several others walking the Camino, each with their own reasons. They became his Camino family. Although this movie begins with news about a person's death, it became a movie about life. It is a lighthearted movie that presents the Camino in a positive manner and how the walk affects different people both spiritually and physically. It does leave out some of the realities of the walk, such as blisters and sore muscles, which are common on the trail.

A common issue for travelers are blisters from the hours of walking. It is important to prepare for this inevitability. Foremost, have the right shoes. I believe walking with trail runners or cross trainers are better than hiking boots, but you need to wear what is comfortable for you. They should be light weight and breathable. Wearing two pair of socks will keep the shoes from rubbing or shifting and causing blisters. Wool socks are better than cotton. They dry quicker and insulate when wet. Use moleskin pads on sensitive areas where blisters may occur.

Bring flip flops or sandals to wear in the evening and allow your feet to air out.

Bring tee-shirts and underwear designed to wick away the moisture and dry quickly.

A tendency for some people taking the pilgrimage is to get up in the early morning for their trek to the next destination. They do this day after day to keep on schedule and arrive "on time." If you walk in peak season, many leave early to ensure they can secure a bed. I believe this 'hurry to get there 'attitude is a mistake for several reasons, physical and psychological.

Walking everyday is a stress on the lower body muscles, legs, hips, etc. When working muscles you are doing damage to the muscle, so it is important to give them a day or two to recuperate. When they rebuild, they rebuild stronger.

A day or two of rest during your walk will help you recover physically and mentally. Change is good. It will take you away from the daily grind. After all, isn't that why many walk the Way of Saint James, to get away from their daily lives. The usual routine and attitude of daily life of home is best left behind. The hustle and bustle of life on the go left behind. Why in such a hurry? Take the time to relax and enjoy the world around you. Even while walking, take moments to enjoy the stroll and see the spectacular landscape, architecture, and most importantly, the people you encounter. It is easy to get drawn into the mundane movements of walking for hours on end with head down step after step. Keep looking around, even if the same scenery is seemingly endless as in long stretches across La Meseta, the interior plateau of Spain. Find the details, the nuances of the world around you. See how the grasses sway in the wind, the beautiful arrangement of the colors on the landscape, the patchwork of farmland and more. Keep your eyes open. You will be surprised at all you can find.

For some, walking the Camino can be extremely painful. Blisters, tendinitis and other issues can arise with such a long walk. This made me think about pain and agony, as a Christian tradition, starting with Jesus Himself who came to earth to save mankind through his sufferings and eventual Crucifixion.

In the past, the some of the strict faithful practiced self-flagellation, maybe some still do today. Self-flagellation is a punishment sinners apply to themselves to atone for their sins. Is the suffering during the pilgrimage a form of self-flagellation or a form of atonement for our sins? Maybe, since medieval judiciary sometimes sentenced the guilty to walk the Camino as punishment for transgressions.

In medieval times, pilgrims made the Way of Saint James to seek plenary redemption, sometimes ordered and sometimes self imposed. If they walked during Holy Years, years in which Saint James holiday falls on a Sunday, pilgrims received complete redemption of their sins and a direct route into heaven when they entered the cathedral through the door of forgiveness. We were walking in a Holy Year, which was actually extended into 2022 due to covid. The Pope can change the rules.

Pain was often required as punishment for sins. Early puritanical settlers of America punished sinners publicly in town squares. Sinners were placed in shackles and the more serious, such as witches, were burned at the stake.

CHAPTER TEN

9/14/2021
Leaving Orlando

Due to the Covid-19 pandemic, there were additional hassles and cost to travel to France and Spain. First, the airline required a negative Covid test within 3 days of departure. I scheduled a test at the Orlando International Airport with AdventHealth CentraCare for 11:50AM Monday, September 13 at a cost of $175. Rick had an appointment for 11:30AM. Dave had to work out his details from his home in New Jersey. We are flying out on Tuesday, September 14. We weren't sure if additional tests were needed to get from France into Spain.

To enter France, we needed to be fully vaccinated against Covid-19. The French government web sites talked about a "health pass." For this, we needed a valid passport, a vaccination certificate, and a return airline ticket with the information emailed to the Interior Ministry. A QR code will be sent upon approval.

To enter Spain, we needed a valid passport, be fully vaccinated, a negative PCR test within 3 days of arrival and the completed form on the Spanish Ministry of Health web site. A QR code will be sent upon approval. As it turned out, this was needed to fly into Spain. Since we walked into Spain, we didn't need all this, but had applied anyway to be sure.

We all managed to jump these Covid hurdles successfully.

When I woke in the morning of our departure, I got out of bed filled with anticipation, the day finally upon us. I got up early, about 3AM. Lisa, Rick's wife, will be driving us to the airport at 5AM.

Today, we leave for what I hope to be an enlightening adventure. I trained for this walk for over a year, longer than originally planned due to the unforeseen delay caused by the worldwide Covid-19 pandemic. This worldwide crisis caused business shutdowns, curfews and closed borders in an effort to contain the spread of this disease that eventually caused the death of millions.

Pharmaceutical companies worked quickly to develop a vaccine. By November 2020, several drug companies had vaccines at a 90% or better efficacy during the randomized control trials (RCT). This was a promisingly high rate. According to a television interview with Dr. Anthony Fauci, the director of the National Institute of Allergy and Infectious Diseases, they would have been good with a 60% effectiveness. According to the Center for Disease Control, the flu vaccine reduces risk by 40% to 60%.[xiii]

In any case, with the vaccine developed. I got my first shot in January and the second on February 6, 2021. I felt comfortable to travel. Once Spain opened its borders, we were good to go.

As it turned out, this comfort waned as we approached our departure date of September 14. With the appearance of a Covid variant, cases began to rise again in the United States with over ninety percent of the cases caught by the unvaccinated. I felt a certain amount of animosity towards those non-vaccinated, those stubborn individuals that refused to get the vaccine due to political, religious or some other reason. We live in a free country and they have the right to their beliefs, but their beliefs were affecting my plans.

On the last few days of August, the European Union brought back restrictions to travel for the unvaccinated, including a quarantine period. So glad I am vaccinated. But, other hoops still existed, including a negative covid test within three days of arrival, a EU Health Pass and a signed affidavit regarding contact with Covid.

Before we leave for the Orlando International Airport, I jokingly suggest to Rick that we should walk to the airport to truly start our Camino from our homes. However, since it would take about 4 to 5 hours to walk the 15 miles and our flight was at 7:40 in the morning, we decide to let Lisa drive us. Besides, if we walked to the Orlando International Airport, it would mean we should also walk from Paris to Saint Jean Pied de Port. We decided to wait until Saint Jean Pied de Port, France to start walking.

We start our adventure flying out of Orlando heading for Paris by way of a connection in New York at JFK Airport where we will join Rick's longtime friend, David. Dave and Rick served in the Air Force forty years ago. We fly standby, since Rick is a retired Delta employee and we are taking advantage of their Friends and Family Program. This was very helpful for me, reducing my cost to about one-third of the published rate.

I try to live in the now. I try not to worry about the future. Yet, preparing for this trip I found myself worrying. I traveled a lot as a hotel sales manager, a least one a month for a week at a time. I usually had some anticipation before leaving, but this was different. Most of the time, I did not sleep soundly if I had an early flight, worrying that I may oversleep and miss the flight. I don't think this is unusual and suspect that many have a certain amount of anticipation. I didn't sleep well the night before our departure and was up an hour or more before needed. I did not want to miss this flight.

This trip is much different than my other trips. For one, my business travel was always domestic. Even flying internationally to Cancun for a vacation a few years ago felt routine. But this is my first time to Europe and the first time I will be away from home for so long, up to 45 days.

Being away so long created the need for extra preparations, such as setting up most of my bills for auto pay and arranging for sufficient cash to be in my checking account to handle the ATM withdrawals in Europe. Although these issues were addressed, I moved on with some lingering doubts that all was done correctly. I value my good credit rating and didn't want any issues to arise.

The most worrisome aspect of my preparation was trying to figure out what was needed to comply with all the new Covid-19 restrictions to travel. Vaccination records, negative test result, French Health Pass, Spanish rules for entry. There was so much that kept cropping up. Requirements changing with less than two weeks before departure. I like to roll with the flow, but this was getting annoying.

I applied for the French Health Pass seven days before departure but did not receive an email confirmation of completion. I thought that this may be a hassle to rectify at the border.

Once we get on the plane at JFK Airport and in the air heading towards Paris, I feel more at ease. At this point, everything is in motion and I will deal with life as it progresses, moment by moment, like I want to do.

Other worries include my two dogs and my roommate. Will they be alright? I have to hope they will be, but, again, some lingering thoughts. All I can do at this point is trust that all will be okay. Once I am off the ground, these worries diminished.

CHAPTER ELEVEN

9/15/2021
Arriving in France

We arrived at Roissy Charles de Gaulle Airport (CDG) in Paris about 8AM. Originally, the plan was to stay a night in Paris to readjust to the time change and relax from the flight, but on a trip like this, plans need to be flexible. Instead, we decided to take the train to Saint Jean Pied de Port and stay there. I cancelled our Holiday Inn reservation. To save cash, I had made the Holiday Inn reservation using travel points earned on my IHG membership card. I'll use them at another time.

Starting our new adventure, we followed the signs to collect our luggage and present our passports. We thought we needed to have a French Health Pass, but found out our proof of vaccination for Covid-19 was all we needed. One situation solved easily after much stress. Then, we needed to figure out where to get the train. You think it would be easy. There is a station at the airport. But simple things can be confusing without an understanding of the language. I knew minimal Spanish and no French.

We asked at an information counter about the trains and got nowhere with the young man behind the counter. He tried to help but became frustrated because he did not understand English and we could not speak French. Eventually, he walked away and ignored us. I heard the French are rude to Americans, but this was the only case I experienced. Everyone else we came across truly tried to help despite a language barrier. Generalizations and labels are dangerous. Did this young man represent the general attitude of the French towards Americans or was he just having a bad day? The counter was busy and he seemed a bit flustered trying to help everyone.

The language barrier was evident when I tried to look for a bathroom. I knew to ask for "el baño" in Spanish, but no idea of the French translation. I asked for help from a woman pushing a janitorial cart who finally understood what I wanted when I moved my hands towards my zipper and acted like I was peeing. Smiling and nodding, she pointed across the terminal hall towards a well-marked sign on the wall above an entry that said "toilettes." I went that way in a bit of a hurry only to return unsatisfied when I learned that one Euro was needed to enter. I was able to get change and finally handled the situation.

Rick and Dave waited for me at a coffee shop. When I returned, we went looking for the trains.

Signs eventually led us to the train station and we thought we had it figured out. From my prior research I knew we needed to take a train from Paris to Bayonne and then transfer to another train in Bayonne to Saint Jean Pied de Port. We found the ticket machine and tried to review the tickets. Looked like we had the right tickets and I tried to buy them using my Mastercard but the transaction was declined. I did check the web site of my credit card company before leaving. It informed me that notification about travel out of the country was not needed due to the advancement of technology. What it didn't say was that transactions needed a two-factor authorization to verify it is me. Unfortunately, I couldn't do this since I did not have cell phone service. My carrier did not have an international plan. I did not have access to phone, text or Internet. Not having access on my phone kept my first few days interesting as I struggled to communicate with Rick and Dave and finding our housing each day.

An attendant hanging out at the ticket machines carrying a clipboard and wearing a dark blue jacket with a train company logo that knew limited English tried to help us. We found out the train from the airport to Bayonne was sold out. She suggested trying to depart from Paris-Montparnasse Station not the airport station. She helped us get the tickets for a train from the airport to Paris-Montparnasse Station, about a forty-five minute ride. Rick paid for the train fair with his credit card.

When we arrived, we learned that the Montparnasse Station was a couple blocks away from the local train station stop. We made our way up to street level looking in all directions for the station. We saw the complex and walked in the drizzling rain to take the next step in our journey.

Fortunately, we were able to book a train to Bayonne and on to Saint Jean Pied de Port for the same day. There was a thought that we may need to stay in Bayonne for a night if the schedule wasn't right.

The ride to Bayonne took about four hours passing through beautiful French countryside, farmland with massive wind mills scattered about in some of the fields and old stone farm houses nestled in hills. I thought about the American and allied armies of World War II marching through this farmland in the fight against Hitler's attempt to rule the world. I also thought of stories about the French farmers' daughters that fell in love with American soldiers as portrayed in many Hollywood versions of the war to end all wars. How wrong was that thinking, the war to end all wars? Will we ever be free of war? At the time of this writing, the Russian army has invaded Ukraine and is threatening the beginning of World War III with Putin's finger on the nuclear button.

On the train to Saint Jean Pied de Port I met my first fellow pilgrim, Krystal, a young lady from the Netherlands. She is also starting her walk in Saint Jean, but will only walk for two weeks since that is all the time she had off. When we arrived at Saint Jean, I wished her a "buen camino," the traditional greeting to fellow pilgrims. I would not see Krystal again since she was leaving in the morning and we are staying a couple nights in Saint Jean Pied de Port. Our planned stay in Paris was now an additional night in Saint Jean Pied de Port. It was a wise decision. I was not that impressed with the little I saw of Paris with its congested big city atmosphere. That is not what I wanted for this adventure. I will give Paris another try in the future. I'm sure it is nice. My older brother George liked Paris and went there often.

CHAPTER TWELVE

9/15-16/2021
Saint Jean Pied de Port

The train stopped at the Saint Jean Pied de Port station, a quaint white building with red window shutters and red tile roof, a sample of the architecture that gives this town so much charm. We grab our backpacks and depart. I wished a "buen camino" to Krystal, a greeting that I will hear and say often for the next five weeks, wishing a "good way" to fellow peregrinos or pilgrims walking the Camino de Santiago, the Way of Saint James.

Dave and I followed Rick as he walked through the narrow cobbled streets with his head down looking at the GPS on his phone, making his way to our residence for the night.

Pilgrims walking the Camino de Santiago will sleep at an Albergue or a hostel. These accommodations, designed for pilgrims, offer the basics, a shared room with bunkbeds and shared showers and toilets. They may be public facilities or privately owned. Privately owned hostels may offer more comfortable accommodations and a few more amenities, such as a private room and bathroom, a washer/dryer, and Internet. The cost for a public albergue is $8 to $15 per person. Private rooms worked out to be close to the same when sharing with three people, $35 to $60 per room. Nicer hotels are more expensive. A night at the Parador in Santiago may be $400 per night.

Our room in Saint Jean Pied de Port was nice. There was a single bed and a bunkbed in the room. Dave took the upper bunk and I was on the bottom. Rick had the single bed. Bunkbeds are common in rooms for pilgrims. Dave and I usually took turns taking the upper bunks. Dave, having empathy for my bad knees, took the top bunk more often.

Once we got settled in, we went out to explore and find a place to eat. We found a small cafe, the Restaurant XOKO, just a few doors down from our albergue. We sat at a table out front under a canopy. The owner greeted us warmly, speaking French at first, then switching to his best English. He gave us a menu and placed a small bowl of mixed nuts on the table then went over the menu of the day. It was difficult to understand the menu. Dave kept it simple and ordered a hamburger and fries. I learned later that Dave's favorite dinner is pizza. We ate pizza more than any other menu. Pizza is not a bad choice. The carbohydrates in pizza provide energy for the walk. I don't remember what Rick and I ordered for this meal. Rick and Dave shared a bottle of wine. I took a taste, but drank water for my meal. I don't usually drink alcoholic beverages. I may drink half a dozen beers at most over a year's time. I don't have anything against a drink or two, but have seen it take over a person's life, even my own in my younger days. I choose to live life without alcohol. I will admit that I smoke marijuana though. I guess that is my substance used to change my mood. Here in France and Spain, I use the Camino to change my mood.

After dinner, we walked around Saint Jean Pied de Port, a medieval walled town on the river Nive in French Basque Country. While now part of France, the town of Saint Jean Pied de Port changed sovereignty several times over the centuries. In the 12th Century it was part of the Spanish kingdom of Lower Navarra. When the kingdom was abolished during the French Revolution, Saint Jean Pied de Port became part of France.

We walked the cobbled *Rue de la Citadelle* to experience the different world of the 16th and 17th century with small shops and eateries, and albergues for pilgrims. Dave and I bought some dried fruit from a small shop to take on our walk across the Pyrenees. I took some photos of a spice shop with open containers and scoops. The colorful spices are sold by weight. Wine and cheese shops, bakeries, and souvenir shops cater to pilgrims and tourist.

We stopped midway across a stone bridge to view the river and the white buildings of traditional Basque Country architectural design lining each side of the river. These charming buildings adorned with colorful flowers in window boxes, red trim, small balconies overlooking the river and red tiled roofs foreshadowed the delightful villages we will walk through in the next several weeks. From the stone bridge we saw the wood bridge used in the film *The Way* with Martin Sheen.

Eventually we made our way to the Pilgrim's Office to pick up our credential, the Pilgrim's Passport. A pilgrim gets the credential stamped along the way as proof they have made the journey and qualify for the certificate of completion at the Pilgrim Office near the Cathedral of Santiago de Compostela. Passports are stamped at the albergue, cathedrals, post offices or restaurants and cafes on the Camino. At least 100 km must be walked or made by horseback to receive this certificate. 200 km are needed if bicycled. On the last 100 km, two stamps per day are required.[xiv] It is important to get the passport stamps on these last 100 km. If stamps are missing on the last 100 km, you will not get a certificate even if you have walked all the way from France and have those stamps. If having a credential is important, be sure to get your credential stamped for the last 100 km walked or 200 km bicycled.

The Pilgrim's office in Saint Jean Pied de Port is small. On the back wall is a map of the Camino Frances. Below the map is a bust of Saint James the Greater. There are two eight foot long tables and four chairs where pilgrims sit to apply for their passport. We sit on one side and staff on the other. We are separated by a small plexiglass stand as protection against covid. With the forms completed, we receive the passport, a list of albergue along the Camino Frances, and a flyer about the Camino. We also get an update on the weather forecast. Scallop shells were available for a small donation, but we already had ours. Rick had ordered them online before we left. We each drop a few coins in the box anyway.

Saint Jean Pied de Port is the most popular starting point for the Camino Frances. About 11% of all pilgrims that complete the Camino start in Saint Jean Pied de Port. Only Sarria is higher with about 26% starting there. Sarria numbers are high because it is the last town for departure within the 100 km needed to qualify for a certificate of completion. According to followthecamino.com, nearly 350,000 pilgrims, arriving from all routes, completed the pilgrimage in 2019 to receive the Compostela certificate. Due to the covid pandemic, the numbers have been much lower the last few years. About 54,000 received their certificate in 2020. In 2021, 179,000 received their certificate[xv]. As borders opened and covid restrictions became less restrictive the numbers increased.

One thing to remember about the Compostela is that the pilgrimage must be made for religious or spiritual reasons to qualify.[xvi] You may walk the Camino for whatever reason you want, but they will ask you at the end why you walked.

The Pilgrim's Office is just a short distance from the gothic architecture of the Notre Dame du Bout du Pont Church (Our Lady at the End of the Bridge) just down the street. The clock on the bell tower, a statue of Saint John the Baptist inset in the tower wall, and a stone arch, the Notre-Dame Gateway, can be seen from the street outside the Pilgrim's Office. We walk down the hill towards the church to continue our tour of the town.

Staying two nights gave us time to see historic Saint Jean Pied de Port, a fortified town at a strategic location at a pass through the Pyrenees and on the river Nive. To protect the town, it was heavily fortified with walls and the Citadel. The Citadel is a massive block fortress built in 1628 by Cardinal Richelieu[xvii] to protect the town following a war between Catholics and Protestants. Now serving as a school the inside is closed to the public, but we could walk around the perimeter.

We made our way up the steep cobblestone path to the Citadel. At the top we are blessed with a spectacular panoramic view over the town and the rolling landscape leading to the Pyrenees Mountains, the mountains we will cross to start our way to Santiago. The view is impressive, yet daunting. Knowing that a challenge lay ahead, I felt enthusiastic excitement and maybe a little apprehension about the days ahead.

CHAPTER THIRTEEN

9/17/2021
Saint Jean Pied de Port - Roncesvalles
Crossing the Pyrenees

Rick, Dave and I left our room in Saint Jean Pied de Port about 6:30 AM to finally officially start walking the Camino de Santiago by crossing the Pyrenees. After two nights in SJPDP, we were excited about starting the adventure. Since it was still dark and foggy, we wore headlamps to see the Camino markers, either a yellow arrow or a scallop shell. If a marker is missed on the Camino, a person could walk many kilometers and many hours in the wrong direction. I experienced this unfortunate situation a few weeks into our walk. It is not fun.

The Camino Frances offers two routes over the Pyrenees, the Napoleon route and the Valcarlos route. The Napoleon route is considered by many to be the hardest part of the Camino Frances due to the ascent of over 1200 meters followed by a 500-meter descent into Roncesville. This route is hazardous in some areas and subject to a sudden change in weather. In the winter months, the Napoleon route is closed. At first, the Valcarlos route was more popular for pilgrims because it was not as steep, however, in Medieval times it was subject to constant attacks from bandits. To stay safe the Napoleon route became the preferred path.

As I headed up a hill on a cobbled street becoming steeper with each step, I already felt the challenge that lay ahead and I just started walking. I also had my first experience of walking alone. Rick, always walking like he's on a mission to get somewhere quickly, pulled ahead with Dave walking just a few feet behind. It wasn't long before they were well ahead. The lights of the headlamps disappeared into the fog. I referred to this distancing in a message home as the guys leaving me in the dust. Right from the start, it felt like I was in a race. With the arthritis in my left knee, I knew I could not maintain the same pace as them. Although I walked daily to train for the Camino, I trained on flat Florida roads. My knees were not ready for the steep climb. My training also told me walking too quickly increased the pain and inflammation in my knee. Rick has titanium knees from two successful knee replacement surgeries. He was having fun trying to show how well his new knees were working and enjoyed telling fellow pilgrims about them. Dave trained in New Jersey mountains and was more prepared for the climb.

The first day foreshadowed how often I will walk alone on my Camino de Santiago. At first, it bothered me when Rick and Dave left me behind. I didn't understand why they were in such a hurry. Occasionally, they teased me by waiting for me when they needed to rest. But, as soon as I arrived, they were ready to go, having had their break. Taking off and leaving me behind again. Instead of stopping for a rest, I felt compelled to try to keep up with them, a fruitless effort. It took a few days for me to get over the frustration of being left behind and to learn how to enjoy my solo walks. My mantra after all, for the last year, was that everyone walks their own Camino de Santiago and through life. I needed to embrace the concept on my own walk.

Crossing the Pyrenees was the hardest walk of my life. As mentioned, I trained for nearly two years by walking eight to ten miles a day in my neighborhood or on a treadmill. Yet, I was ill-prepared for the great change in elevation. The degree of elevation on my treadmill was maybe ten percent of what we experienced. Rick commented on our first evening that the day's walk was harder than his hikes in the Grand Canyon. All of us hurt from the difficult climb and descent. Dave thought the descent was harder than the climb. They were both hard for me and a stress on my arthritic knee. A discomfort I would encounter, off and on, for the next thirty days, but never to a degree to keep me from walking.

As hard as it was, I think everyone should cross the Pyrenees as part of the Camino. The experience is amazing. We enjoyed the majestic views from the Pyrenees when we finally walked out of the fog and above the clouds. I looked down to a small group of buildings nestled in the hill side. It may have been Saint Michel. We also enjoyed hills littered with sheep, cattle and horses. Many wearing their bells chiming a symphony in the countryside. The mountains were alive with the musical sounds of cow bells in the distance.

I met Ginette from Idaho and later, her friend Lori from Biloxi. Ginette seemed to know a little about the sheep since she was involved with a sheep rescue program in Idaho. She was surprised not to see a shepherd nearby, explaining that a shepherd is needed to help the sheep survive, protecting them from danger and moving them to fresh pasture to keep them from getting sick.

I meet up with Rick and Dave again at Orisson, about 7.5 km from Saint Jean Pied de Port. Many pilgrims stay the night at the albergue Refuge Orisson to break the hard walk across the Pyrenees into two days. On my next walk on the Camino Frances, I will do this, too.

The Refuge Orisson offers a cafe for pilgrims to buy drinks, lunch or snacks. The albergue offers a communal dinner and breakfast for those staying there. Many pilgrims start building their Camino family in Orisson as they go around the table at dinner to introduce themselves. Some of these folks become the family you walk with or dine with along the Way to Santiago. If you are lucky, you may make some lifelong friends.

Across the path from the cafe entrance is a large wooden terrace with tables and umbrellas and a spectacular view of the Pyrenees Mountains. The morning sky was now blue and bright giving us a clear view of the mountains. We rest for about thirty minutes with a drink and a snack, enjoying the beautiful day. I took some photos. A fellow pilgrim took a picture of the three of us with the mountains in the background.

About an hour past Orisson, I come up on a gravel parking lot and was surprised to see a food truck selling snacks and beverages. Laying on the grassy mound across the lot from the food truck were Rick, Dave and about a dozen other pilgrims enjoying the beautiful weather and relaxing in the sun after a tough climb. A good place to take a rest, I take off my backpack and set it on the ground near Dave. I buy a drink and snack from the food truck and return to enjoy my break on the grassy hillside.

Behind me is the Vierge d'Orisson, a ceramic statue of the Virgin Mother holding the baby Jesus, was brought from Lourdes by shepherds to watch over pilgrims. She stands atop a rocky peak with a panoramic view of the the Pyrenees Mountains.

Soon after the Vierge d'Orisson I walk through an open pasture among remnants of the Chateau Pignon, a castle built by the Spanish in the 16th century and ironically destroyed by the Spanish in the 17th century during the Napoleonic wars. To me it was just scattered rocks or boulders on the hillside exposed by erosion with grazing sheep moseying among the rocks. I didn't realize it was a ruin until I did some research for this book following my walk.

Next, I experience my first cow parade. A Jeep driving slowly up the path with the driver holding a bucket of feed out the window. Ten or twelve cows followed behind, moseying their way to another pasture for grazing or back to the barn. I stepped aside to let them pass. After they passed, I realized I could have filmed the parade with my iPhone. I caught the tail end, literally, on video.

It wasn't unusual for horses and cows to block the path, slowly moving out of the way as you approached. I stopped for a few moments at the Fountain of Roland to scratch the nose of a huge stout horse, a breed strong enough to pull farm equipment. I later learned it was a Pottok, an ancient breed of semi-feral ponies accustomed to the harsh conditions of the Pyrenees. It was a gentle giant, hanging out with several other horses at the water stop taking turns for a drink, sharing with pilgrims. Along the Camino, fountains provide water for pilgrims to fill their bottles. It is important to stay hydrated. Most fountains are marked as potable or not-potable to let the pilgrims know if the water was safe to drink.

The Fountain of Roland is near the Roncesville Pass, the sight of several historic battles. In 778, Charlemagne was returning from his campaign against the Moors. Roldån (Roland) leading the rear guard of Charlemagne's Frankish army across the Pyrenees, was attacked by the Basque on August 15, supposedly, in retaliation for the destruction of the walls of Pamplona. Everyone was killed and the battle became the basis of the 11th century epic poem, *The Song of Roland*. Myth is that Roland was instructed to blow a horn for help from Charlemagne, if needed. Due to his pride, he waited too long. When he finally blows the horn, he blows it so hard he burst his temples and dies. At nearby Puerto de Ibañeta there is a chapel and monument to Roland.

Another historic battle took place in 1813 between French Napoleonic troops and Anglo-Portuguese during the Peninsular War. It ended in the defeat of the Anglo-Portuguese. This battle led to naming this section of the Camino across the Pyrenees as the Napoleon Route.

Leaving the Fountain of Roland, I continued my walk through a less steep forested area and come across a marble Templar-shaped cross memorial for Antonio Jorge Ferreira. Across the top it said "Por todo dad gracias a Dios" (Thank God for everything). Dates on the memorial were 29-8-53 – 13-1-02. Just 49 years old. Beneath the dates were written "Peregrino, Brazil" Beneath that "Oct - 94" and another October date under that which was obscured by stones, trinkets and scallop shells. I assume these were the dates he walked the camino. This was the first of many memorials I encountered walking the "Way of Saint James."

I come upon an emergency shelter, a stone building with red tiled roof about fifteen-by-fifteen feet in size. A sign on a plaque says "Refugio para emergencias" with instructions in several languages: "Use shelter material only in case of emergency, thank you." On the timber beam above the door is carved the word "Izandorre." Inside, the walls are covered with graffiti. It is a shame that some people feel a need to deface these ancient structures. No telling how many lives this shelter has saved. Weather in the Pyrenees is unpredictable and severe storms can come up suddenly.

The walk down the Pyrenees proved as hard or even harder than the climb. In one area walking down rocky wet river ravines. The pounding on the knee felt like a pile driver setting a pylon for a bridge. I get relief when I return to an asphalt or gravel path.

Along this section, I met Anika, a pretty young lady from

Germany. She is very friendly, speaking English with a charming German accent. She slows her pace to walk with me for a while. We had a pleasant conversation. She moves on, but then I see her again a while later resting on a grassy slope. We wave at each other as I pass. I will see Anika several more times in the next few weeks.

The asphalt path comes up to a T in the road, a junction with highway N-135. This is the convergence point of the Valcarlos route with the Napoleon route. To the right is the Iglesia de San Salvador de Ibañeta. A modern style construction from the 1960s, this church is on the site of an ancient monastery from the 11th century which had been destroy by fire. Legend is that monks would ring the bell of the church to guide pilgrims on the Camino. Archeologist have found remnants of the original monastery, as well as some Roman artifacts.

Across N-135 from the church at the end of a field at the edge of the forest is the stone Monument to Roland. "Roldan" is carved at the top of this block of stone. At the bottom are carved the years 778 and 1967, the year of the battle at Roncesville Pass and, I assume, the year the monument was placed.

I get a little confused here thinking that I should follow the road, then I see pilgrims ahead of me open a cattle gate and enter a pasture. At the church there are people at the entrance and I head that way for information. I yell up asking if I should enter the field and they signal to the affirmative. Three cows are at the gate move aside to let me enter. I thank them and follow the trail across the pasture and into the woods.

The skies are starting to darken and I am not sure how much longer I need to walk. The enthusiasm I had this morning changed to worry and uncertainty. Would I be sleeping in the woods tonight?

After more than ten hours of walking and the skies darkened into night, I finally exited the woods. Before me stood a massive block building, ominous and foreboding under the dark skies. An ancient gothic monastery, like something you would see in a Frankenstein movie, stood before me, the Real Colegiata de Roncesvalles.

Exhausted, confused and even a bit scared with no idea where Rick and Dave were, I felt truly alone. I had no idea where I would sleep that night. I had not expected to be walking alone. I thought we would walk together like the pilgrims in the movies and videos I had watched. It was the end of the first day walking and nothing like the joyous Hollywood version of the Camino I expected.

Across the path from the monastery, a man was setting up a small tent. I later learned this was for his dog. Dogs are not allowed in most albergue. I learned from him that this was a monastery that served as an albergue. I could stay there for the night. The Real Colegiata de Roncesvalles offers 183 beds divided into three rooms. That's where I would stay whether Rick and Dave were there or not. I could go no further.

I tiredly climbed the stone stairs off the dirt and gravel path towards a few people standing outside a side door smoking cigarettes or just getting some fresh air. They stopped me from making the strenuous climb all the way to the top by signaling to me to go back down. Telling me how to get to the main entrance around back in the courtyard. I descended and found my way around the side of the building and into the courtyard to the entrance. Walking in tentatively, I encountered other pilgrims checking in for the night. I dropped my backpack beside a couple others, relieved to be rid of the weight. Not sure what to do, I observed the other pilgrims to determine my next step. A girl leaving a room to the left saw that I was confused and told me I needed to fill out a card and bring it with me into the next room. She pointed at a table along the wall with a stack of cards and a few pens. The card asked for my name, country of origin and the reason for my camino. The reasons listed included religious, spiritual, adventure, the challenge, and a few others I don't remember. I marked off spiritual. It also asked for your religious affiliation. I marked off Catholic. I went into the next room with the completed card and registered for a bed, dinner at 7PM and breakfast in the morning. They also told me lights out at 10PM and lights on at 6AM with the room vacated by 8:30. Assigned a bed on the third floor, I left the office and grabbed my backpack when I saw Dave coming down the hallway. I was happy and relieved to see him.

Dave led me to an elevator up to the dormitory, a huge room filled with cubicles, each with two beds and a small cabinet at the head of each bed just large enough to hold a backpack. Dave and Rick were sharing a cubicle about ten spots away. I was sharing with Claudio, a man from Brazil, who warned me right off the bat that he was a snorer and apologized in advance. Little did I know then how annoying snoring could be when trying to sleep. I slept so soundly that night I didn't hear Claudio's snoring.

Claudio and I talked for a while about the pilgrimage and religion. He told me he studied many religions over the years, but recently decided to go back to his Catholic roots. He asked if I was going to the Pilgrim Mass at seven. Unfortunately, I did not know about the Mass or I would have selected the 8:30 time slot for dinner. The Pilgrim Mass, a traditional start of the Camino walk, includes a blessing for the pilgrims for safe travels. I hoped the blessing included those not in attendance.

Rick and Dave chose eight thirty for dinner. Par for the course, I was on my own for dinner.

In order to accommodate all the pilgrims, several locations served dinner. When you registered for dinner, a ticket was issued with the location for your meal. I was assigned to a meal room on the outer side of the monastery on the second floor. To get there I cut across the courtyard diagonally and through an arched tunnel, then up the stairs on the right. Atop the stairs was a large terrace with tables for outside seating and the entrance to the restaurant. Inside, the hostess took my ticket and seated me with two frenchmen, Jason and Sebastian. Jason spoke English and translated our conversation to Sebastian when needed.

I learned Jason started his Camino in La Puy and already walked about five weeks before arriving in Roncesville. He pointed out to me that the real Camino Frances starts in La Puy, not in Saint Jean Pied de Port. He was also very proud to point out that it only took him five hours to cross the Pyrenees from Saint Jean. It took me over ten hours. I guess he was in a race, too.

After dinner, I returned to the dorm, chatted a bit with Rick and Dave, then went to bed. Tired from a hard day of walking across the Pyrenees.

CHAPTER FOURTEEN

9/18/2021
Roncesville - Zubiri

At six o'clock, the *hospitalero* turned on the lights and walked the aisle between the cubicles announcing it was time to get up, breakfast at seven, and everyone out by 8:30.

Breakfast in the common room consisted of toast with butter and jam, coffee and juice. Just enough to get started for the day.

Donning our backpacks with the rain covers on, we head out in drizzling rain for another day of our walking adventure. Looking back, I took a few photos of the monastery's exterior. In hindsight, I wish I spent more time visiting and appreciating this historic site.

This ancient monastery has served as a pilgrim hospital and hospice since 1127. Built to assist pilgrims walking through the Pyrenees by King Alfonso the Battler. He convinced the Bishop of Pamplona to permit the construction of this first pilgrim hospice[xviii].

Later, in the 13th century, King Sancho VII (Sancho el Fuerte) built the French Gothic Royal Collegiate Church of Roncesvalles, modeled after the Cathedral of Notre Dame. The tombs of King Sancho VII and his wife, Clemencia, are housed in the Chapel of San Augustine. In the church is a sculpture of the Virgin of Orreaga, a wood carving of Mary and Child. A library at the monastery contains many historic documents and Charlemagne's Chess board. Other buildings in Roncesville around the monastery include a chapel dedicated to Santiago, a Monument to the Battle of Roncesvalles, and the gothic house Itzandegia.[xix]

In between Roncesville and Burguete-Auritz, the next town on the Camino, is the beech and oak Sorginaritzaga forest, also known as the "oakwood of witches." The area is known for witch covens of the 16th century and nine people burned at the stake. During that time, a white cross was erected to ward off evil in the area. This cross is also known as the Cruz de Roldan, the Cross of Roland, to commemorate where Roland may be buried.

Burguete-Auritz became known for a visit from Ernest Hemingway in 1924 when on his way to Pamplona for the Feast of San Fermin and the Running of the Bulls. While there, he heard about and participated in a trout fishing tournament in the River Irati. Hemingway stayed at the Burguete hostel and that evening for dinner, he enjoys trout and a hot bowl of vegetable soup. His experience with the town, the fishing, and the soup is recreated in his novel *The Sun Also Rises*. At the hostel, the soup became known as Hemingway Soup and remains on the dinner menu for current pilgrims to enjoy.

Despite the drizzling rain, the walk through the quaint quiet village of Burguete-Auritz is pleasant. I passed attractive whitewashed buildings with colorful window shutters, colorful flower boxes and red tiled roofs.

Next, I enjoyed a walk through Espinal, another quaint small town with similar whitewashed buildings and window sills adorned by potted geraniums.

Even with the rain, the walk so far has been easy, mostly on a gravel or an asphalt path along highway N-135 and through these beautiful villages. Following Espinal, though, we start a climb up to the Alto de Menkiritz mountain pass then back down for walks through the villages of Viskarret and Linzoain.

Following Linzoain, is another climb to the Alto de Erro. Near the Alto de Erro, I exit the forest to cross an asphalt highway, N-135. Across the road is a food truck and I spot Rick and Dave sitting on plastic chairs at a folding table. I buy a coke, an apple and a banana to get some sugar and extra energy. After ten or fifteen minutes, we are on our way back into the forest.

The rain doesn't stop and the descent to Zubiri from the Alto de Erro mountain pass is treacherous, a steep decline on a loose slippery river rock ravine. Rain water flowed steadily over the exposed rocks. The continuing rain made this section dangerous and tough on the ankles and knees. My walking sticks kept me from falling a couple of times. If not for them, I may have tumbled down the ravine. The uneven terrain caused my heels to shift around in my shoes leading to the one and only blister of my Camino. A dime size blister formed on the bottom right side of my right heel. Fortunately, it drained overnight, but the skin became tender and caused discomfort when walking. In the following days, I tried to avoid unnecessary pressure on my right heel which in turn led to a slight limp and extra pressure on my left arthritic knee. To combat the tenderness, I used a Compeed blister bandage for a few days and doubled up my socks for the extra cushion and to tighten the heel area. In a few days the tenderness dissipated. I continued wearing doubled socks for the rest of the Camino. I also started putting petroleum jelly on my feet. Petroleum jelly is slick and helps reduce friction. The petroleum jelly also keeps your feet from drying out. Dry skin results in more friction.

I am lucky. Dave had blisters on the bottom of his foot for several weeks and Rick had a blister under one of this toes and black toe for most of his Camino. Eventually, his toe nails started coming off even after returning home.

Even though the rain was nasty and the walk uncomfortable, people can find humor in any situation. Walking ahead of me were three elderly grandmotherly ladies, two from Canada and one from Ireland. Talking and laughing, and having a grand time as they made their way down the ravine. One lady, struggling to get around a log on the rocky terrain, snagged her poncho on an overhanging branch. "Shit," she said when the rain cover tore, then I heard her giggle and say, "I said a dirty word on the Camino." I had to smile at the childlike innocence of this grandmotherly figure.

Zubiri is about half way between Roncesvalles and Pamplona. It is the main town in the Esteribar Valley and sits on the Argo River. I crossed the Argo River on the gothic bridge of Puente de La Rabia, the Rabies Bridge. According to legend, medieval farmers believed that animals are cured of rabies, the rage of animals, and other illness by going around the center pillar three times.[xx] They would circle their herd around the pillar to cure them of Rabies and other diseases.

I make my way to the Albergue El Palo Del Avellano, our lodging for the night. It is in a long stone three story building with a small check-in desk just inside the entrance to the right. Near the front desk was a closet for our shoes. Pilgrims are required to remove shoes and store them in a cubby hole. This rule helped keep the albergue free of muddy footprints. To absorb the moisture from shoes pilgrims stuffed them with paper from stack of newspapers beneath the cubby holes. Beyond the reception desk is a large common area with couches, pool table and dining area for guest to enjoy. A wide staircase leads to our bedroom on the second level furnished with bunkbeds. Bunkbeds aren't the most comfortable, but they work for our needs.

Later, while discussing the day's walk, I found out Dave slipped on the ravine rocks, scrapping his left arm. He was fortunate the injury from the fall was minor. I found out weeks later when discussing this part of the walk again that a Camino friend, Linda from Holland, that she had froze up descending the same ravine. Learning this surprised me. Linda had become part of our Camino family and I knew that she

Iturgaiz Bridge leaving Irotz 9/19/2021

was a tough pilgrim. But here, she needed help from another pilgrim to guide her, following his footsteps to the bottom. This was just one section of the Camino presenting a real challenge to pilgrims, especially in rainy weather. Linda's story exemplifies how a pilgrim will help another pilgrim in need.

In our room were several bunk beds and we shared the room with a couple other pilgrims. A friendly Italian man offered us some candy. He didn't speak any English, so I didn't get to know him, but whenever I saw this short stout man walking with a staff a foot taller the him, he always greeted me with cheerful "Heyyy!!"

CHAPTER FIFTEEN

9/19/2021
Zubiri - Pamplona

We have a simple breakfast at the albergue and head out in the rain for Pamplona. Just outside of town we circle around an unattractive industrial zone with a magnesium mining operation. After that, our walk goes through more quaint Spanish villages and through forest as we follow the Arga River.

Shortly after leaving Zubiri I come up on the Abbey of Eskirotz & Ilarratz in the Valley of Esteribar. The Parish Church, known as the Church of Saint Lucy (Santa Lucia), is listed as a UNESCO World Heritage Site.[xxi] The church was closed, but on a table outside the entrance was a stamp for our credentials and a donation box. Rick and Dave were there stamping their credentials. Their backpacks leaning against the building.

I stamped my credential, dropped coins in the donation box, and immediately started up the hill towards Eskirotz leaving Rick and Dave behind. I thought I would get a head start since I knew they would soon catch up and pass me. They called out to me to turn around for a picture. I held both walking sticks in the air like a snow skier raising his poles in celebration when crossing the finish line. This picture was later used as proof they didn't always leave me behind.

I crossed another Roman stone bridge over the Arga River near Larrasoaña know as the *Puente de los Bandidos*, the bridge of bandits. Unlike the positive myth of the *Puente de la Rabia*, this bridge was noted for bandits that robbed pilgrims. From Larrasoaña, I head towards Akerreta. A scene in the film "The Way" with Martin Sheen was filmed in Akerreta at the Hotel Akerreta where he joins a communal meal and meets the character Sarah.

After Akerreta, I cross another arched stone Roman bridge, Puente de Iturgaitz, back over the Arga River when leaving Irotz.

Finally, I cross the Puente de la Magdalena into Pamplona. The Magdalena Bridge is part of Pamplona Riverside Park system, *Parque Fluvial de la Comarca De Pamplona*, running along the banks of the Arga, Elorz and Sadar rivers. At the end of the bridge is a cross with the images of Saint James encircling the base of the cross. I soon pass the massive towering walls of the *Baluarte del Redín*, the Bulwark of the Redín, a triangular fortress. The triangular design allowed cannons to cover all angles.

Pamplona is the first major city of my Camino. I walked the narrow cobbled streets following the scallop medallions placed in the walkway. I walked with a scattered parade of pilgrims heading into town.

I admired the architectural style of the four to six story buildings. The buildings are connected together, but have slightly different roof lines. Each building's facade is painted in different, but complimentary colors. Most have narrow balconies with rod iron railings. Many cafes and shops on the ground floor line the road. I asked a local for directions to the Hostel Plaza Cathedral. Fortunately, I was at the right intersection. He pointed down the street. At the end of the narrow street I saw one of the two bell towers of the Cathedral de Santa María la Real de Pamplona. The hostel was on the left just before entering the cathedral plaza.

Arriving in Pamplona about two thirty gave me time to relax a bit before going out to explore the town with Rick and Dave. It was nice to have time to see the city. The city has a European charm about it and I can see why Hemingway liked visiting Pamplona. He made the town more popular with his novel *The Sun Also Rises* about British and American expatriates visiting from Paris for the *Fiesta de San Fermín*, the Running of the Bulls, held July 6 to July 14. The event features a daily running of bulls through the streets of Pamplona to the bullring for the daily bullfight. The tradition of running the bulls through the streets began with herders moving the animals through town to the city square for sale or for bullfights. The festival is named after Saint Fermin of Amiens[xxii], the first bishop of Pamplona and the city's patron saint. He was persecuted and martyred for his faith, beheaded on September 25, 303 AD.

While exploring Pamplona, we stopped in the Cafe Bar Gaucho for some tapas and drinks. The main kitchen was closed but on the counter were prepared tapas. There was the traditional Spanish Omelette (egg and potato mixture served like a pie), a couple types of bocadillos (sandwiches) on baguette, a french style bread, and a few other options. I order a sandwich with prosciutto ham and a slice of hot green pepper, aqua to drink. I usually drank water or iced tea. The English word of iced tea is not usually understood when ordered as such. You need to order Nestea. Later, in Galicia, I noticed the brand changed to Lipton.

At one point, we end up in the *Plaza del Castillo*, the central square in Pamplona's Old Town. In the center of the square is a raised bandstand with a domed cover. The plaza has a very family friendly atmosphere with children playing and running about the plaza. The Hotel La Perla[xxiii] in one corner, opened in 1881, is the oldest hotel in the city. Bars and cafes line the perimeter of the square with tented or canopy seating outside. Hemingway visited many of these establishments in the 1920s, including the Café Iruña. In the cafe is a statue of the author leaning against the bar. Bull fights were held in the *Plaza del Castillo* until the mid-1800s.

Tomorrow we head off to Puente La Reina. This walk is also about thirteen miles. Rick and Dave leave a couple hours before me to secure the albergue reservation phoned in by the clerk at the Hostel Plaza Cathedral. Due to language barriers, we sometimes solicited the help of our current host to call for us. In this case, we needed his help because the Hostel's web site was only available in Spanish and we were unable to make the reservation online. After the clerk confirmed the reservation, he told Dave that we needed to check-in by two thirty or they may give the beds away. He said we could call them if we were running late, but we didn't want to take a chance since there would still be a language barrier. Many albergue sell out due to the fifty percent occupancy restriction brought on by Covid.

I leave later to mail home my camera equipment and other things to lighten my load. The Post Office doesn't open until eight thirty. Over the last couple days I realized my pack is way too heavy, causing neck pains and making the walk unnecessarily challenging. Except for the couple days in Saint Jean Pied de Port, I haven't used my 35mm camera. It is much easier to use the cell phone while walking. The camera and a few other things I am sending home will reduce the weight about ten pounds.

So, tomorrow I walk alone. Maybe I'll find a walking companion. However, since I walk slowly, most of the peregrinos (pilgrims) pass me by. With lighter weight I may be able to walk faster. I can only hope. I am not in a hurry though and will walk my own Camino. I like to enjoy my surroundings and stop often to take pictures. I took about 150 today.

CHAPTER SIXTEEN

9/20/2021
Pamplona - Puente la Reina

Up at 6AM, we gather our things to head out for the day. By 7AM, we are out of the room and downstairs. Rick and Dave leave for Puente de la Reina. I wait behind for the Post Office to open so I can mail items home to lighten my pack. I set my backpack on the floor in the hostel's reception area, lean my walking sticks against the wall and get a coffee from the kitchen area. I sit on a couch to enjoy my coffee, my backpack at my feet. About thirty minutes later I grab my backpack and head out to find the post office. I have a tourist map of the area given to me by the front desk clerk yesterday. The hostel and the post office locations are circled. Only a few blocks away, it didn't look too hard to find. It shouldn't take too long.

This is the first day I start off completely on my own and I feel a little uncomfortable, a little insecure and maybe a little impatient because I wanted to get my package out and be on my way. Usually the guys are ahead of me by less than thirty minutes. Today, it may be a couple hours. I know it's not good to be too dependent on other people but it can be the easy way out. Just following Rick and Dave was the easy way out for me. I let them plan the walk each day, the distance to travel, the accommodations for each night. I didn't bother looking at the guidebook or at any maps. I just followed the backpacks and Camino markers. Which was fine by me. I didn't want any responsibility. I just wanted to enjoy the walk.

Today was different. Partially because we were in a city, not a quaint rural community with one main road in and out. Usually, we walked together to the edge of the community, then the guys pulled ahead. Pamplona is a large city, not a small hamlet. There are many ways in and out of Pamplona.

Even with a map, the ten-minute walk to the post office took me 45 minutes to an hour. The streets in Pamplona are narrow and run in many directions. It is not a grid pattern. I found it hard to follow the simple tourist map. It took the kindness of non-English speaking locals doing their best to send me the right way. One kind resident actually walked a half block with me to point out the cement stairs leading to the post office, oficina de correos.

I climbed the stairs, pushed through the glass door and walked towards the counter windows. Before I made it to the window, someone instructed me with a pointing finger to pull a number from a machine near the entrance. I turned around, pulled the paper ticket from the machine, and waited for my turn. The postal clerk didn't speak English and I struggled explaining my needs, including the need for a box to pack my items. I showed her the camouflaged fanny pack I used to carry my camera and lens so she could see the size needed. She retrieved the proper size box from a shelf on a side wall. Before I could pack the box she needed to see what I was sending. She saw the spare battery for the camera and indicated I could not send this due to a possible fire hazard. I could only send the battery already in the camera. I stuck the spare in my pocket and put the rest of the items into the box.

I wrote my address on a piece of paper she gave me. I handed it back and she entered the information into her computer and printed the labels. With everything weighed and packed, my package was sent back home for about €44. That evening, I called home and told my roommate Joe to keep an eye out for it.

Now I needed to get back on the Camino and asked several people for directions. The language barrier again made this difficult. Some people did not understand what I was talking about. I wished I paid more attention in my high school Spanish class. My limited knowledge helped me find a bathroom (el baño) or order water (aqua), but that's about it. Despite my best efforts to get my point across, I was often greeted with blank stares or shrugged shoulders. In cities the Camino is not the main focus of the residents. Small hamlets depend on pilgrims for their survival and anticipate their needs. Cities have many other interest. When someone did understand me, they would point in the general direction and tell me in Spanish what I needed to do. Since I couldn't understand the instructions, I thanked them and walk in the direction they pointed, then asked someone else for directions at the next corner. Somehow, I kept getting turned around. Eventually, I spotted the familiar scallop medallion markers in the sidewalk. Relieved to be back on track, I headed on my way with my head down watching for the silver medallions embedded in the sidewalk. All was now good. Carrying a lighter pack and happy to be on my way.

After about fifteen minutes of walking though, I sensed something wasn't right. I thought it might be the lighter pack. I walked for a while longer glad to be carrying the lighter pack, yet something didn't feel right. It took a few moments before I suddenly realized I didn't have my walking sticks. I left them at the albergue. My heart sunk and panic took over. Now I needed to backtrack, to find my way back to the hostel. I hoped they were still there. I needed the walking sticks for support on steep climbs and descents. Again, I struggled to get directions I could understand and often turned the wrong way down the narrow cobbled streets looking for the cathedral I knew was just a few blocks away, but obscured by the buildings. It took me another hour to find my way back to the Hostel Cathedral Plaza. I was really getting frustrated with this new delay.

The hostel was locked. I knocked, but nobody there. Then, I thought of the code they gave us at check-in. Fortunately, the code for the door still worked and I could enter the lobby. Hope came back when I saw the walking poles were right where I left them. I grabbed them and left.

About every ten feet, scallop shell medallion markers in the sidewalk guide the pilgrim's way. I am on my way again, following the medallions until, suddenly, I didn't see any more medallions. I looked around, walking in different directions to see if I missed a turn. I didn't see any more medallions. I was lost once more, feeling frustration and some panic. Looking around, I spotted a young lady standing on the corner across the street waiting for the traffic light to change. Wearing a backpack, I knew she was a fellow pilgrim. I hoped she could get me back on the Camino. When the light changed, I crossed the street and asked her if she could point me to the Camino. I explained how I couldn't find any more medallions and didn't know which way to go. She looked at me, smiled and pointed up to a blue sign hanging on the light post with the Camino Scallop Shell logo and a yellow arrow pointing in the direction she was headed. I had been walking with my head down looking for medallions in the sidewalk when I needed to look up.

They say that "the Camino provides" and today God gave me Laura to save my Camino. A very special person with a kind heart living in London but originally from São Paulo, Brazil. She too had some issues walking and stayed in Pamplona an extra day to rest her muscles. Without her I may have never seen the sign. I was too focused on looking for the medallions in the sidewalk. I could have roamed for hours more, but I was saved by God and Laura.

I asked if I could walk with her for a while. She kindly agreed. Laura's muscles were still sore, even after a day at rest. So, we navigated the confusing streets of Pamplona together. We made a wrong turn when we misread the direction of a yellow arrow. Seeing we were pilgrims, a city worker corrected us when we started to walk past him. We made our way past the University of Navarra, through the suburbs of Pamplona and finally back into the countryside. We walked slowly together to Puente de la Riena, a thirteen mile trek. At one point, I noticed Laura, still limping, was not using her walking stick and I suggested it might take some weight off her sore hip.

Laura and I walked well together as we climbed about three hundred meters to Alto de Pardon. We watched out for each other. When one needed a break, the other stopped and waited. We also took breaks a couple times for a café con leche or something to eat. We walked slowly and carefully.

We didn't talk much. Just light banter here and there. Laura would answer a question, but kept many thoughts to herself, not really offering up much personal information. Eventually, I did learn a little about her. She was a corporate tax consultant currently between contracts giving her time to walk the Camino. I felt she was a good person with a good warm heart. I also believed part of her heart was hidden or suppressed not wanting to reveal too much. I could tell she was a private person. Yet, I could feel a symbiotic relationship forming during our walk together. I was getting a crush on this beautiful person, enamored with her beautiful smile. Yes, even an old man with arthritic knees can have a crush on someone but in a much different way than when one is young. Perhaps it is inevitable to become attracted to someone when you spend so much time with them. The Camino emits so much positive and loving energy.

Once out of Pamplona, we walked on a gravel path through fields of plowed farmland, dry brown dirt with towering stacks of hay bales, or fields of dried sunflower plants. On the horizon I see a line of windmills across the El Perdón mountain range. The regular winds of the El Perdón range resulted in the first wind farm in Navarre in 1994. It started with 6 windmills. Now, there are 40[xxiv] collecting energy for Navarre. The windmills take advantage of the constant winds to harvest about twenty-three percent of Spain's energy needs. This compares to 8.4 percent in the United States as reported by the U.S. Energy Information Administration[xxv]. With today's concerns about global warming, perhaps the United States should take more advantage of this source of energy.

Seeing the windmills made me think about Miguel De Cervantes Saavedra's Don Quixote. Quixote mistakes a field of windmills for giants and, as an imagined knight, attempts to battle them. He travelled throughout Spain with his squire, Sancho Panza, to seek adventure. Are we seeking adventure on our pilgrimage to Santiago de Compostela? We are in many ways, both internally and externally. We challenge ourselves mentally and physically. We challenge our spirit and we challenge the limitations of our bodies.

Across the fields I see a building that looks like a castle I later learn is the Palace of Lord Guenduláin with the abandoned village of Guenduláin within its walls. There are thousands of abandoned villages or ghost towns throughout Spain many brought on by Spain's Industrial Revolution. Many residents, especially the young, left the small villages for work in the bigger cities and did not return. Some of these abandoned villages in Spain can be purchased for under $100,000.[xxvi]

As Laura and I made the tough climbed to Alto de Pardon, the Hill of Forgiveness, we heard a woman from South Carolina and her daughter behind us chatting away. At one point, I asked Laura if she thought they would ever stop talking. She laughed and told me she was thinking the same thing. We often walked in silence throughout the day. There is just not that much to say to talk for hours on end.

We reach the peak and the life-size metal sculpture of medieval pilgrims, the "Monument to the Pilgrim's Way" created by Vicente Galbete in 1996. The text at the sculpture says "Donde se cruza el camino del viento con el de las estrellas," "Where the path of the wind crosses that of the stars". According to [xxvii], the sculpture represents the pilgrimage from Middle Ages to present. The first figure, a lonely pilgrim, finding its way. Next is a group of three representing the growth of popularity of the Camino. Then, a group on horseback depicts merchants and tradesmen. With a gap between the tradesmen, the next figure shows the decline of the Camino due to unrest at the time. At the end, two pilgrims show us the rise of popularity in the twentieth century.

The talkative lady from South Carolina offered to take pictures of Laura and I in front of the sculpture. When she handed our phones back, she joyfully told us she even captured our wind blown hair. And she was right. My long hair was waving in the wind. Laura, as well, but most of her hair was under her cap. She also told me she wanted to take our pictures together because she was under the impression we were a couple and was surprised when I told her we just met that morning. Maybe we were a couple, if just for the day. I was very comfortable walking with Laura and had grown fond of her over the last several hours. I hoped that I had found a lifelong friend.

Have faith and the Camino and God will provide. Laura is the highlight of my trip so far. When we split up in Puente la Reina heading for our perspective albergue, I hoped we would cross paths again.

CHAPTER SEVENTEEN

9/21/2021
Puente La Reina - Estella

Puente La Reina, the queen's bridge, is the name for the town and the bridge in honor of Queen Muniadona who commissioned the bridge so pilgrims could cross the Arga river. Built during the reign of King Sancho the Great, the Romanesque bridge spans 110 meters and has 6 arches. The pilgrim's path is a cobbled road through the center of town leading to this bridge. Leaving town I cross this thousand year old historic bridge.

Once out of town, I pass a small cemetery protected by an eight foot white wall with an iron gate and an intricately designed iron cross above the gate. Along the Camino, many small cemeteries hold on hallowed ground the remains of villagers and possibly pilgrims. I look through the bars at the grave markers and contemplate how short life can be and about the insignificance of many of our problems. Life is short. Yet, we waste our precious life filled with negative thoughts, intolerance of our fellow man, or concentrating on material things. On the Camino, you will realize how unimportant these material things can be or the danger of negative thoughts. How faith needs to become part of your life. How belief in God and yourself will move you forward.

I move on and am soon walking again through plowed farmland.

Enjoying the beautiful day. Along the way, I am blessed once more, meeting and walking again with the beautiful Laura. This is how I envisioned my Camino, walking with someone and feeling the grace of their presence.

Laura and I come upon a peaceful rest area, the "Olive Gard Zen." A wood sign on the right says "Rest Area / Zona Discanso." We follow along a stone wall and up a few steps to a shaded area with a few tables and chairs. They even had a few books you could read. Relaxing transcendental music plays in the background. Snacks, fruits, and beverages are set up on a table under a crudely built open sided pavilion made with two-by-fours and pieces of plywood for the roof. We take a break to enjoy a beverage and some fruit before continuing on our way. It was a peaceful zen-like place to rest in the shade.

About forty minutes later we go through a tunnel under the highway and then continue our way through more farmland and small villages until we reach Estella. Sadly, Laura and I go our separate ways to our respective albergue.

Estella was established by King Sancho Ramírez in 1090.[xxviii] The city is noted for its palaces, mansions and churches. The 12th century Church of San Pedro de la Rúa built in the Romanesque style, is the oldest church in town. Across from the church is the Palace of Kings, home to the Gustavo de Maeztu 'Museum.

These churches represent a mixture of architectural style due to the time it took to build them. Started in the 12th century and finished in the 14th or 15th century. Different sections of each church may represent the Gothic, Romanesque and Baroque styles. This is the case throughout Europe. Medieval churches took centuries to build and represented the style of different architects.

The first church I see is the Iglesia del Santo Sepulcro (Church of the Holy Sepulcher)[xxix] started in the 12th century. It was left unfinished in the 16th century. The arched Gothic entry way of the north wall has twelve flared archivolts. Beneath the peak of the arch are detailed cravings, including Jesus on the cross, the Blessed Mother, angels and the Last Supper. Inset in the wall on each side of the arch are detailed carvings of the twelve apostles, six on each side. The church was not open when I passed. The church offers examples of the Romanesque and Gothic styles of architecture.

The rest of the day in Estella was quiet and relaxing.

CHAPTER EIGHTEEN

9/22/2021
Estella - Los Arcos

Breakfast at 7AM consisted of oatmeal, toasted bread, coffee, juice, apple and yogurt. I took the apple with me for the walk.

Each day, the sun rises later and we leave in the twilight hour with the cobbled streets of Estella lit dimly by the street lights. Rick and Dave were well ahead of me within a short period of time. I began to walk alone following other peoples 'backpacks to make sure I was headed the right way. It was a method that failed days later, causing me to walk miles out of the way.

There were times when walking by myself I felt a sense of abandonment, as if Dave and Rick didn't really care how my walk was going. I suppose a form of jealousy crept into my thoughts. A form of loneliness when you thought you'd have your friends around to walk with you, like the friends that walked together in the movies. Is this a sign of insecurity? At other times I was glad to be walking alone in quiet solitude with my own thoughts. Walking slowly to keep my knees and the blister on my heel from getting worse. Although parts of me were hurting, I used the time to enjoy the scenery, the sounds of nature and the crunching of the gravel from each step. There is so much beautiful scenery. I stopped often to snap a picture or two on my cell phone. I couldn't help but think how much Rick was missing by walking so quickly. I found out later that his pace today also left Dave behind, perhaps intentionally. Maybe, Dave slowed down intentionally to walk on his own for a while. We all need a bit of separation at times. We all walk at our own pace, sometimes together, sometimes alone, sometimes with friends, sometimes with new Camino friends.

Walking through Ayegui, I passed a monument built into a stone wall of a church. I noticed the stone wall was constructed differently, using what I thought was an Adobe style. The other stone buildings had the stone stacked to form the wall. This looked like stone plastered into the wall and the color was that of red clay. An arched inset in the wall had three crosses on a rock mound, a representation of the three crosses on Calvary. Above the crosses, a white arch. On the arch it said "padre entus manos encomiendo mi alma" (father in your hands I commend my soul). Beneath that, just above the crosses, it said "hoy seras conmigo en el paraiso" (today you will be with me in paradise).

After passing this inspirational monument, I came upon the Bodegas Irache, a winery. On the wall facing the Camino is the Fuente de Irache. This fountain was very different than the other fountains on the Camino I used to refill my water bottle. Like all the others, this fountain offered refreshing cold water. Unlike the others, this fountain had a second faucet offering a taste of wine. The Fuente de Irache is also know as Fuente del Vino, the fountain of wine. The sign above the fountain states "¡ Peregrino! Si quieres llegar a Santiago con fuerza y vitalidad de este gran vino echa un trago y brinda por la Felicidad." (Pilgrim! If you want to get to Santiago with the strength and vitality of this great wine, have a drink and toast to Happiness) According to another plaque, the fountain was inaugurated in 1991 to continue the tradition of the Benedictine monks. The Fuente de Irache is a popular stop for peregrinos offering an experience unique to the Camino.

Across from the Bodegas Irache is the 8th century Benedictine Monastery of Santa Maria de Irache and the Iglesia de Santa Maria la Real de Irache.

In the distance, atop a mountain outside Irache are the ruins of the Castillo de Monjardin. The castle overlooks the town of Villamayor de Monjardín. Many of the stones from this castle were use to build the Ermita San Esteban.

The remainder of the walk to Los Arcos is relatively flat through woodland, fields and vineyards. As I walked through the wooded path I occasionally stopped to pluck half a dozen or so wild blackberries to enjoy. They were sweet and juicy, quite tasty and refreshing.

Walking alone today I often thought how I missed walking with Laura. Most of the time we walked in silence. Yet, she was a pleasure to walk with. Just having her around felt good. I was fortunate to have someone so kind to walk with me. Her sore muscles hurt as well so she needed to walk slowly, too. We had empathy for each other as we struggled up and down the hills. We walked well together.

The last time we walked together, I noticed she wore earbuds throughout the walk, listening to music. I had sent my headphones back home with the camera to reduce weight. We were walking quietly for a while, when I finally asked what type of music she liked. She is open to anything, she told me. Had seven hundred songs on her phone set to shuffle. I learned she likes rock from the 90s, blues, and jazz. In fact, she went four years in a row to the New Orleans Jazz Festival. She knew I was from New Jersey and mentioned Bruce Springsteen's performance at one of the festivals, especially enjoying a set he did with Dr. John. Bruce Springsteen, if you didn't know, hails from the New Jersey shore.

Walking along vineyards again, I looked around to see if anyone was behind me before pulling a bunch of ripe purple grapes from a vine. I felt guilty in a way because I was stealing. I didn't have the owner's permission to take those grapes, but they were delicious and thirst quenching. I thought no one would know I took the grapes until I looked at my hands. My fingers were purple. I'm sure my tongue was too. Evidence of my crime. I used a little drinking water to rinse my fingertips.

A little while later, now out of the vineyards, I met Rachel, a wonderful Asian lady from Canada, carrying a red umbrella for shade. We were walking through an area with only a few trees. Rachael is doing the Camino with her husband who, she said, was far ahead. She told me she didn't mind that he was ahead. I mentioned my friends were up ahead, as well. When I told her I lived in Florida, she said she was a little jealous because it's too cold for her in Canada. She actually moved from Montreal to British Columbia because, according to her, that's the warmest area of Canada. Unexpectedly, she volunteered that we were about 2 km away from Los Arcos. I was glad to hear. I was getting a little tired. Today, though, was relatively easy because we walked along flat roads through flat fields. Rachel and I walked together for five minutes or so before I pulled ahead. She walked slower than I did. I seldom met people that walked slower than me.

Los Arcos sits on the banks of the river Odrón. The town features the Iglesia de Santa Maria in the main square. Construction of the church started in the 12th century and completed in the 18th century has a mixture of Baroque and Gothic architecture.

I made my way through town to the Albergue Casa Alberdi, also known as Taxi Los Arcos since they provide taxi service for the Camino. Rick and Dave were sitting at a table out front. A small white dog was laying on a white plastic chair outside the entrance. I set down my pack and sat to rest a few minutes before Rick showed me the way to our room. I followed him through the beads hanging in the doorway. I was told the beads help keep the flies out but allow the breeze to pass through. We went through the front room, then back out a side door to the backyard and up a stairway to a patio. There was a table with chairs, a couple of lounge chairs, and a clothesline strung between the post of the patio overhang. Two guest rooms opened up to the patio. We were in the room to the right. I put my bag on a bed. Rick told me the bathroom and shower were back outside to the left. This shower and bath was shared with the other room. I went through my usual after walk routine, shower and change, then went back downstairs to sit with Rick and Dave to enjoy a Nestea.

It wasn't long before I spotted Laura approaching and my mood brightened. The sight of her lifted my heart. By the way she was walking though, I could tell she was suffering some pain. She hobbled her way to our table. We greeted each other with big smiles and I introduced her to Rick and Dave. She told me all her muscles were sore and had a blister on her left foot. I felt bad for her. We all have painful days and can empathize with another's pain, especially if you like that person. She is a trooper though and I knew this would not keep her from making it to Santiago. After a few minutes chatting with Rick, Dave and I, Laura moved on to get checked into her albergue and attend to her blister.

After sitting for a while, I decided to take a walk about town. I became fascinated with all the old wooden doors of the ancient buildings along the cobbled streets. I took photos and thought about creating a photo album about the Doors of Spain.

I ran into Laura again at a supermercado when I went in to buy snacks for the following day. I liked bringing fresh fruit and snacks to munch on while I walked. I asked Laura if she wanted to walk together again the next day. Although she was wearing a mask, I saw the smile in her eyes. We usually start our walks early each morning, about 6:30, before sunrise. This was too early for her, so to walk with Laura, I agreed to leave at 7:30.

CHAPTER NINETEEN

9/23/2021
Los Arcos - Longroño

Dave and Rick left at 6:30 and I waited for Laura at the table outside the albergue. I didn't mind waiting. The guys are always ahead of me anyway and this was an opportunity to walk again with someone whose company I enjoyed. Walking with Laura was more important to me than keeping up with the guys. I also believed Laura was happy to have someone walk with her. I thought how nice it was for her to help me out of Pamplona. Seeing her after her rough walk yesterday, I wanted to be chivalrous, like the Knights Templars charged to protect pilgrims, and help her out of Los Arcos. Not that she needed any help. She could very well take care of herself. This was just a thought that floated around in my thoughts.

The sun was coming up as we walked through flat farmland, some plowed, some with rows of grapevines. The early morning walk offered blue skies with a scattering of wispy clouds.

We walk through a quiet street going through Sansol, stopping for a break at the Tienda - Colmado, a small cafe in a stone building. The counter, just inside the door about three feet, blocked access to the rest of the room. Outside the entrance were a red card table and two plastic chairs under a rod iron-barred window. Next to the window hung an old wooden wagon wheel flanked by clay flower pots. There were a couple clay pots on the ground. All of the plants looked like they needed attention. I enjoyed a ham sandwich. Laura had a café con leche and a Spanish Tortilla.

After our break, we continue on to Torres del Rîo where we come upon the Parroquia Iglesia del Santo Sepulcro (Church of the Holy Sepulcher). The church is different than other churches I've seen with an octagonal floor plan. On each side of the octagonal center section are cylindrical sections. The left side higher than the main building, the right half as high. Atop the left tower is a bell supported in a metal frame with a metal cross at the top. In the past, a lantern in the center peak guided pilgrims on the Camino. The church is known as a funerary and many pilgrims are buried in the grounds around the church. The shape of the church suggest Mudejar influences and the style is known as Mudejar Romanesque[xxx]. The design is similar to the *Iglesia de Santa Maria de Unate*. Both are believed to have a Templar connection.

On the way out of town, I pass a small stone-walled cemetery. An iron gate secured the cemetery. The inscription on the gate reads, "Yo que fui lo que tu eres, tu seras lo que yo soy," (I was once what you are, and you will be what I am). I wondered if this was a pilgrim cemetery.

Walking again in farmland, I passed a Camino stanchion. At the foot of the stanchion were a pair of black boots. Occasionally, people leave worn out boots and shoes or uncomfortable boots and shoes at Camino markers. This walk is tough on shoes and feet. If your shoes are causing blisters or other issues it is best to be rid of them.

Near Bogota we pass a small stone building with a colorful tile plaque on the side depicting the Blessed Mother and Child. *Nuestro*

Señora del Popo (Our Lady of Poyo) scrolled across the top and *Bendice al pueblo de Bargata, protege a los peregrinos* (Bless the people of Bargata, protect the pilgrims) at the bottom. Just past the hermitage are stone steps leading to a stone alter.

The walk through this area has several ascents and descents with spectacular views of the Spanish farmlands with olive tree groves and vineyards. We will soon enter the Las Riojas region of Spain noted for it wines.

Approaching Viana, we stop briefly at a small six-foot by eight-foot shoddy-built wood shack on the forest trail with Bar Casita Lucia stenciled on the front panel below the wood countertop. Across from the wood shack are a wooden bench and couple of card tables with red plastic chairs displaying the Estella beer logo. As we rest, I snap a photo of Laura wearing her purple windbreaker, light tan cap, sunglasses, and her beautiful smile.

The town of Viana and the bell tower of the Church of Santa Maria are seen on the horizon from the hilltop. When we arrive, we walk through a stone archway to enter the town. Above the archway is a banner celebrating Viana 1219 - 2019 with an eight-hundred-year history. The typical narrow streets of the medieval town lead us pass the Gothic Parroquia de Santa Maria de la Asuncion. On the tympanum above the door is a relief of the Virgin with child with an angel on each side. Above that in a dome inset is a scene of the three crosses at the Crucifixion with the blessed mother praying at the foot of the center cross. Below that, the body of Christ is carried away for burial. Other detailed reliefs, too numerous to describe, adorn the building.

Outside of Viana, we walk through a passageway and find graffiti, a scallop shell wishing pilgrims a Buen Camino. I usually don't photograph graffiti since I don't wish to promote the defacing of public properties or gang activities, however, this shell rendering was colorful and welcoming. I took a picture with Laura standing beside the artwork, then she used my phone to take my picture.

From here, we walk along a gravel path through farmland until we reach the main road into Logroño. The gravel path follows the road and soon we reach the Ebro River.

Laura and I crossed the bridge over the wide Ebro River to enter Logroño, a town vibrant with activity. We were out of the country and back in a city. In Logroño, Laura helped me once again. Using the GPS on her phone to direct me to my hostel, Pensión La Bilbaina - Albergue Longroño in the city centre. Laura walked with me following directions on her cell phone before needing to split off for her own albergue. She gave me last minute instructions and then headed on her way. I was sorry to see her go. It's curious how quickly you can befriend people on the Camino. Some more than others.

The albergue was just off a street lined with eateries and bars with indoor and canopied outdoor seating. The street was busy with many people enjoying the evening for dinner, drinks or a stroll in the comfortable weather. A few blocks away a band played in a courtyard or square between the buildings for the festival of San Mateo (Saint Matthew) celebrated each year on September 21.

I was about to turn a corner onto the street with the albergue when I spotted Rick and Dave at a table enjoying a beverage. I sat with them for few moments to enjoy an iced tea and then Rick walked with me to the albergue. I'm glad he did. It would have been hard to find. The entrance was just a door set back in one of the downtown high-rise buildings, just a small sign hanging outside. I walked up four marble steps to the double doors decorated with stained glass windows. The small foyer inside had black and white checkered floor tile and a marble staircase. I carried my pack up the staircase to the reception area on the second floor to sign in and get my credential stamped. Our room was at the end of a hall. There was a shared bathroom for our use.

After a shower and change of clothes, I used the Internet in the hotel and my phone to find an Orange Store, a local telephone provider offering prepaid plans. I went back to the corner bar to let Rick and Dave know I was heading to the Orange Store before they closed at 7PM. Over the last five days finding the albergue at the end of each day was a real challenge without GPS. It was difficult communicating with locals for directions. As helpful as they tried to be, I often did not understand them and they did not understand me.

I headed out using a screenshot of the storefront and address when asking for directions. I found someone that spoke English to help me on my way until I saw the lit orange frame around the door to the store. After stumbling through the conversation with a couple store employees, I managed to get a prepaid card for 28 days and 65 Gigabits of data for twenty Euros. Since 28 days ended before the end of the Camino, I asked about renewing the data plan. I would need to visit an Orange Store again to renew, they told me. This seemed inconvenient, thinking I could renew online, but decided not to worry about it until closer to the end of my 28 days.

I went back to the corner cafe bar, but Rick and Dave were no longer there. I walked up the busy street looking at the outside seating and inside the different restaurants to spot the guys, but couldn't find them. I texted Rick to find out they were at an Irish Pub. This was a little funny to me since Rick and his wife Lisa were partners in an Irish Pub and Restaurant in Orlando. Maybe he was looking for some familiar foods.

On my next Camino, I may decide to stay an extra night in Logroño to enjoy the city for more than one night, to be a tourist for a day. The city is rich with the flavor and history of Spain.

Logroño is the second largest city on the Camino Frances and capital of the province of La Rioja. La Rioja is known for its vineyards and fine wines.

The Church of Santiago el Real is the oldest church in Logroño, begun in 1513. It has two statues of Saint James. One portrays Saint James as a pilgrim, the other is an equestrian statue of Santiago Matamoros, Saint James, the Moor-slayer. The church was used as a meeting site for the Municipal Council and where the important council documents were stored.

Next to the Church is the Fuente de Santiago, the pilgrims fountain. A place for pilgrims to stop and rest.

There is the famous monument of the "*Juego de la Oca,*" the "Game of Goose" beside the Albergue Parroquial and the Church of Santiago el Real in La Plaza de la Oca. The monument is a rendition of the game board using mosaics on the ground. The initial game, some believe, was created by the Knights Templar as a spiritual map played for spiritual awareness. Others believe the game contains secret codes of the Knights Templar disguised in the game. The map in La Plaza de la Oca features different stages of the Camino, such as Burgos, Sahagún, Ponferrada and more. The Game of Goose is a race game along a spiral track with 63 spaces, movement along the track determined by a roll of one or two dice. Starting on the outside, players move towards the board's center. Landing on a goose allows the player to move an equal number of spaces again. Landing on a space marked with a bridge allows the player to cross to a specified location on the board. A penalty space results in moves backward or a lost turn. If you land on the one space marked with a skull (death), you return to the start. To end the game, a player must have an exact roll. If the number is higher then the number needed to reach the end, they go back to the beginning to complete the roll count.

CHAPTER TWENTY

9/24/2021
Logroño - Najera

Last night I purchased a prepaid SIM card for my cellphone, 65 Gigabits of data for 28 days for 20 Euros from the Orange Store, a cellphone service company in Spain. Now I have access to Google maps, email, Facebook and more through the data plan and wireless access in an albergue or restaurant. It will help keep me connected. Especially the access to Google maps to help find my housing each night. Until now, I walked around asking locals that rarely spoke English for directions to an albergue they may not even know existed. Some Camino purest suggest leaving all electronics behind, including a cell phone, but there is no sense in making your life miserable on purpose. Mine was miserable at points, like when I was lost in Pamplona or when looking for the albergue each night without a map. It is nice to have GPS, which I will soon appreciate even more.

We left about 6:45AM and made our way through the streets of Logroño, around a traffic circle at the Plaza Alferez Provisional, a few more turns, a couple more traffic circles and eventually into the Parque de la Grajera y la Barranca on the outskirts of Logroño maintained by the Logroño City Council. The Camino goes through this beautifully landscaped park which includes a reservoir, bird observatories, a playground, picnic areas, sport fishing, and a club house with restaurant overlooking the reservoir.

Walking through the park is a little tough today due to soreness on my right heel from the blister I acquired a couple days ago. The tenderness makes it difficult to walk confidently. I'll get through it. Just need to slow down a little bit more and continue doing my Camino slow walk.

Since I haven't seen any markers or yellow arrows for a while, I turn to Google maps for the first time, glad that I now have GPS. I'll soon see if Google maps is correct and puts me back on track to the yellow arrows or Camino markers. I make a left as instructed by Google. I don't see any other walkers but just hope I'm going the right way, putting a lot of trust in a mapping program. I know I'll get to the programmed destination; it just may not be on the Camino path. Google just knows I'm walking. It doesn't know I'm walking the Camino de Santiago.

Finally, after winding my way through a warehouse and industrial area, Google leads me to a dirt path through a vineyard. Still no markers but at least walking on a dirt and gravel path feels better than walking past warehouses.

A few minutes later this path ends at a T with another gravel path. I see a couple backpackers walk the cross of the T and know I have returned to the Camino. I missed the turn for the correct path but Google kindly set me right. I turn off Google maps to save power on the phone. I will just follow the path. I'm on my own again.

I stop for a moment at a Camino marker stanchion to take off my jacket because it was getting a little warm. I removed my backpack and lean it against the stanchion when I hear Dave's voice behind me.

"How did you pass us?" He repeated the same question several times. "How did you pass us?" It gave me great satisfaction. I guess Google did me right by showing me a shortcut, putting me ahead of Rick and Dave. I was ahead of them for a change. But, as expected, before I even had my backpack back on, they pulled ahead of me again. We are on our separate ways to the Santiago Cathedral.

There was a section of today's walk on a ridge about twenty feet up that ran along a highway. A chain-link fence on the right protected the pilgrims from the drop off to the highway. Twigs and sticks intertwined the chain's links to form crosses as memorials to loved ones. Some were tied with colored ribbons or had a card or note attached. Crosses serve as memorials to loved ones throughout the Camino de Santiago.

From here I saw the back of a huge billboard in the shape of a massive bull. I found out it was an Osborne Bull, the Torro de Osborne, originally used to advertise the Osborne Company's Veterano brand of brandy.[xxxi] The marketing campaign began in 1956 with the Azor advertising agency with the bull designed by Manolo Prieto. The first billboard was placed in Cabanillas de la Sierra (Madrid). At one time there were over 200 billboards throughout Spain and the Torro de Osborne soon became an iconic symbol for Spain. Today there are about 90 bulls. The first bull was about four meters high, but grew as high as 14 meters as Spain's billboard laws changed, moving the advertising further from the road. A 1962 law required billboard advertising to be 20 meters from the roadway. In 1974, this was increased to 50 meters. Hence, the growth of the bull's size.

From this raised walkway above the highway, I saw the town of Navarrete with the bell tower of the Church of Santa María de las Asunción, a parish church in the historic district, dominating the skyline.

Entering Navarrete, I pass the ruins of the Antiguo Hospital de Peregrinos, San Juan de Acre founded in 1185.[xxxii] Just past the ruins is the Don Jacobo Winery.

Making my way up a hill I come upon the Bocateria cafe with Rick sitting at an outside table drinking a café con leche. As soon as I walk up he told me Dave had to go to the hospital, taking a taxi back to Logroño. Seems he had blood in his urine. Rick thought it was because of dehydration and went on for several minutes about how he warned him about not drinking enough water. I hoped he was okay and that it would not end his Camino. If he can, he will take a taxi to meet us in Nájera. Later, I learned the doctors thought he passed a kidney stone. Tests showed no infections and his urine was clear at the hospital. That was good news. He can continue his Camino.

Leaving the small hamlet, we passed a small cemetery. I stopped to take pictures of the entrance and I went inside to photograph the ornate gravestones. I believe this cemetery used the facade from the Antiguo Hospital de Peregrinos for the entrance. Rick was in front of me and I watched him plow ahead pushing himself to maintain his pace of about 3 mph. I don't even know if he saw the cemetery. I believed he was missing so much by walking so fast. Not sure why his goal was to push so hard to reach Santiago. My goal is to see Spain, to take pictures of Spain's beautiful landscape and buildings. But, Rick is walking his Camino and if he wants to push himself that is his choice. I don't have to understand, I just need to let him be who he is. I know he is enjoying his experience and that is the important thing.

Leaving Navarrete and walking through vineyards, I thought about Laura again. I thought about her several times during this morning's walk. I missed walking with her. For some reason I felt a connection with her. I hoped we will see each other again.

If she decides to stay an extra night to recover from her difficulties of yesterday, I'm afraid I may never see her again. We will be distanced by days of walking. Like relationships with many friends in the past, life will move on as we walk a different Camino. The friendship remains, but will change as distance and time move along.

Yet, I continue to think about her and hope she is okay. I hope she discovers and finds what she's looking for on the Camino de Santiago. I believe we all discover something of ourselves along such a long journey.

When I started the Camino, I didn't see a need for self-discovery. Wasn't something I worried about. I have known who I am forever. I have always been me. Someone not easy to describe in simple terms or a simple label. Physically and psychologically, I am who I am, an ever-evolving me. I don't know if Laura was walking for self-discovery, but that's the best time to find yourself, when you are not trying. People learn quite a bit about themselves walking many hours by themselves and testing their resolve. I look forward to whatever self-discovery I may encounter.

More grapevines line the path and I pull another bunch off a vine. While munching on grapes, I saw a truck with field workers harvesting these grapes. Feeling guilty again for stealing grapes, I held them down to the side cupped in my hand so the workers wouldn't see them. I don't think they cared but that's what I did.

My fingers sticky from eating the grapes, I wasted some water to rinse off my hands. I didn't want my phone getting sticky or the screen smeared with grape juice.

On this stretch, I met Elizabeth from Sarasota Florida and walked with her for a short while. She told me she had also lived in the Catskills and other areas. Also a slow walker, I enjoyed her company. When I stopped to remove another layer of clothes because it was getting warmer, she moved on. I'll see her down the road. That's how it goes. Not everyone stops when you do. Another reason why I missed Laura. She stopped when I did and I stopped when she did so we could continue walking together.

About six or eight feet in front of me a small animal ran across the road. It was quick and I didn't get a good look. I thought I saw a white patch on its back, I'm tempted to think it was a skunk, Pepé Le Pew perhaps, but that would be in France, not Spain.

I did see Elizabeth again passing through a small corner park. Pacing back and forth in front of a picnic table she asked with panic in her voice, "have you seen Les. He is an older man with a white tee-shirt. I heard that he became sick or had an accident." She was very concerned about a fellow pilgrim she befriended. Pilgrims build relationships of all kinds and the family grows as we cross northern Spain. Unfortunately, I couldn't help Elizabeth find Les. I didn't recall seeing anyone with that description and didn't know who he was at the time. I did meet Les a few days down the road and many times afterwards. He is a good man, walking to bring attention to the need of a young child with a terminal illness. Trying to get people to donate on a GoFundMe web page to help the family with their expenses. When I mentioned Elizabeth's concerns, he told me he did have some issues, but got through them. He had fallen at the totem pole rest stop where the man was giving out cold watermelon slices. When he looked up, he saw a priest and thought he was dead, he joked. The priest helped him to his feet.

I crossed a wood slat pedestrian bridge over the rio Yalde. In this area, it is just a small stream flowing around river rocks.

I walked for a few more hours before entering Najera for the end of this day's walk. Our reservation for Najera is at the Albergue Nido de Cigüeña.

Nájera sits along the River Najerilla in the La Rioja region with vineyards and monasteries. Nájera was once the capital of the Kingdom of Navarre.

Another tale about Roland occurred outside Nájera. It is a tale of a 3-day battle between Roland and the Islamic giant Ferragut,[xxxiii] lord of the Castle of Nájera. Legend says that Roland was challenged by the giant when he passed through Nájera on his pilgrimage to Santiago. Ferragut was known for his superior strength and skills in battle. After two days of battle there was a short truce. During this time, the giant admits that his only weak point is his navel. Remembering this, Roland stabbed him in the navel when the battle resumed, killing the giant.

The Monasterio de Santa Maria la Real is a monastery of Cistercian nuns built near a natural cave. The site of the monastery is based on the legend of The Hawk and The Partridge. In 1044, the Navarrese king Don Garcia IV was hunting. His falcon entered a cave chasing a partridge. When the king entered the cave to find his falcon an image of the Virgin Mary appeared with a lit lamp, a bell, a vase of flowers, the falcon, and the partridge at her feet. King Don Garcia built a monastery and pilgrim hostel at the site. Santa Maria la Real is also known for its Royal Pantheon, the burial site of numerous Navarre kings.

CHAPTER TWENTY-ONE

9/25/2021
Najera - Santo Domingo de la Calzada

Dave decided to walk with me for a while today. Rick walked ahead. It was a pleasure to have someone with me. Not as pretty as Laura but still a good person.

Dave is cool and I can relate to his viewpoints since I am from the same area of New Jersey and also politically conservative. At times, I believe Rick had a hard time understanding that smart ass, wise-cracking attitude of some people from the metropolitan New York/New Jersey area. Plus, Dave is politically conservative and Rick is liberal or left of center. I am politically conservative, or right of center, and having grown up in New Jersey, I understood Dave's viewpoint and attitude. The New York/New Jersey attitude can be blunt. For a lot of people from there, being a smart ass is a way of letting people know you like them. Giving someone a hard time or a rough teasing is a sign of friendship. I could be wrong. Maybe we are all just A-holes. I have personally toned this down a bit since moving to Florida over forty years ago, but I still reserve the right to revert back to my New Jersey attitude when needed.

On the way out of Nájera, we pass the monastery before climbing up a hill to start walking through the countryside again. Woodland, vineyards and fields are the scenery for the day.

Azofra, a village we pass through on our way to Santo Domingo de la Calzada, is located in the valley of the river Tuerto, also known as Valle de Cañas. The village is believed to be of Arabic origin. The etymology of the name is derived from an Arabic word as-suxra which means "the tribute" or "to work for the lord."[xxxiv]

Entering the village, there is a Y in the road and I follow the markers to stay on the Camino. Dave and I met up with Rick and we stopped for breakfast. After breakfast, the walk through town is quiet. Rick pulls ahead but Dave stays back to continue walking with me. We pass a small community park with benches and shade trees. Nobody is in the park. Before leaving town, Dave and I enjoy a café con leche. I am soon back walking on a gravel path through country fields. Then, I begin to climb again.

Going around a curve in the climb, I discover a golf course, the Rioja Alta Golf Club. Built into the mountain in the middle of nowhere it is an unexpected find on the Camino. The sign on the clubhouse entrance welcomes pilgrims by offering *Precio Especial*, Special Price in the Cafeteria Restaurante.

I'm not a golfer, but imagine this is a tough course. I also wonder how many pilgrims had the energy to play golf after walking for hours or was this course busy with local golfers. It's hard to tell how far civilization is when walking through the mountain's paths. A five-hour walk may only be a twenty minute drive.

Today, for some reason, while walking through the woods, I am being tormented by flies buzzing around my face. The annoying insects make me feel like the cow in a picture I took in the Pyrenees. A dozen or more flies crawling around his eyes and nose. Maybe I'm starting to stink like a cow and that is why they are flying around me. They just won't leave me alone. I need a cow to get their attention and get them off of me.

The walk is soon on a dirt path through kilometers of a quilted patchwork of undulating farmland up to a horizon with blue skies and

Rick, Dave, and John in Grañón
Photo taken by a passing pilgrim using my iPhone

fluffy clouds. A wonderful day to enjoy a walk through the countryside. Eventually, I come over a rise to see, far ahead, the redroof tops of Santo Domingo de la Calzada. Seeing the town ahead is uplifting but deceiving with an hour or more walking still to go. The pilgrims ahead of me are just specs.

Santo Domingo de la Calzada sits on the banks of the Oja River and is named after the saint that maintained the area for pilgrims. He lived as a hermit in the forest where the town now stands and saw how hard it was for the pilgrims. Wanting to help them, he built a bridge across the Oja River, a pilgrim's hospital, and a church. He dedicated his life to maintain the roads to help pilgrims pass through the area. The church no longer exist, but his efforts were honored with the building of the magnificent Cathedral of Santo Domingo de la Calzada.

I follow Dave up the cobbled street to the Carpe Viam Hostel. We rented a nice size room. There were four single beds in the room. Much more comfortable than climbing up onto a bunk bed. The fourth bed was extra space to hold our stuff. The room was on the second floor with a window that opened up to a decorative narrow balcony with a view of a cobbled street below. A pot of red flowers hung on hanger screwed into the brick. Rick took advantage of the plant hanger and hung his stinky sneakers outside to air out for a while.

On a wall inside the hostel's entrance is a poster in a gold frame of a long-bearded pilgrim with a staff. At his feet on each side is a hen. Below the figure are the words "*donde canto la gallian despues de asada,*" "where the hen sang after roast." This is in reference to a miracle attributed to Santo Domingo de la Calzada (Saint Dominic of the Road). The story tells of a German 18 year old boy traveling on a pilgrimage with his parents. The innkeeper's daughter at the hostel makes sexual advances to the boy which he rejects. She gets angry and to get even with him, she hides a silver cup in his pack. After they leave she tells the authorities the cup was stolen. When leaving the area, the boy is searched by authorities and the silver cup found. The boy is immediately found guilty and hung for his crime. When the parents examine the body still hanging on the gallows, they hear his voice saying that Saint Dominic had saved his life. They go to see the magistrate to let him know their son is still alive and to have him taken down. The magistrate, who was eating dinner at the time, laughingly told them their son was no more alive than the rooster and hen on his plate. At that moment, the two birds jumped up, grew back their feathers, then crowed and danced around the table. In memory of the miracle, a rooster and hen, supposedly decedents of the originals, are kept alive in a pen at the Cathedral of Santo Domingo de la Calzada.

CHAPTER TWENTY-TWO

9/26/2021
Santo Domino de la Calzada - Belorado

I photographed the Cathedral of Santo Domingo de la Calzada in the early twilight on the way out of town. The church is not open at this early hour and I could not visit the rooster and hen they kept in the church. I missed another opportunity to explore this sacred path.

Just before crossing the Puenta de Santo Domingo, I pass a tiny chapel, the Ermita del Puente. On the arch above the doorway it says *"Costeada por Dña Cecilia Marin,"* financed by Ms. Cecilia Marin. Inside the arch, above the door, is a relief of a tree with a rooster and hen at the base. Under the tree is says, *"Año de 1917."*

I cross the bridge and am back to wheat fields with scattered giant stacks of hay bales.

Today was a good day walking with cool temperatures and no rain. Finally, after nine days, we walked together the entire day. Rick and Dave slowed down. My knee was feeling better and I walked a little faster to keep up. We had time to stop and enjoy the scenery, the sunflower fields and much more.

Several Spanish speaking pilgrims passed us playing Johnny Cash's

Ring of Fire. Obviously, American country music fans. Dave suggested they check out The Highway Men, a musical group with Cash, Willy Nelson and Kris Kristofferson, all big country music stars.

The walk was going well with only an occasional reminder from my knee to pace myself, a little throbbing pain, especially on the uphill climbs. All in all though, my knee treated me better then I expected.

After walking many kilometers through farmland, I see a domed bell tower in the distance, the Church of San Juan Bautista. We soon enter the village of Grañon, the last town in La Rioja. At the village entrance is a wall with cartoonish renderings of Camino life. One is the *Ermita Nuestra Señora de Carrasquedo*, a donativo parochial albergue named for the patron saint of the village, the *Virgen de Carrasquedo*. Next is a traditional bearded pilgrim wearing a brown rob and hat bearing the Templar cross. He also wore sandals and walked with staff and gourd. Then, there is a modern female pilgrim sitting on a bench reading a map. She wears hiking boots, shorts and a sun hat. Her walking sticks lean on the wall behind her. There is a coat of arms for Grañon, a castle tower, two crosses on each side, and a horse at the base of the tower, on a light blue background encircled with a white border. Below the coat of arms in the white border is the name of the village. At the top is a scallop shell.

There is a break in the wall for stairs, then the wall continues with more paintings: the back of a pilgrim with a backpack and staff, a sign pole with arrows pointed to Santiago, Logroño, and Roma with kilometers listed, and finally, a pilgrim walking through wheat fields with mountains in the background.

We climbed the stairs to an aqua blue food truck at the top. Rick waits in line to order us café con leche and pastries. Dave and I wait patiently at a table nearby. It is a long line.

While we enjoyed our break, Dave became serious for a few moments. "You know, John. You may want to get a knee wrap. I can

Bell Tower at the Monasterio de San Juan de Ortega
Illustration © Gene Russell, GRussell Creations

see in your face it is hurting." "I guess you're right," I answered then quickly forgot the conversation.

After the break, we are back to the trail. Before leaving Grañon I take pictures of the Renaissance Church of San Juan Bautista, the parish church and a municipal albergue. I learned that this albergue provides lodging to pilgrims for a donation, whatever they can afford. For a small donation, pilgrims get the privilege of sleeping in the bell tower on mats on the floor. Maybe bunk beds are not so bad after all. I might be missing out on the fun, but I do appreciate a bed over a floor.

Once through Grañon we are back on the Meseta walking through a patchwork of plowed farmland and dried sunflower fields. Again, massive stacks of hay bales from the fall harvest dot the expansive landscape.

The next village we pass through is Redecilla del Camino, the first town on the Camino Frances in the autonomous community of Castile and León. It is a small community of about 150 people. The streets were empty, like most small communities we passed through. The only people you saw were other pilgrims and the cafe operators. We stopped for a café con leche. Am I getting addicted to this drink? It is a good way to get a little caffeine charge before moving on.

I passed a small garden. On a wooden sign in yellow lettering, it says "Huerto Ecologico," ecological garden. We then passed the Romanesque Iglesia de Nuestra Señora de la Calle, Church of Our Lady of the Street.

We checked into the Hostel B in Belorado. A nice place, well kept and very friendly with a very accommodating host. It looked like it may have been recently renovated. With a marble tile exterior wall it look more modern right from the start. Inside was welcoming with wood beam ceilings. A young lady at the desk just inside the entrance to the right checked us in. I assumed she was the owner's daughter. These small hostels were usually family owned and operated. Across from the desk was a small pantry with bottles of wine, pasta, jar fruit, can tuna and other packaged items for pilgrims to purchase. Past the front desk is the dining area for breakfast and dinner. We purchased the pilgrim's dinner and breakfast.

After going through the routine of showering and getting cleaned up from a day's walk, we went out to explore the area. We found an open cafe in the town plaza. Rick and Dave ordered a beer and I ordered my usual Nestea.

Almost immediately, a drunk old man sitting outside the cafe entrance started laughing and speaking to us in Spanish. I shrugged and told him, *no hablo español*, I don't speak Spanish. I didn't understand what he was saying. He continued laughing and talking to us. I tried to ignore him. He was drunk and it became obvious he had a low regard for us and was making fun of us. Whether it was a low regard for pilgrims, Americans, or just us was hard to tell. While we sat at a table outside the cafe enjoying our drinks, the old man started laughing again when he saw Rick pull out money to pay for our drinks. Rich Americans, he laughed disdainfully. That's the only English he spoke. The rest of his ranting continued in Spanish.

I took some pictures of the rose window in the cathedral tower across the plaza. When I looked back down I caught the eye of a young girl sitting with another girl at a table in front of the next building. Both girls were dressed in dark goth clothing. The one that saw me take a picture had metal in her nose and eyebrow and was giving me the finger. I smiled. I guess she thought I was taking pictures of her and her friend. Dave later suggested that they were hookers. I didn't consider that at the time. I just thought they were young girls trying to look cool. Looking back though, they could have been working girls.

Rick turned his chair around to face the entrance to the cafe, because he thought the young guys at a table behind us might be working with the old man to rip us off. He actually turned so his back was to them, but he could see their reflection in the cafe window. The situation seemed to be bothering Rick and he was positioning himself to keep an eye on them without being obvious. He was preparing to defend himself, if needed. Dave suggested that he calm down. He didn't think there was an issue or didn't want anything to escalate. I wasn't worried about it at all. I was enjoying the show. Someone did eventually come over and admonish the old drunk man. Don't know what was said, but the old man did calm down.

We decided to head back to the albergue to relax before dinner. While we waited, Dave looked through the Wisepilgrim app guide book on his phone. He did this to review our stops for the next couple days. He noticed that Wisepilgrim app warned of the poor neighborhood attitude toward pilgrims in this town. It suggested keeping away from the town's main square.

Annika, the friendly young German girl with blue eyes and blond hair I met in the Pyrenees, sat with us during communal dinner. She had walked slowly with me for a while. It was good to see her again. She is a vibrant and cheerful young lady. At dinner, it came up that she was a little tired and had a rough walk that day. It turned out that yesterday was her birthday. She stayed up late and partied too much, she said. Ah, to be young again.

Annika is an intelligent person with a young European viewpoint on the world and somehow the conversation turned political. She told us the feelings of many German people about our past President

Trump and how they hated his rudeness. They don't necessarily support Biden but do believe relationships between our countries will be much friendlier. We also discussed the difference in healthcare systems and tax codes between our countries. There is a trade-off between universal healthcare and other social programs and tax rates. Many Americas believe we have the best systems for our people, but much can be learned from democratic European countries. I believe in low taxes, but also know that a major medical emergency can wipe out a life's savings. Should one of the richest countries in the world have citizens suffer due to a lack of healthcare? Should the choice be between healthcare and poverty or a lowered standard of living? Something to think about as we move forward in the American experiment.

Heading back to our room, I grabbed a couple of ear plugs from a basket on front desk. We all snore and they would come in handy.

I laid in bed propped up on a pillow looking through my phone at the photos of the day. At the end of each day I post photos on my Facebook page. Dave reminded me that some of his family signed up for my blog at www.johnseegers.com. I had not posted recently and were asking him when I may be posting an update. I explained it is easier to post photos on Facebook than posting on the blog. That night, I posted to the blog requesting that followers visit www.Facebook.com/jfseegers for updates. I suggested they do a friend request, as well. I'll be happy to except the friendship request. Some people don't use Facebook, but I also didn't want to spend my Camino on the Internet. I told myself, I would update my web site and blog when I got home.

About 22 more days to go.

CHAPTER TWENTY-THREE

9/27/2021
Belorado - San Juan de Ortega

Our breakfast was excellent, much more than expected. Usually, we just got a piece of toasted bread with butter and jam and a café con leche. If we were lucky, breakfast included orange juice. Today we had a buffet with a selection of meats, cheeses, fruits, hardboiled eggs, yogurts, breads and pastries. The host even made us fried eggs and bacon. It was a hearty meal and set us off right for the day.

After breakfast Annika asked the attendant to fill her water bottle with hot water to take with her. The attendant didn't completely understand and began filling the bottle with tap water. I saw Annika was having a hard time explaining what she wanted so I was happy to translate with the little Spanish I knew. Annika wanted hot water, Agua Caliente. She wanted to use it later for tea. My high school Spanish classes saved the day.

Today we leave Belorado without our backpacks. We decided to use a company called JacoTran to ship them to the next overnight. Giving it a try and hoping they end up in the right place on the other side. The cost was 5 Euro each. It felt weird not having a backpack strapped to my back when I started walking. It felt too easy. I did have my pockets packed with my needs for the day. I had a banana, an apple, two bottles of water and a large candy bar. Hopefully, without a backpack today's walk will go a lot easier and relieve some of the stress on my knee. I did have my walking sticks. They were not sent ahead with the bags. I looked forward to another good day of walking. We head to San Juan de Ortega.

The weather is cool with no chance of rain. The winds blow strongly and threaten to steal my hat. I lower my head walking into the wind to keep the hat from lifting off my head. I have already chased my hat into plowed farmland like a character in a slap-stick comedy.

When I passed through Villafranca Montes de Oca I saw a donkey with leather saddle bags on its back, a few articles of clothing thrown atop the saddle bags. He was tied to a tree in the road medium across from a cafe. I did not see who owned the donkey. He was probably inside the cafe. Later, I found out from Rick that the man walking with the donkey was wearing a kilt. I wondered how he handled the donkey going through cities like Leon. Going forward from here I noticed many piles of donkey poop. Along with yellow arrows and scallop shells, I now had donkey poop to guide my way to Santiago.

After a couple hours walking, I felt my knee getting a little tight and slowed down. I can usually get two or three hours of good walking before my knee stiffens.

I considered how I used to think about traveling to Europe. I wanted to visit Germany or Lithuania, the countries of my family roots. My father's family heritage is German. My mother's is Lithuanian. I also considered Great Britain and France, both deep-rooted in our American history. I never thought about Spain as an option, even though they have a history with America's beginnings, as well. Now, traveling through Spain, I am falling in love with the country. It is a beautiful country filled with a gorgeous landscape, fascinating history and the wonderful hospitality of its people.

I learned walking slowly along the Camino is a blessing for me. Although my knee occasionally hurts, I enjoy the walk, enjoy the country and the people I meet. For me, enjoying the journey is more important than reaching the destination. It's the experiences leading to the destination that make the trip enjoyable and memorable, truth that applies to your journey through life, as well. Enjoy your walk through life, even if your knee hurts. Enjoy the world around you and the people you meet. That is what the journey is all about.

As I walked, I thanked God for my arthritic knee, for slowing me down to enjoy the countryside, for giving me an opportunity to photograph His wondrous works.

Walking slowly along the forest path, an older gentleman came up alongside me. He seemed to be struggling so I asked how he was doing. Not well, he told me. I suggested he take it easy, to walk more slowly. He replied gruffly, if you walk slowly, you don't get anywhere. He moved on still struggling. I begged to differ with his opinion but didn't have the opportunity to debate his hypothesis. I later found out his name was Barry, a publisher and author from Holland. A few days later, we did walk together, slowly, and had a great discussion about his history in the publishing business and being an author. I'll get back to this later.

Along the forest trail I came upon a rest area decorated by carved totem poles and a stand filled with fruits, beverages and pastries. As I approached, a man walked up to me, handed me a piece of ice-cold watermelon, and wished me a Buen Camino. It was a perfect treat at just the right time, sweet, refreshing and delicious. I came upon a donativo stand.

Donativo stands provide free drinks, fruit and pastries for weary pilgrims through the kindness of locals. A box is usually available for a voluntary donation. Each pilgrim determines how much to donate, if anything at all. You come across these stands every once in a while on the Camino. Some use simply built wooden structures; some just work out of a cooler. I came across one set up in an open-sided barn in the owners backyard. The barn and yard decorated with Camino memorabilia. Lawn furniture in the yard, cushioned couches and chairs under cover in the barn.

I joined Rick and Dave already at the rest area. I sat on a log across from the stand to rest and enjoy my cold watermelon and a drink. Regular breaks keep you going, giving you a chance to recharge. But you don't want to break for too long or you will stiffen up, making it harder to get started again.

I mentioned the grumpy old man I met and his odd remark about getting anywhere. Rick told me the old man said he saw me. Many fellow peregrinos knew we were traveling together without walking together because they saw us together at night.

After a few minutes break at the donativo, I move on. There is a sense that you shouldn't stay too long anywhere or you will never get anywhere. Maybe the grumpy old man was right.

A short while later, I came upon a man lying on a slight incline in the grass on the side of the gravel path propped up on his elbow. I asked if he was okay. He told me he pulled a muscle but will be alright, just wanted to rest for a while. I started on my way, walked about ten yards, then stopped. I realized I just couldn't leave him there. I should do something to help him. I walked back and offered to carry his backpack explaining that we had shipped ours ahead so I could carry his if it would help. He said it would not be necessary and moved to get up. I reached out a hand to help him up.

We walked together very slowly, slower than I usually walked, to San Juan de Ortega. His name is Eldad. A biblical name, he told me. He was from Israel, twenty-four years old, a student studying to be a social worker and currently working with teenagers. Another good person I met on the Camino. He was doing a partial Camino to Burgos with the time he had.

I arrived at our accommodations for the evening, Hostel El Descanso de San Juan. Next to the hostel is the Monasterio de San Juan de Ortega built in the 12th and 13th century in late Romanesque style.

Rick and Dave were sitting at a picnic table in front of the hostel when I arrived. I sit down and asked Eldad to join us. He was going on to the next town, but knew he needed to rest again. I went inside, had my credential stamped and ordered a pizza and Nestea for lunch. When the pizza arrived, I offered a slice to Eldad. He asked if the meat on the pizza was pork. I didn't know. I told him it was salami. He took a slice.

After a short rest, Eldad got up to leave. Before he did I gave him a business card I printed for the trip. I asked him to keep in touch and let me know he was okay.

Rick took this time to lighten the load in his backpack by setting items on the table for other pilgrims to take, items he realized were not needed. The *hospitalero* said they would be kept available for other pilgrims.

After lunch I walked around to take pictures of the monastery. When I went inside there was a man putting pamphlets on the pews so I asked if there was a service tonight. A pilgrim's Mass will be offered at 6PM.

At 6PM I returned to attend the pilgrim's Mass. Although the service was spoken in Spanish, I was able to follow along with the familiar Catholic ceremony I remembered from going to church during my twelve years of Catholic education. A part of the service is dedicated to the pilgrim blessing with the priest pointing to different attendees to tell him where they came from. People from around the world.

I felt good after leaving the Mass. I felt the good intentions and sincerity of the Pilgrim's Blessing. I am glad I experienced the Mass. I had missed the pilgrim's Mass in Roncesville.

While I was gone, Dave asked the hospitalero for help finding accommodations for September 30 in Hornillos del Camino. Dave was having a hard time confirming reservations because of the language barrier. Hospitaleros were usually very helpful when needed to translate for us. He was happy to call and confirmed arrangements. Perhaps the Pilgrim's Blessing was already kicking in.

The food and the hospitality of this albergue was excellent. The sleeping quarters, however, were tiny and we started referring to it as our submarine hotel. The room had bunkbeds with only a couple feet between the bed and the wall. There was hardly any space to put your backpack. The bath and shower was also tiny. In fact, it was so tiny that when I bent over to wash my feet, my butt would press against the handle and turn off the water. At first, I thought the water flow was on a timer. Some albergue do this. But it was my butt, not a timer turning off the water.

San Juan de Ortega is a very small community of about 20 people. The hamlet named after Juan Velazquez who later became known as

San Juan de Ortega.

San Juan de Ortega or Saint John the Hermit, a disciple to San Domingo de la Calzada, planned routes and built bridges to ease the pilgrim's way through the region. San Juan also built an Augustinian monastery later known as the Monastery of San Juan de Ortega.

His dedication to pilgrims resulted from his own pilgrimage to the Holy Land. On his return journey home, his ship wrecked. Praying to San Nicolas de Bari, a prominent Bishop in Turkey, he promised to dedicate his life to fellow pilgrims if saved. He chose the mountains around San Juan de Ortega for his work building the Saint Nicholas chapel to honor the bishop.

If you are fortunate enough to be in San Juan de Ortega on the Spring Equinox or Fall Equinox, you will experience an amazing event. Around 5pm a ray of light will shine through a stained-glass window to light up one of the Romanesque capitals of the temple moving across three carvings from the Annunciation to the Visitation then to the birth of Christ.

CHAPTER TWENTY-FOUR

9/28/2021
San Juan de Ortega to Burgos

Each morning when we start, I find myself racing to keep up with Rick and Dave. It starts before we even leave the room. They are often out of the room before I even have a chance to go to the bathroom. Once I start walking, I realize how foolish that is and slow my pace. I take the time to look around. See the beautiful country, the landscape, the medieval buildings, some well preserved, some crumbling. I try to find a beautiful scene or subject to photograph.

Leaving the small community of San Juan de Ortega, we were back on a dirt track and into the woods within a few minutes. Up ahead I see three workers in bright yellow jumpsuits clearing tree limbs with a chain saw and powered pole saw. I nod at one of the workers as I walk by.

For the most part, the Camino paths are well maintained, often by volunteer organizations supporting the Camino. This concept started centuries ago with the example and efforts of Santo Domingo de la Calzada and San Juan de Ortega. The Knights Templar protected the pilgrims' passage and built hospitals to aid them. Recent efforts include Father Elias Valiña Sampedro who promoted the Camino in the 1980s and his efforts led to it becoming a UNESCO World Heritage site in

1993. Father Elias also began marking the trail with the yellow arrows we now use to stay on the correct path. Today, groups of associations and members of the Associations of Friends of the Camino de Santiago are non-profit organizations dedicated to the restoration and maintenance of the Camino de Santiago.

While walking I went to scratch my beard, to stroke my beard. I was surprised that it was wet. It had collected the dew.

I departed the woods and returned to farmland. Across fields I saw the triple bells in the tower of the Iglesia de Santa Eulalia in the small community of Agés. When I walked through, I saw many crumbling buildings held together by large, warped beams. It appears the builders had to work around the weathered timber. It was like having a home designed by Dr. Seuss.

The crumbling buildings, especially the doors, offered classic photographic opportunities. I come up on a barn with the green doors framed in weathered timber that contrasted well with the fading tan or peach stucco. The red tile roofs completed the Spanish rustic look. This scene has an interesting addition, a photo of a sheep framed in the old wood. At first, you may think it is a window.

As I approached Atapuerca, a man I recognize from dinner last night came up on me. He is a young man in his twenties from Germany. His name was Alex. Annika pointed him out to me last night at dinner at the hostel. She thought he was writing a book, too. When I asked him about it though, he said he wasn't quite sure. He moved on since he was walking at a faster pace than me. It didn't seem like he wanted to talk about it. I wish him the best if he is planning a book. I'm finding it is a big project putting the experiences of the Camino into a coherent book. There is so much information to process and then put forward for an enjoyable read.

Just outside Atapuerca a sign with a rendering of a prehistoric man announces *"yacimientos paleotologicos patrimonio de las humanidad,"* a paleontological site of human heritage. Across the road from this sign are large stone structures reminding me of Stonehenge I had seen in photos. Near Atapuerca is a cave called Sima de los Huesos (Pit of the Bones) where human fossils 300,000 to 600,000 years old were found, the oldest known hominin in Western Europe. Atapuerca is a World Heritage paleontological site. On my next Camino I hope to take the time to visit these caves. The caves are a couple kilometers from the Camino path. To visit them you need to take a detour.

Rick and Dave were enjoying a café con leche at the Cantina de Atapuerca and I joined them for a mid-morning break.

In a small park near the cafe, a concrete bust of the prehistoric man with a spear sat on a pile of rocks. The sign at the bust stated *"Hace mas de 300,000 anos el humbre ya vio amanecer desbe este mismo lugar"* (More than 300,000 years ago, man already saw the sunrise from this same place). A spider web beaded with the morning dew hung between the spear and the face. A wonderful opportunity for a photo.

Much of the walk today and most days is through woodland, plowed farmland and dried sunflower fields. Mountains in the distance hinted at the walk coming up. The communities I walked through are small and quiet except for the pilgrims stopping at cafes.

I had a lot of time to think while walking. Having walked a couple days with Laura and being smitten by her made me think about relationships. Wondered why I chose to live my life on my own. Maybe because it's been that way since I was young, on my own. When I was young, my thoughts about relationships were selfish and centered on sex with a young man's raging hormones. I made it about me. What I wanted. Not one hundred percent about what I wanted, but a lot. I was selfish. Now, I think about relationships differently. It is about caring for another. Finding someone that you care for. Finding someone that you want to make happy, not caring about your own needs, or at least, not as much. It is about companionship.

There is a certain magic in the air when walking the Camino. I felt that magic when I walked with Laura. I know that may sound foolish, but walking alone again I think about how she made my walk enjoyable. She is intelligent, determined and kind. I would like to know her better. I hope that I will see her again along the Camino. Maybe try to keep up by email when the Camino ends.

Besides Laura, another common theme that keeps popping up in my mind the last few days is that I have no hatred in my heart. I believe hatred and anger just sucks the energy out of you. The Camino is about love, companionship and caring for one another, caring for fellow pilgrims. We should live our lives learning how to care for other pilgrims throughout the world. We are all walking our Camino through life. It would be good if we walked our daily life Camino the same way we walk to Santiago de Compostela.

When you get lost in your thoughts, you can get lost on your walk. I got lost for a few moments as I came upon a small town. I thought I was following the yellow arrows. Must have missed one. Thank goodness for other pilgrims that sent me in the correct direction. Another example of pilgrim helping pilgrim. Now, I'm on my way again. In some ways though, I think it is good if we get lost every once in a while. It creates an opportunity to learn about yourself, your ability to see a need for a change. Like a lost sheep making its way back to the fold. It feels really good to be back on the right track on the Camino or in life.

My metaphysical thoughts are interrupted when I begin to feel some pain in my right groin area. Still have about three hours to walk so I hoped it will work out and go away. Eventually, it did. For both young and old, the Camino can come to an abrupt end with an injury. It is important to listen to your body and my body started talking.

My discomfort did go away. I was able to walk it out. But when I caught up to Rick and Dave at a cafe in Atapuerca it was nice to have a break.

Dave mentioned during our break that the trail had a choice up ahead with one path avoiding a walk through the industrial area on the outskirts of Burgos. Dave's guide book warned, however, that the intersection with the alternate path was not well marked. The book was right. Luckily, Dave spotted the faded yellow arrows painted on the street at an intersection. One was pointing left, the other straight ahead. The paint was very faded and easily missed. The guide book suggested going to the left, which we did. This took our walk around a very small airport. I didn't realize it was an airport until Dave said something. It was just an empty field to me. I didn't see any planes.

As I walked the dirt path along the airport's fence line on my right, Rick and Dave started pulling ahead, so I made my way into Burgos without them. I don't recall how many times we entered our destination together, very few that I can recall. It's not necessary that we arrive together. I know that now. After all, I am walking my own Camino. However, I did think it would be nice if we walked into Santiago together. I was hoping we would.

I walked through the suburbs and a short time along the busy streets of Burgos. After a few turns, I crossed the rio Arlanzón and into a beautifully shaded park running along the river. Joggers and bicyclist enjoyed the wide paved walkway. Although I was tired, a very peaceful walk along the river led me towards the historic district.

I followed my GPS back across the rio Arlanzón. I passed a statue on a pedestal on an island in the road, a monument to Rodrigo Díaz de Vivar, better known as El Cid, a national hero of Spain from the 11th century. This imposing warrior with a long flowing beard rides his war horse, a white stallion called Babieca, welding his raised sword with his long cape flowing behind him. El Cid, his wife Doña Jimena, and other prominent Spanish leaders are entombed at the Burgos Cathedral.

I soon arrive at the Hotel Mesón El Cid, an elegantly appointed hotel built in 1961 that overlooks the Burgos Cathedral Plaza.

In order to sleep three people, Rick booked a suite with a king bed in the bedroom and two single beds in the large parlor area. Rick took the private bedroom. He said so we could have a break from his snoring. We all snore, but Rick's is definitely the loudest. I recorded it one night so I could play it back to him later. Dave and I each had a single bed. It was good to have Rick in the separate room. I finally had a good night's sleep. Just kidding, Rick.

We were living it high on the hog here at the Hotel Mesón El Cid. The suite had fine wood furniture, comfortable beds with a real mattress, not just a pad. A spacious room with a breakfast table with two chairs, a cushioned side chair and nice decor made the stay enjoyable. The marble tiled bathroom was also spacious, a delight when compared to the submarine size showers at some hostels. At the end of the parlor room, wooden paned doors opened up to a grand view of the cathedral plaza and the amazing Gothic architecture of the Burgos Cathedral with its intricate spires reaching to the sky.

The suite even had a private reading nook. In the hall leading to the master bedroom, across from the bathroom, a small enclosed balcony served as a reading nook. A small wood bench in a wood-paneled room with wood-paned windows on three sides illuminated the room. It was only big enough for one person to have some private reading time.

We took our turns for the daily end of walk shower and change to clean clothes. We stuffed our dirty clothes in Rick's laundry bag and set out for the laundromat just down the street, according to the desk clerk. Rick was the man when it came to laundry. Each day he found out where we can wash our clothes, then made his way with our laundry. He said he used the time to put together his daily Facebook video. For me, it was another opportunity to take the easy way out. We found the laundromat easily, right next to Bar La Babia, an establishment we visited a few times in the next couple days.

Bar La Babia is across from the Albergue Municipal de Peregrinos de Burgos. As we sat outside the bar, we watched fellow pilgrims walking down the street to check into the albergue. I am happy Rick booked us into the Hotel Mesón El Cid. Much nicer than suffering through shared dormitory rooms in an albergue.

At Bar La Babia, we had the pleasure of sharing drinks with Ludwig and Stefan, two gentlemen from Germany, recounting their tales of previous Caminos. Ludwig walked the Camino with his daughter in 2010 after her break up with her fiancé. She was to walk with her fiancé, but when they broke up, Ludwig offered to walk with her, starting the Camino in Germany. This year Ludwig set out alone. Stefan is walking for two weeks, adding to his previous Camino walks. He started where he left off last time.

Many of the people I met started alone. A few, like Bob and Cindy and Phil and Marcel, walked as couples. Then there was Rachel with her husband, who was far ahead. Once I saw a group of 5 or 6 college age young adults walking together. When I saw them they were laughing and having fun like I saw in the movies. I was jealous. The Camino, however, is a personal journey for most people, a time for self-reflection and discovery. I was not as brave as the solo walkers. Although most of my walk throughout the day is alone, I did not start the Camino on my own and may not have started without the encouragement from Rick and his infectious enthusiasm for this adventure. I am glad I started this journey and at the end of the day we are together. I look forward to arriving in Santiago in about 20 days, hopefully together. Perhaps on my next Camino, I may go on my own.

Burgos Cathedral 9/29/2021

CHAPTER TWENTY-FIVE

9/29/2021
Burgos

Since we were staying an extra day in Burgos to rest, there was no hurrying this morning. Nonetheless, we were all up early, creatures of habit.

I was resting on my bed when Rick called me over to the window that overlooks the cathedral plaza. He showed me a picture he had just taken, a spectacular view of the sun rising behind the Gothic spires of the Burgos Cathedral. I immediately grabbed my iPhone and took a couple shots, but because I was a minute or so later, I believed that Rick's picture came out better. The colors of the sky just a little different and, to me, better.

Burgos is a big city filled with Medieval architecture and art. The Burgos Cathedral is magnificent and we are fortunate to have a hotel room overlooking the cathedral plaza. I spent a good portion of the day walking around and photographing the buildings and statues throughout the Burgos historic district.

I sat at a table outside the Bar La Babia eating the pilgrim menu (salad, half roasted chicken, potatoes, and ice cream for dessert). The bar is across the sidewalk from Albergue de Peregrinos. As I ate, I watched pilgrims walk up the slight hill to check in to the albergue for the night. I could tell most were tired from the long walk. I watched hoping that I would see Laura come into view. She had replied to yesterday's email that she would be in Burgos today and would let me know when she got here. When my meal was finished, I left with Rick to get our credentials stamped at the Burgos Cathedral.

I heard from Laura and we agreed to meet in the Cathedral Plaza. When I went out to meet her, the plaza was being set with an art display of life-size silhouette figures of pilgrims. I watched from the top of the stairs thinking it would be easier to see her from there. I spotted her and descended the stairs to greet her with a welcoming hug. We walked around for a while then stopped for something to eat. It was good to see her. Little did I know, this was the last time I would see her. I was hoping to see her again in Leon or Santiago, since we would be staying extra days in those cities, as well.

CHAPTER TWENTY-SIX

9/30/2021
Burgos - Hornillos del Camino

This morning Rick and Dave left the suite in Burgos to head down for breakfast before I was ready. When I arrived and tried to sit with them the waiter stopped me to tell me in English that the breakfast was for hotel guests only. I pointed to Rick and Dave and said "I'm with them." I thought he understood so when they waved me over, I walked away from the waiter and sat at the table next to them. When I came back from the buffet line with my food, the waiter came up to me again repeating the same thing. Breakfast was for hotel guests only. I said I am a guest. I don't know why he didn't understand or believe I was a hotel guest. I ignored him and ate my breakfast. Rick later went up and explain the situation, showing a copy of the hotel bill for three people. I suppose the waiter understood, but he did not come over to apologize. I believe that he should have apologized for the misunderstanding. I probably should have, too. I did walk in with an attitude since I was upset about being rushed again. I walked over to Rick and Dave like I owned the place. "I'm with them" is usually understood. I later learned from Bob and Cindy that they were questioned as well. Bob and his wife were sitting a couple tables away. He was wearing his walking clothes, a bandana on his head, well-worn shoes, shorts and shirt. He looked like a pilgrim ready for his walk. He did not look like the senior tour group in the restaurant that morning wearing their well-kept stylish attire. I suppose pilgrims do look a little out of place in a higher end hotel like this and I suppose they may have had pilgrims trying to sneak in for a free buffet breakfast.

During the walk out of Burgos I realized I wasn't following my own mantra that everyone should walk their own way to Santiago. I was getting angry about feeling rushed every morning and considered breaking off from Rick and Dave to book my own albergue and be on my own. We didn't walk together anyway and today, they didn't even wait so we could enjoy breakfast together. Again, I didn't understand the constant hurry.

Since hotel reservations were made through October fourth, I will stay at the accommodations already booked, but then planned on making my own reservations for the rest of the Camino. I can walk at my own pace and stay where I want to stay. I'm sure we will see each other regularly maybe staying in the same albergue. I was tired of feeling like a third wheel and this was the way it needed to be.

I continued walking alone and at my own pace. I wasn't trying to keep up with Rick and Dave. They walked together sharing memories of their time in the Air Force. These were memories I didn't share. I needed to walk my own pace with my own thoughts and memories.

You don't always walk alone when you decide to walk alone. You meet fellow pilgrims and enjoy their company for short periods. I walked a few moments with a Dutch lady that spoke English very well. When I commented about how well she spoke English, she thanked me and replied that in Spain and in Germany, the television shows and movies are dubbed in the country's language explaining why it is difficult for many to understand English. On the rare occasion I saw a television, I did notice American shows are dubbed. I don't expect everyone to speak English. That would be presumptuous. In fact, I'm impressed with the number of people that do speak English. In the hospitality business it is nice to try to communicate with your guests. I often made a feeble attempt to use the little Spanish I did know and tried to learn new words as we made our way through their country. It made me think of the experience Rick had at an Orange store yesterday when the young girl helping him became frustrated and upset. She stated that Americans needed to learn Spanish before coming to Spain. She knew how to say that in English to get her point across. I understand the frustration she felt. I hear many people in the hospitality industry in Florida wishing our international tourist spoke English. But, in a service economy, these frustrations must be contained, as difficult as it may be. It can take years in the service industry to perfect the customer service attitude. Not everyone is cut out for the field. She is young and perhaps will learn more patience in time. Sometimes people just have bad days.

An hour or so later, while walking through a small town, I found the arrows confusing about which way to go. When I saw Bob and Cindy again resting on a bench, I asked them to point me in the right direction. They walked the Camino three previous times so I trusted their directions. They said I was going the right way. The arrows were winding me through the side streets of the small hamlet. Taking me off the main road. I suppose this is done on purpose to let pilgrims experience their town since I ended up at the main road.

A few minutes later a local walking her dog, seeing my hesitation at an intersection, directed me to the correct path. Gracias, I told her.

Walking through the small village of Rabé de Las Calzadas, I stop to take pictures of a small church, the Ermita de Nuestra Señora del Monasterio. The church is situated at a fork in the road, a dirt road passing each side. After taking pictures of the outside, I went inside to look around. To the left sat two church sisters. When I saw the nuns, I pulled out my credentials to get a stamp. While one sister stamped my credential, the sister on my right motioned for me to lean forward and she put a small necklace with the figure of the Blessed Mother on the medallion over my head. Then the sister that stamped my credential took my left hand holding it with both of hers. She started to pray. She hesitated at the end of the first line and looked at me. She said the line again indicating that I was to repeat the words. She said another line of the prayer and I tried to repeat the words I did not understand except for the word Camino. Finally, the prayer was finished. I put a few coins in the donation box across from them on the side wall. I went on my way feeling blessed. I later learned that the prayer blessed my Camino and asked that I light a candle at the tomb of Saint James in the Cathedral in Santiago in honor of their church.

I arrived at Hornillos del Camino, a tiny community dependent on the Camino for survival. The Camino de Santiago is the only road through town and there are just a couple short side streets. The town's name translates to Stoves of the Way and derives from the town's beginnings, a community known for ovens used to bake tiles.

We checked-in to the Albergue El Alfar Hostel about 3PM. We get a room on the second floor with six bunk beds. After we settle in, we explore the town and meet Les at the Bar Casa Manalo off the town square.

I later find a gothic church and photograph the splendor of the inside with dozens of carved figures, several gold gilded altarpieces, buttresses and arches.

We rest for a bit before heading downstairs for dinner. We pass through a small dining room and through the beaded curtained door to a patio out back. Off the patio area was a covered room with a twelve-foot wooden table with a twelve foot bench on each side. For dinner we sat around this table to enjoy a wonderful community dinner that will be one of my fond memories of the Camino.

There were eight of us at dinner. Dave, Rick and I sat on one side of the table. A Dutch couple, a retired man and a boat operator sat on the other side (sorry, don't remember the names). Phil and Mariel sat together at the end. The hostess served plates filled with a paella made with rice, chicken, and pork. She dished from a large wok type pot on the counter along the side wall. Several bowls of mixed salad and baskets of hard-crusted bread were on the table for self-service. There was plenty of food for everyone. A delicious lemon parfait for dessert was the final course.

We already started our meal when a young woman comes hurriedly into the room apologizing for being late. She just arrived at the albergue. To accommodate the new arrival, our hostess brought in another chair and utensils for a seat at end of the table near the entrance. The last to join us for dinner was Marta Marciano, a 34-year-old blues and jazz singer from Italy, full of energy and spunk. She again apologized for running late. She made an impressionable entrance filled with her special energy and infectious enthusiasm. As a blues and jazz singer from Italy, she had a natural ability to entertain.

During dinner we took turns introducing ourselves and telling why we are walking the Camino. I don't remember everyone's reasons. I do remember some. A widowed man walked grieving for his late wife. I told everyone that I hoped to write a book about my experience that might be motivational and of some help for others. The Dutch woman wished that I find the inspiration for my story. When it came around to Rick, he told us he wanted to walk with his deceased sons. Sadly, Rick had lost two of his sons. One of them had visited Spain for a while and loved the country. Marta told us she wanted to walk the Camino since age 18. Her husband did the Camino last year by bicycle.

This was the first time I met Phil and Muriel, a French husband and wife. I saw them often over the next few weeks. They are really good people. Phil always greeted me with a warm smile and an interest in my recent photos. We became good Camino friends and have maintain contact as Facebook friends.

We were getting ready to leave when Rick suggested for Marta to sing a song. She jumped at the occasion and was ready to entertain. She thought for a moment for the appropriate song. Then snapping her fingers gave us an upbeat Jazzy song. Just right for the moment. A surprising treat that complimented a wonderful communal meal with several pilgrims we would encounter many times over the next thirty days. The Camino family was growing.

The Way into Hontanas 10/1/2021

CHAPTER TWENTY-SEVEN

10/1/2021
Hornillos del Camino - Castrojeriz

Woke up at 5AM. Everyone else in the room was still sleeping. I quietly dressed and packed my backpack. Breakfast was available at 6. When I came downstairs the table was already set with prepackaged muffins and bread for toast. I started the coffee machine. When done, I made a cup with sugar and milk. I ate a couple small muffins, drank some coffee, then sat on the couch in the room to finish my coffee, read my email, check Facebook and make my notes.

The others started coming down about 6:30. Rick and Dave came down about 7. Shuffling around, everyone finally found a place at the table. I was standing off to the side leaving table space for the others since I had already had a couple muffins.

Marta was there with as much energy and enthusiasm as last night and greeting everyone cheerfully. Someone asked her to sing for us again. Sitting at the table, she thought for a moment then started tapping her foot and snapping her fingers to an uplifting song for the morning. She rose to her feet and finished with a theatrical arm to the air and a slight curtsy. Marta was made for the stage. You can see she enjoys performing. This time I made a video to post on my Facebook page. I wanted to share her beautiful voice for others to enjoy.

Originally, when I woke up early, I thought about leaving early, before the others got up. I would get a head start and let Rick and Dave catch up with me for a change. I know, childish thoughts. I'm glad I didn't. I would have missed Marta's beautiful song.

We walked along ancient block buildings on both sides of the one main street through Hornillos del Camino. It felt like walking through a tunnel. Overhead, the sky gradually began turning light blue. Once past this row of buildings, I walked along a low stone wall with a view of the spectacular orange clouds of the sunrise. A couple of windmills became visible on the mountain range as the sky lightened.

The dirt and gravel trail of the Camino ran through a wide expanse of plowed wheat fields. Nothing but light brown dirt for kilometers. In the far distance, tiny stick figures, which were windmills, lined part of the horizon. The dozens of windmills appeared to grow as we got closer, the blades turning slowly.

I passed an iron cross about ten foot high covered with an assortment of stickers, most of them faded. A small arrangement of dried flowers were tied about two-thirds up the post.

Barry, walking at a good pace today, passes me. As he did, he told me his belt broke and needed to string together shoelaces to make a new belt otherwise his pants would fall down. At times, resourcefulness is important to keep moving along the Camino.

After Barry passed, I ate a nice juicy peach I bought at a mercado yesterday. The juices began dripping down my beard. I wished I had a napkin but didn't so I guess that's what my pants are for. I just wiped my beard with my hands and wiped my hands on my pants. They will get washed eventually, in a few days, hopefully.

About three hours into the walk I saw Hontanas and the bell tower of the Iglesia de la Inmaculada Concepción which dominated the skyline of red-tiled rooftops. I made the steep descent into the town past a tiny stone church built into the side of the hill. It was maybe ten foot by twelve foot with a stone beehive dome. It was the Church of Saint Bridget of Sweden. Saint Bridget[xxxv] is the patron saint of Sweden and founder of the Bridgittines (Order of the Most Holy Savior). Saint Bridgett was a mystic whose visions of Christ were influential in the Middle Ages.

Just past the Church of Saint Bridgett, the first building on the left is the Albergue Santa Brigida with a restaurant-bar. Rick and Dave were there and I stopped to enjoy a café con leche. After a comfortable break we descended the main street through town past the 14th century church. I took several pictures of the block and stucco buildings, trying to capture the essence of this small medieval community. There was a crooked bench and a slightly curving round red brick chimney that caught my attention. Great photogenic subjects.

About thirty minutes outside of Hontanas is a ruin, a ruble of stone with a solo corner piece of the building, a stubborn remnant that refused to fall.

About an hour later, I walked around a bend and am surprised by the 15th century Ruinas del Convento de San Antón. The road passes under a pair of stone arches with the entrance to the convent between them. A functional part of the complex became the Hospital de Santa Anton Refugio for Peregrinos.

The Convento de San Antón provided care to pilgrims, especially those suffering from Saint Anthony's Fire[xxxvi] or ergotism, a disease brought on by eating rye grain contaminated by the ergot fungus, *Claviceps purpurea*. The name comes from Benedictine monks sometimes using relics of Saint Anthony to cure the disease. Sufferers of Saint Anthony's Fire experience a burning sensation in extremities caused by impeded blood circulation. This can possibly lead to gangrene and loss of limbs. Hallucinations and convulsions are brought on by the pain.

I passed through the convent's ancient arches and follow the road running along the ruins of the medieval convent. This long stretch of paved road leads into Castrojeriz. From the road, I can see the 9th Century Castle of Castrojeriz sitting on a hilltop overlooking the city and neighboring towns. At the base of the hill is the Iglesia de Santa Maria del Manzano.

Walking down the road towards Castrojeriz I saw Bob and Cindi again, fellow peregrinos we meet regularly along the way. He asked where we were staying. I told him the Iocubus Hostel. Bob told me it was a nice place. He was right. It was a nice place.

Rick, Dave and I stopped for a few moments at the Iglesia de Santa Maria del Manzano. A long stone bench is built into the stone wall across from the entrance. I grab a photo of Rick and Dave laying head to head on the bench. I continue photographing the church with is combination of Gothic and Romanesque architecture.

When we arrived at the Iocubus Hostel, we find the lobby entrance locked. We go around to the left and down the stairs and through an iron gate to the restaurant patio in the back. At the bar, we checked-in and the hostess gave us a quick tour on our way to our room, showing us the laundry area, the elevator to the lobby and our rooms. In the lobby we were given instructions on how to get in after hours. Across from the front desk, an elegant wide wood banister staircase led up to the rooms. A three-foot wide paisley designed carpet ran up the center of the eight-foot wide polished wooden steps. A shiny knight's armor stood protectively at the base of the stairs.

We took the elevator to our room. Cleaned up and then Rick took laundry down to put in the machine. Afterwards, we went to the restaurant for a drink and something to eat.

The Iocabus sat on a hill. Castrojeriz is a narrow community curving along the side of a hill. Block stairs led up and down to the different streets that curved around the hill. The restaurant at the back of the hotel had an outside patio overlooking part of the town and the mountains beyond. We enjoyed our beverages while enjoying the view. Then, we took a walk about town. We walked down a street to a small mercado and I bought snacks and fruit to take on tomorrow's walk. We made our way back up the street and stairs to find a cafe bar. At the Bar La Plaza, we saw a man we knew as California and his friend. Rick, Dave and I sat nearby so we could chat with our Camino friends.

California told us about how he prepared for the Camino by walking 2-3 miles with his grandkids twice a week with the goal of crossing the Golden Gate Bridge. He would park at one end of the walk and the kid's mom parked at the other end. I don't remember how far he was from the bridge and how many weeks he trained, but thought it was a cool way to have an adventure with the grandkids.

CHAPTER TWENTY-EIGHT

10/2/2021
Castrojeriz - Fromista

We made our way following the curving cobbled road through Castrojeriz. Overhead, the sky is pink from the rising sun reflecting off the clouds. As usual, Rick and Dave move ahead.

I soon cross a wooden bridge over the rio Ordrilla and along an old Roman causeway leading to an ascent to Alto de Mostelares. If you look to the right just before the ascent you may see the remains of a Roman Mica mine.

It is a steep ascent to Alto de Mostelares. During this climb, I met Katie and Marie. Katie is from California and speaks English. Marie speaks French and very limited English. Somehow, they communicate with Marie's limited English. They are wonderful women walking slowly since both are elderly. Katie has arthritis in her right knee. I have arthritis in my left knee. I jokingly suggested we try walking together just using our two good legs. Then I moved along wishing them a Buen Camino. I don't recall running into them again. Some people you just know for a few minutes. Yet, somehow a bond develops with pilgrims. You wish them well, Buen Camino.

At the top of the Alto de Mostelares is a simple monument, a five by six foot pedestal of stone about six feet high. Atop the pedestal is a pyramid with a flat top, also about six feet high. It is a larger version of the cement stanchion markers along the Camino. A relief of a scallop shell is on the front and back. Beside this monument is an iron cross planted in a pile of stones. This is a small version of the Cruz de Ferro with stones left in memory of others. The sign says "*cruz de la suerte*," lucky cross. On top of the cross is Saint James with a staff in his right hand and a bible in his left.

The view from the Alto de Mostelares is a long and winding dirt road through an undulating valley landscape. The road stretched through a quilt pattern of cut fields and terraced lines of olive trees on the hillsides. The view went on for miles. This is the path I needed to traverse. It seemed to go on forever to a horizon of white fluffy clouds hanging in bright blue skies. To the left I see windmills on distant hilltops.

I descend to the bottom for the long walk across the plowed farmland. During this part of the trek, I had the pleasure of meeting DJ from Alaska and enjoyed walking with her for a few minutes. She was wearing a sleeveless blouse and shorts. When we started this morning, it was 48°. I'm wearing a long sleeve tee-shirt, a short sleeve tee-shirt on top of that and a rain jacket. With all that, I'm still cold. For me, it takes a little while getting used to the cooler weather but for her the weather was perfect. We will be starting out in even cooler weather as we move into October and back into the mountains.

As we walked and talked, I noticed a wrap around her left knee. I considered getting a wrap for my knee. DJ also told me she recently had a hip replacement. I find a commonality in people undertaking the Camino with some physical discomfort. They are stubbornly determined to overcome their issues to continue their journey. I feel that way about the arthritis in my knee. I refuse to allow the discomfort to keep me from reaching the Cathedral de Santiago. It is easy to let a little discomfort stop you from achieving a goal. Life isn't easy and to succeed you need to be stubbornly determined.

Walking the way through this wide expanse of farmland I find the San Nicolás de Puente Fitero, maintained by the Confraternita di San Jacopo de Perugia (Italian Pilgrims 'Association).[xxxvii] This simple 12th-century rectangular block building was once part of a larger complex. Today it serves as a hostel for a small group of no more than eleven pilgrims willing to experience the conditions of centuries ago. The albergue has no electricity, using candles in the evening for light. There is a shower for pilgrims to share. A dining table in the church nave seats twelve people, eleven pilgrims, and one host. In the evening, the confraternity offers pilgrims traditional foot washing as Jesus washed the feet of his disciples. Those that stay here are experiencing the life of a medieval pilgrim.

I crossed the rio Pisuerga on the Puente de Itero, a beautiful medieval stone bridge with 11 arches. The bridge offers a peaceful scene of small islands of assorted grasses and the fall colors of trees reflected in the water.

The rio Pisuerga forms the boundary between the kingdoms of Castilla and León and the province of Palencia. A stone marker at the end of the bridge marks the border. I passed by a cultivated forest of birch trees lined up in rows about ten feet apart. The view down the row of trees is like looking through a long tunnel.

There is a four-foot stone wall on the left at the entrance to Itero de la Vega. The name of the town is painted on the whitewashed wall over a colorful flowery background. At the end of the wall is painted a comical looking yellow-haired, big-eyed, wide toothy smiling pilgrim wearing a red shirt, green pants and backpack. He stands beside a

Camino marker stanchion with a shell and yellow arrow pointing towards town. Near the pilgrim it says, "Buen Camino, Peregrino." Behind the wall is a two-story crumbling building, windows broken and boarded, tile roof caving in. I believe this is the Ermita de Nuestra Señora de la Pi.

I passed the Ermita and into the village of Itero de la Vega, a small community with a few shops, a supermarket, and a couple of albergue. Crumbling buildings, except for two renovated buildings of red brick instead of stucco or stone, lined the narrow street. At the edge of town is a building painted with Buen Camino Peregrino on a light blue background with mountains and clouds. A yellow arrow points to the left, the direction I need to go. After the arrow, the painting depicts another comically painted white bearded pilgrim with a staff, cape, sandals, and scallop shell chain. The three four-pained windows on this side of the building are blocked on the inside with red brick.

Back in the countryside, the winds picked up and caught the rim of my hat, lifting it off my head. Fortunately, the strap hanging below my chin kept me from a chase through the grain fields to get it back. I pulled the hanging hat off my back and pushed it back onto my head. To keep the wind from getting back under the rim, I walked with my head tilted down.

I heard music coming up from behind and was soon passed by a young couple holding hands walking to the music. It made me think about different relationships on the Camino, I was somewhat jealous. I thought how nice to have a partner to walk with you. Someone on the same wavelength. Someone to walk with hand in hand on occasion. Enjoying life, the walk, and the beautiful Spanish countryside. I believed that Phil and Muriel had such a relationship. Whenever I came across them they appeared happy to be with each other. In a way, I felt that joy on the days I walked with Laura. Walking with someone I liked very much made me feel good.

I meet up with Rick who is walking with our Dutch friend Barry. They tell me about an Irishman they met pulling a luggage cart going in the other direction. I remembered seeing him but didn't think anything of it. Maybe I should have. Every once in a while you come across someone walking in the opposite direction. Not everyone is walking the Camino heading west. Sometimes locals walk from town to town. Sometimes someone needs to backtrack to get something left behind. There are even a few that walk back to their origin once they arrive in Santiago. Rick talked with the man and said he learned the meaning of the Camino from his encounter with him. The man had no money. All he owned he picked up along the way. He was grieving the loss of his parents, the loss of a sister to stomach cancer, a brother committing suicide, and other negative events in his life. He blamed God for all his problems. Rick said he connected emotionally with the man, sharing his grief with tears. Rick walks partially in the grief of the loss of his two sons and could relate to the man's sorrow. Not having spoken with the man and feeling his grief, I had a different opinion of the situation. Maybe a little cold-hearted, but I thought that he needed to get over it, move on and stop blaming God for the things that went wrong in his life. It's good to grieve, but at one point, it is time to move on and continue walking your Camino, continue living your life. Death is a part of life, a sad part for the survivors, and very difficult to get past, but, I believe, it is good to do so. It is good to get past the sorrow so that you can remember the person you knew in life. Remember and bring that joy with you as you walk through life. I hope this man finds some peace and decides to move on to a happier life.

Next, I walked along the Canal of Castilla constructed in the 18th century as part of a network to transport cereal, barley and other products to northern Spain. The canal also supplied ancient aqueducts used to irrigate the fields. The canal runs 207 kilometers through the provinces of Burgos, Palencia and Valladolid in the Autonomous Community of Castile and León. Today, railroads transport the grains and the trails along the canal are used for pleasant scenic walks. The dirt path along fields on the left and the canal on the right is lined with poplars, willows, and other shade trees. The fresh green plants along the canal are a welcome change from the brown plowed fields of the Meseta. A small dock on the canal has a sign offering pilgrims an enjoyable boat ride down the canal. No boat was there at the time.

I head towards Frómista which is still about an hour away.

When I reach the Frómista end of the canal I see the tour boat at the dock. The boat has five large windows on each side for passengers to view the countryside. On the side, under the cabin window, it says, Juan de Homer. I assume he is the operator of the boat.

Shortly after the boat dock are canal locks with four flights that drop 15 meters to the valley of the rio Ucleza. With the gates missing, the locks are no longer functional. Nonetheless, the locks offer a great photographic opportunity.

I walk down the steep path alongside the canal. A group of 5 or 6 bicyclists that arrived about the same time as I did stop to decide which path to take, the bridge to the road or the dirt path I was on. I watched them cross the bridge.

Located in a productive agricultural region, Frómista derives its name from the Latin word for cereal, *Frumentum*. At the entrance into Frómista is a building with "*Almacenes de cereales abonos minerales y pajá*" painted on the side - Warehouses of cereals, minerals fertilizers and straw - followed by the proprietor's name and phone number. This reminded me of the smell of fertilizer I often encountered walking through the Spanish farmlands.

In the main square of Frómista is a statue of Saint Elmo, the patron saint of sailors, born here in 1190.

The Church of Saint Martin, built in 1066, is another beautiful Romanesque church. Additions made throughout the years actually damaged the original building. The church restorations between 1896 and 1904 eliminated the additions to bring back the original structure. Under the eaves on the inside are over 300 stone carvings of human and animal faces.

Another monument in town is the Iglesia Santa Maria del Castillo built in Gothic style. Its altarpiece includes 29 religious paintings. The church also hosts the Vestigia, Leyenda de la Camino, a multimedia museum about the history of Frómista and Jacobean legends.

When I walked with Barry from Holland that day, I had a chance to learn more about him. He retired as a publisher and writer. In his day, he started a Dutch version of Rolling Stone Magazine and had the pleasure of interviewing many of the rock stars of the 1970s for articles, rock stars such as Peter Townsend from The Who, Ron Woods from Faces, and others. Contacting rock stars then was much more informal, he told me. You could find their home phone numbers and often meet in their living rooms for a casual talk. It's not that easy now, he said. He also wrote a couple of crime novels. Unfortunately, the novels are only available in Dutch so I won't have an opportunity to read his works. I would if there were English versions.

 I walked with Barry into town and it turned out we were staying in the same hostel. That evening, we met Barry again for dinner at a restaurant around the corner from the hostel.

At the Hostel San Pedro, we had a good size room with three beds and a sofa, however, it was an attic room with low ceilings at one end of the room. My bed is near the front of the room with the lower ceiling and a cut-out for the skylight window. I needed to be careful getting up to avoid bumping my head. I only stood fully upright with my head in the skylight cut out until I moved to the center of the room.

I remember reading many times during my research that hot water for showers was at a premium in some albergue. I had not experienced that until today. Rick and Dave were out of the room when I took my shower. It was the coldest shower I had ever taken in my life and the quickest, as well. I was in and out in just a few seconds not even bothering to soap up or wash my hair, I rinsed off as quickly as I could and got out shivering. Spain seems to have especially cold water which is refreshing when filling a water bottle, but a real horror in the shower.

When Rick and Dave returned, I told them about the issue. The hostess was called. She didn't live in the hostel but was just a few minutes away. She came to the hostel riding a bicycle. She wasn't sure why the water was cold and said she would call a plumber to have it checked out. Somehow Barry heard of the hot water situation and told Rick that we could use his shower if we wanted. His room was on a level below ours.

After our hostess left, we also realized that the lights were not working in the room. I didn't notice this because the skylights lit the room. Dave figured out we needed to put the electronic room key in a slot by the room's entrance to turn on the power to the room for the lights and, apparently, for the water heater. Rick and Dave got to take nice warm showers. When the hostess came back to give us an update on the plumber's arrival, Rick told her we got it figured out.

The front skylight window opened to a view of the Iglesia de San Pedro across the street. To the left, on the corner, was the restaurant where we enjoyed dinner with Barry. If you stuck your head out the window and looked to the right there was a plastic owl to keep the other birds off the building.

After an enjoyable meal with Barry, we head back to the hostel. Back in our room, Rick mentions the forecast is for rain in the morning and suggests taking a taxi to our next town if it is raining hard. Dave was of the opinion he would walk regardless of the weather. I didn't care either way. I did think that a taxi would be cheating in a way but also didn't want to walk in heavy rain. The discussion becomes a little heated after going on for a while and began to irritate Dave. Finally, I suggested we wait until the morning and see what it's like. It didn't make sense to worry too much about it at this time. I try to keep worry out of my life. It is hard to do and requires the belief that everything works out in the end. Besides, it is good to keep your plans a little loose while walking the Camino. We didn't need to make a decision right then.

CHAPTER TWENTY-NINE

10/3/2021
Frómista - Carrión de los Condes

When I woke I heard the sound of rain dancing on the skylight window and considered that we may be in for a wet day. Rick, Dave, and I talked last night about taking a cab to the next town if the rain was too hard. Dave insisted he would walk regardless of the weather. We went through the morning routine of brushing our teeth, getting dressed, and packing our packs. As we readied for the day, Rick realized he was missing his jacket. He left it hanging off the back of his chair at the restaurant last night. Looking out the window to the restaurant on the other corner, you can see it was closed. Yet, Rick left the hostel after eating breakfast to check if anyone was there. Perhaps someone was inside working and he could get his jacket. Dave and I waited at the hostel enjoying the continental breakfast while he checked. Unfortunately, no one was there. Fortunately, he had another jacket he could use for today.

We left in the drizzly rain. The rain was light enough to be tolerable and a taxi unnecessary but a rain jacket was still needed. Just outside of town, a couple of people walking in front of me wore Mickey Mouse ponchos from one of the Disney Parks. The mouse is known worldwide.

I expected most of today will be an easy walk on a gravel path running parallel to a two-lane country road. Although it is rainy and cold and I often needed to step around puddles, an overall nasty day, I did not have to struggle up or down steep rocky terrain. I try to look at the positive.

I walked alone. I have become accustomed to walking alone and enjoying the experience without distracting conversation. I see more. I enjoy the landscape. I try to walk with a photographer's eye, looking around as I walk, making a point to get some great photographs. Walking alone allows me to keep my eyes open for a great scene without worrying about keeping up with the other guys. I realized a few days back that we always meet up again at cafes along the way or at our accommodations for the night.

Although the rain stopped I kept my hood up because of the wind. I didn't need to develop ear problems while walking the Camino. And, it was still cold to me. The wind causes me to walk with my head down and forget, temporarily, to find a photograph.

I passed a business with a massive cement sculpture of a human right hand, palm facing down, fingers bent with the fingertips touching the ground. An interesting find. The sculpture was at least six feet high and maybe thirty feet long from fingertips to wrist. It is hard to imagine what the sculpture was for, just art perhaps. I didn't see a sign with the business name so not sure what they did.

I walked through Población de Campos. I passed its small town square with a fountain in the center of the plaza, water streaming from a massive six foot high flat rock. The town is quiet. No one in sight. When I walk through these towns, I wonder where are all the people. So many towns feel deserted. This one was in good shape. Not so many crumbling buildings, yet no one is around.

The community is small and the Camino soon takes me back to the countryside to walk past dried-out sunflower fields and massive stacks of baled hay in naked plowed fields.

Barry and I come across each other on the path and we walked together for a little while. I had another chance to learn more about him. I brought up his smart-ass comment from a couple of days ago when I suggested he walk a little slower when I saw him struggling. He retorted at the time, if you walk too slowly you don't get anywhere. He said it was the first smart-ass remark he could think of at the time. During our casual walk, we talked about the existence of God and other spiritual thoughts until we came upon a little café in Villarmentero de Campos and stopped for a break.

I entered the property through a gate in the stone wall. In the front yard, three geese strutted around keeping an eye on the comings and goings. I saw Dave and Rick were there. I often caught up with them when they stopped for their break. There were other pilgrims I knew and chatted with during the break. It was a comfortable place to stop. I enjoyed a café con leche and a banana, then walked around to take photos, starting with the geese up front. They didn't like the attention and attacked my legs when I got too close. I backed up quickly to get away from them. An angry goose is nothing to mess around with.

Behind the cafe is a fenced pasture. In front of the fence were two tall stone statues of naked women on six-inch high, four-by-four cement platforms. The well-proportioned female figures were about ten to twelve feet high and interesting works of art to see at a pasture at a cafe in Spain.

Behind the pasture fence were a dog, sheep, chickens, more geese, and a donkey. Heading that way, I watched the dog chase off a sheep laying by the fence to lay in her spot. The dog is at the top of the barnyard hierarchy. I saw this several times during my Camino when watching them help farmers move their livestock. The dogs intuitively guided the animals and kept them moving in the right direction. Being a dog person, I admired them at work.

After a short break, I'm back on a gravel path running along the highway passing through kilometers of flat brown plowed fields. Soon, in the distance, across a cut field, I see Villalcázar de Sirga and the Iglesia de Santa Maria la Blanca. Almost cathedral size, this church was built in the 12th-13th centuries. Seeing the church and its large gothic rose window, I thought about all the churches I had already passed. Most churches are small and feature a bell tower. At times, I heard the bells ringing to summon parishioners to service.

I passed through the small community without taking time to visit the church. I did this a lot. Although I was a slow walker, I failed to stop all too often. On my next Camino, I plan to spend more time visiting these historic sites. It would add days to the trip, but I believe worth the extra time.

Finally, I see Carrión de Los Condes in the distance below blue skies with scattered clouds. I follow the pilgrims ahead of me and make my way into town. I checked in to the Hostal la Corte.

Inside, a couch sits along the back wall of the tiny foyer. A small desk for check-in is built into the right wall. There are two staircases to the left of the couch. The first staircase descends to the restaurant. The restaurant's main entrance is on the street behind the hostal. The next staircase leads up to the rooms.

Later, Rick and I went down for dinner. Dave wanted some personal space and did not join us. We recognized fellow pilgrims and were invited to join them at their table for another great opportunity to meet some new Camino friends. I had the pleasure of enjoying dinner with Mika, Linda, Randel, Les, Barry, Rick, Lynn (Westfield, NJ) at the Hostal la Corte Restaurante. This was the first time I met Mika, Randel and Lynn. I learned later that Lynn had to cut short her Camino due to an injury. I'm not sure how serious, but enough to send her home. I've said it before, an injury can end your Camino.

I learned that Randall, an American living in Costa Rica, lost his passport and money. A situation he was still working on. He did get money wired to him and was working with the embassy for a replacement passport. He did not seem too worried and was confident that everything would work out. It would not be a major issue for him to get home, he claimed. He had a great Camino attitude. The Camino will provide.

Dinner tonight turned out to be a real treat for me because they had steak on the menu. This was the first real steak I found on any menu I encountered so far. I was Jonesing for a steak, not the thin slices of Jamon (ham) you received when ordering steak. I wanted a real steak. Barry told me my eyes lit up like a Christmas tree when I saw the waitress carrying the steak toward our table. It was a perfect medium-well strip steak, juicy and full of flavor. I was in heaven.

Monasterio de San Zoilo on rio Carrión 10/4/2021

CHAPTER THIRTY

10/4/2021
Carrión de los Condes - Terradillos de los Templario

The day started with breakfast at the Hostal la Corte Restaurante. At last night's dinner, we agreed to meet Barry again for breakfast. None of us remembered. When we met up with Barry later, he told us he had waited for us. He appeared to be annoyed that we were not there. Oops, I thought.

When leaving Carrion this morning it was a brisk 41°. For this Florida man, it felt really cold. My hands were drying out. My nose started to dripping. I'm glad I bought an ear muff headband from a sporting goods store a few days ago to cover my ears and protect me from the wind. I had the hood on my rain jacket pulled tight over my head. Only my eyes, nose, mouth, and a small part of my beard stick out. I remembered my Camino friend, Phil, suggesting there may be snow once we get into higher elevations of Galicia. I hoped not, this Florida guy does not like snow unless it is in a photograph.

Leaving Carrión de Los Condes, we cross the rio Carrión on a 16th-century bridge and pass the 10th-century Benedictine Monasterio de San Zoilo. Pink and purple clouds of the sunrise hang in the skies above the monastery. The building is currently run as a Parador, a state own hostel.

The Meseta is flat and long. According to my research, we will be walking over an ancient Roman road built to link Burgos with Astorga. The road didn't look too ancient to me with the construction equipment laying a fresh layer of asphalt. The odor of the Camino changed from a mild pungent manure fertilizer to the chemical gas odor of fresh asphalt. I think I prefer fertilizer. At least, the smell of fertilizer is more natural.

Eventually, I am back to the traditional dirt and gravel path to walk many kilometers through flat farmland, most of it turned over and plowed at this time of year. I wonder how many photos I may take since the scenery all around me is similar. I decided to use my photographer's eye. The left one I jokingly thought since I use that one when I look through the viewfinder on my digital camera. I'll see what I can make of this land of plenty.

After a couple of hours of walking, I spot the "El Camino Food Truck" parked in a cut-out in the plowed fields in the middle of nowhere. Rick and I stopped for a pastry and café con leche. We sat at one of the four folding tables set up behind the food truck next to a woman trying to contact Jacotran, the baggage transfer service. She was having problems connecting with them through her phone service. She had left some underwear at her last albergue and was trying to figure out how to get them, hoping that Jacotran could bring them to her next hostal.

With the SIM card in my phone changed to a local carrier, I let her use my phone to make the call but she still had problems. When she did get connected to one of the numbers for Jacotran, it was the wrong one. They were transporting luggage to a different area. Jacotran had different offices to handle sections of the Camino. She mentioned taking a taxi back, but since we were in the middle of a field, she didn't know how to let the taxi service know where she was. She may need to make her way to the next highway and we didn't know how far that was. After thinking about it for a few minutes, I suggested that it might be cheaper and easier to just buy new underwear at the next town. The issue was still unresolved when I moved on.

Down the road, I stopped again at a small lean-to rest area. Several other pilgrims I know were there, including Phil and Muriel. Phil cuts off a two-inch piece of Chorizo sausage and hands it to me. Dave hands me a chunk of French baguette bread. The Chorizo was tasty and the bread came in handy for wiping the grease from my fingers since there were no napkins. These are the simple experiences of a sharing fellowship enjoyed while walking the Camino.

Discovering my Camino family is part of the charm of the Camino. The family grows as you walk. Changes as you grow. Took me about 10 or 12 days before I realized I enjoyed walking alone, but I also enjoyed walking for short periods with someone else, someone from my Camino family or someone new to the family. Along the way my Camino family grows. My introverted self is starting to get out. I am finding pleasure in meeting more people on the Camino de Santiago.

I look behind to find a scene to photograph. I realized there is no one behind me, just miles of farmland. Everyone passed me. That's okay. With a feeling that I have nothing to prove, I enjoy following the pack. I consider it leading from behind. Walking slowly and seeing this wondrous Mesata.

Walking with my thoughts, I met a new Camino friend, a little field mouse hurrying across the path. The mouse didn't even know I was there. I pulled out my phone and took a few minutes of video of him scurrying around and munching on something it found to eat. I wondered why it didn't run off. I was holding the cell phone just a couple of feet from it. Then, I saw its eyes were closed and wondered if it was blind. One of the three blind mice. Where were the other two?

In the community of Calzadilla de la Cueza, I laughed as I passed a cement fountain featuring a toddler peeing and wearing a blue surgical mask.

On a rocky path along a two-lane paved road, I noticed a stone with a message written with white chalk - 6 km until the next town from here. There were several other stones with words, some of the words worn out and unreadable. The next one I could read said, I am high like the sky 420. 420 was outlined by a box. 420 is a term that represents smoking marijuana. Different people catch the Camino spirit in different ways.

A little further along, someone formed Camino arrows with the stones on the path. Someone also spelled out "Ultreia." Ultreia is another pilgrim greeting. Translating from Latin roots it means "beyond." [xxxviii] Maybe the person enjoying the 420 wanted to be "Ultreia."

From a distance, I see the Church of Saint James in Ledigos. Built with brick instead of stone, it sits at the top of a hill. In 1028, the church and town were donated to Santiago by Doña Urraca, mother of King Bermudo II of Leon.

At the town's entrance is a blue sign with the town name, a yellow Camino scallop shell logo, and the distance to Santiago, 373.870 kilometers. I walked through the narrow streets of the small village knowing how much further I have to walk.

Once through Ledigos, I continued through fields of dry sunflowers and fields of mowed wheat until I reached the outskirts of Terridillos de los Templairo, a town that derives its name from the belief it was once owned by The Templars.

I arrived at the Albergue los Templario near the entrance to town. The albergue is a lone building at the edge of a field. I made my way up a long paved sidewalk lined on each side with orange carnations. On the lawn on the left stands a red templar cross, homage to the town's previous owners. Tables with red plastic chairs are scattered about the front lawn. After getting settled in the room, I go back out front to join Rick and Dave. They are sitting with a person named John who is a Camino de Santiago tour guide. He is telling Rick and Dave about the origin of the yellow arrows marking the Camino, explaining the yellow color started with leftover paint from a road project.

The albergue had a large dining area just inside the entrance to the left where meals are served and where pilgrims can buy snacks and drinks. A television hung on the wall, the first one I had seen in a while. I did not miss watching television while walking the Camino. The news was on when we went in to grab something to eat. They were reporting on an eruption at the Cumbre Vieja volcanic ridge on the Spanish island of La Palma in the Canary Islands. The same story popped up several times again when I saw the news in a cafe or in our rooms if it had a TV. The volcano was active until mid-December.

That evening, I posted on my blog at johnseegers.com. It had been a few days since I posted anything and I felt obligated to do so since a few people were following the blog for updates. I started off with an apology for not posting often and explained the difficulty of using the cell phone to make posts on the blog and on Facebook. It is very tedious for me to type on a cell phone with my fat fingers. I post photographs every day on my Facebook page www.facebook.com/jfseegers and asked my blog followers to follow me on Facebook instead. I let them know I was posting photographs on Facebook daily.

I go on to say this is one of the greatest experiences of my life and am enjoying the trip. Although it is not always easy, it is very rewarding. Rick, Dave, and I are getting along. Yet, there are times we get on each other's nerves, to be expected when you're with someone so many days in a row.

Dave and Rick are doing an excellent job finding places to stay each night, booking two or three days ahead then eventually they booked through the entire route when it started getting difficult to find accommodations. Some nights were a challenge with many facilities sold out. Fortunately, we haven't had to sleep in the street, yet. Booking ahead provided a little peace of mind. Overall, the places we stayed were nice. Some places are better than others but the staff is always very accommodating.

We're getting pretty close to the halfway point of our adventure. At Sahagun, we can get a halfway certificate. According to the guide, we get this at the Santuario de la Virgen Peregrina on the way out of town. We should be at Sahagun by Thursday.

Since Sahagun is the halfway point, it should be downhill from there, right? Not quite. We will be leaving the flat lands of the Meseta (the plains of Spain) and into the mountains of Galicia with its ups and downs. They won't be as hard as the Pyrenees, but I'm sure they will offer a challenge. A change from the last few days walking through flat farmland, most of it cut or plowed under. The scenery is very similar everywhere you look. Yet, it is always beautiful.

We have formed a Camino family of fellow pilgrims from around the world. I usually walk alone with my own thoughts, but meet up with our special Camino family at little cafés or restaurants when stopping for breaks or dinner. I hope after this we can maintain lifelong contact with them.

One of the special people we walked with is Les. He's from Great Britain and walking 500 miles to Santiago on behalf of a little 6-year-old girl named Isla suffering from Infantile Neuroblastoma, a cancer that attacks the nerve tissue of infants and young children. She went through treatment and it helped until a relapse with a brain tumor. The tumor was removed, but it then moved to her bones and the doctors say she has only three months to live. The family has sold everything to pay for treatments not covered by the National Health System. To help them, Les set up a Facebook page at https://www.facebook.com/caminoforisla to journal his walk and make people aware of Isla's situation. He also set up a GoFundMe page to help the family cover some of the costs of her care. He wears a white tee-shirt with his "Walk for Isla" logo and her photo on the front. Les was given a second chance having survived brain surgery when he was 12 and wanted Isla to have a second chance, too. Unfortunately, I learned a few months after my return home that Isla did not make it and is now at her home in heaven.

Another gentleman we met is Barry. Barry is a retired publisher and writer. Years ago he started and published a Dutch version of Rolling Stone Magazine. He became connected in the music industry, interviewing many stars such as Peter Townsend from The Who. He's also written some crime novels which unfortunately for me are only in Dutch. I would like to read them.

During the Camino, I met people of all nationalities, including French, German, Dutch, British, Irish, Canadian, and American, of course. They all have their own stories to tell and their own reasons for walking the Camino.

I arrived at Terradillos de Los Templarios (Terraces of the Templars), as the name suggests, once under the protection of the

Order of the Temple, Knights Templar. It is a small community of under 100 people.

The town of Terradillos de Los Templairios claims that the story of the goose that lays the golden egg originated in their town. A priest of San Esteban de Terradillos de los Templarios brought golden eggs to the council meetings until one day the council said they did not want any more eggs, but wanted the hen. The hen was killed and buried in Torbosillo so no one could bring her to Santiago de Compostela.[xxxix]

At the Albergue Los Templario I stand out back to survey the farmland I just walked, thinking about how far I have come. I thought about the people I had met and the amazing experience I have enjoyed so far.

CHAPTER THIRTY-ONE

10/5/2021
Terradilllos de los Templario - Bercianos

Making my way through the empty streets of Terradillos de los Templairo I passed the Albugue Jacques de Molay. A beautiful mosaic tile sign on the side of the building shimmers in the early morning light. The sign portrays the last Grand Master of the Knights Templar wearing a white robe and cape with Templar crosses emblazoned on the robe's chest and cape's shoulders. In his right hand, he holds a medieval sword with the tip planted in the ground near his foot. Both Rick and I stopped to photograph the beautifully detailed sign.

On the wall at eye level, a framed whiteboard provided information about the albergue. On the left was written the *Menú del Día: Platos Combinados, Ensalada Mista, Pincho de Tortilla, Empanadas, Bocadillos Variados* (Combined dishes, Mixed Salad, Tortilla Skewers, Empanadas, Assorted Sandwiches). The right side listed the albergue's amenities: *Literas, Camas, Hab. Privadas, Lavadora, Secadora, Cocina Privada* (Bunk Beds, Beds, Private Rooms, Washer, Dryer, Private Kitchen).

On the way out of Terradillos de los Templario I turned a corner following a marker on the side of a building. I saw Barry up ahead. He was walking slowly again. He has some foot issues. I recalled how he made a comment a couple of days ago when I suggested he should walk slowly. At the time, he made a wise-ass retort about not getting anywhere if you walk too slowly. Just then, a policia car passed by. I rarely saw cars in the little hamlets I passed through and this was the first time I encountered a police car. When I caught up with Barry I told him I thought he might be getting pulled over for speeding. Not today, he said.

The weather has been cool for the last few days. As I walked I noticed the trees showing more fall colors. I thought we might have some beautiful scenery coming up, especially when we get to the Galicia mountains. Or, should I say, 'more 'beautiful scenery. The views on the Camino are amazing.

Acres of dried brown sunflower plants lined the path on this part of the Camino. How wonderful these fields must look when the flowers are in bloom with their bright yellow faces slowly following the sun's movement across the sky.

I passed through the small community of Moratinos. Its hillsides dotted with bodegas built into the mounds. Bodega translates from Spanish to English as cellar, bodegas as wine cellars. All that is visible are old wooden doors framed into the cave entrance, usually with red brick. A sign at the base of one of the hills jokingly lets visitors know they are not Hobbit holes but were used in the past to store locally made wine. Some are still used to store wine, vegetables, hams, and cheese. Many are abandoned. I climbed the wood plank steps to the left of the sign leading to the top of a mound for a view of the town. At the top is a lone chair for the adventurous pilgrim to rest and enjoy the view. I took photos of the tiled rooftops.

Continuing my walk through Moratinos I spot a few colorful doors to photograph, one painted red, the other a bright blue. Both doors are set in crumbling stucco walls. Many of the buildings in Moratinos are crumbling. The bright painted doors contrasted with the fading tan stucco. I found the ancient doors across the Camino to be interesting and very photogenic.

I walked again through farmland until I reach San Nicolas del Real Camino. The small hamlet is a municipality of Moratinos. No one around, of course. Walked through taking a few photos of the doors and windows of the crumbling buildings. Doors, windows, and crumbling buildings seemed to be the theme for today's photos. I thought about putting together a photo album on my website called "Doors of the Camino."

I passed an old John Deere tractor at the edge of the hamlet that may have plowed the barren dirt fields I walked through.

In the middle of these fields, just past a short two-arch stone bridge over the Valderaduey River, is the Ermita de la Virgen del Puente - Hermitage of the Virgin of the Bridge. It is a small church built in the Mudejar architectural style, with a single nave and small semi-hexagon apse. While I was taking photos, Phil and Muriel came up. We talked for a few moments. Phil took some photos. Then they moved on.

I followed the footpath from the church to two large statues that flanked the path at the property's edge. Carved into the pedestal of the left statue it said, *sahagun centro historico de la orden de cluny* - Sahagun historic center of the order of Cluny. The statue on the left was a religious figure wearing a monk's robe tied with a rope around the waist. A cross hung from the rope. In his right hand, he held a handle to a rope tied to a bundle of wheat. In his left hand, he held a book to his chest. The cover of the book read "ora et labor" which is Latin for "pray and labor." I later learned this was Bernardo de Sédirac, the first archbishop of Toledo following its takeover by Alfonso VI. The statue on the right was the medieval king, Alfonso VI. In his right hand, he held a sword with its point in the ground. In his left hand, he held a scroll.

It started to drizzle as I left the church to walk through the fields to Sahagun. I pulled up the hood on my jacket.

When I reached Sahagun, the halfway point on the Camino Frances, I am not initially impressed with the town as I walk past warehouses and industrial buildings. I see the Sahagun rail station and the rail line running alongside my path. I prefer the crumbling buildings of small hamlets with their interesting doors and windows. After many miles of enjoying the beautiful Spanish landscape, walking past the industrial areas of larger cities is a letdown. Sahagun did improve when I reached the historic town center.

Up the street from the train station was a walking pilgrim statue with a backpack and staff made from sheet metal. It was an interesting futuristic look for an ancient tradition. Along the Camino, I have seen other metal machines made to look like pilgrims. They made pilgrim souvenir coins. Just put money in the slot. They are Camino commercialism.

I was taking photos of the Mudéjar-styled architecture of the Iglesia de San Lorenzo and the bronze statues in front when Phil and Muriel walked up. It was good to see them again. We walked together towards the town square when Phil and Muriel break off to find a pastry shop they heard about. I thought about going with them. My sweet tooth was calling for a treat. I decided against it though and told them I would see them again later. I wanted to find the Santuario de Virgen Perigrina, a church and museum, to get my halfway Compostela. I started towards the Santuario after looking up the location on Google Maps. The church and museum sat atop a steep hill. I was tired from walking for the last several hours but trudged up the hill anyway. The halfway certificate would be a good memento of my journey. Due to my limited knowledge of Spanish, the attendant at the door had no idea what I was talking about when I asked if I was in the right place for the certificate. He did know how to tell me it cost 5 EU to enter. He eventually went into the building and came back with a young lady with a better understanding of English. From her, I learned that the Compostela was now issued from the town library in the center of town. She pointed back in the direction from which I just came. Since I still had another two hours of walking ahead of me, I didn't want to backtrack. I decided the halfway Compostela was not that important after all and continued on my way to Bercianos.

On the way out of Sahagun, I took the Puente de Canto (Singing Bridge) over the rio Cea. Below me, I spotted a man wearing shorts wading in the water and taking photos of the bridge. The bridge was stone with several arches. A water view up to the arches was a different angle for a photo. I took my photos from the top of the bridge and from its banks. It was too cold for me to be wading through the river for a picture. Although, the thought did pass my mind. I guess I'm just not a dedicated photographer.

After crossing the bridge, I walked a gravel path along the street lined with trees providing good shade. Names and initials were carved into the white bark of several trees. A yellow arrow on the white bark of one tree directed my walk.

The shaded walk didn't last long enough. I was soon back to farmland and walking past miles of corn fields and more plowed fields.

Approaching Bercianos I spotted the church bell tower, a structure different from the many medieval church towers I had seen on my Camino. This was a six-story steel frame structure with a modern design. The stairs to the top are visible through the open sides. It actually looked out of place to me. It looked like an observation tower like those used by forest rangers. I did not look like a bell tower from a distance.

Bercianos is a small farming community. The sign said population 250. It appeared much smaller. They have a couple of albergue and a very small market with some snacks, canned or jar products, and a few essentials like laundry soap.

Our albergue, Bercianos 1900, was at the entrance to the village at a Y in the road. Umbrella tables outside and an open-sided restaurant was a relief to see after a few hours of walking. I didn't realize I was at the albergue right away. I saw Dave and Rick and sat with them. I thought they were taking a break and I asked how much further was the albergue. Rick said I was there and led me back to our room through sliding doors at the back of the restaurant to another outside area with additional tables and chairs. To get to the rooms, we went back inside a side entrance. The rooms were nice. There was a set of white bunk beds built into each side of the room. There were two cabinets under each bottom bunk. The bunks had curtains for added privacy. A small cubby hole with power, light, and a shelf for the phone at the head of each bed was an extra bonus.

After settling in, I went back out to the restaurant. The dining counter along the wall had stools with bicycle pedals for footrests. I ordered a hamburger for lunch then went back to sit with Dave and Rick. Shortly after I ordered, I saw the waitress bring out a steak for another customer. A good steak was hard to find so far on this trip, so I asked if I could change my order. She said it was okay and I am glad I did. It was a delicious meal.

For dinner that evening, we found another albergue about a block away with a restaurant. We had pizza for dinner. Pizza was Dave's favorite meal and we ordered pizza many nights on the Camino. While there, an Italian peregrino we met in Zubiri came in with another fellow, someone else that spoke Italian. It was good to see him talking with an Italian friend. He gave us his usual wide smile and a shout-out of "Heyyyy!!!"

CHAPTER THIRTY-TWO

10/6/2021
Bercianos del Paramo - Mansilla de Las Mulas

Started walking today at about 8 AM in heavy fog. As I walked I felt the dew collecting on my beard. It's 43°. No place was open to get coffee, so we made our way out of town which was easy since in this small community there was only one main road that led to the Camino Francés.

After about a ninety-minute walk through fog-blanketed farmlands, I entered El Burgo Ranero. The Cafe El Camino was open and I was able to order a café con leche, hoping it would warm me up. I also ordered toasted bread and jelly. I bought an apple and a Special K bar, sticking them in my pocket for later.

On the way out of town, I saw the steeple for the Parroquia de San Pedro Apóstol (Parish of Saint Peter the Apostle). From my distance, I thought I saw thin white lines painted on the shingles forming an arrow. I wondered if it was a Camino arrow. A strange place to put an arrow. I laughed at myself when I realized the thin lines I saw were an antenna, a standard rooftop television antenna.

Also, on the way out of town, in a small grassy area, I spotted an older couple walking around looking at the ground. Maybe 6-12 feet from me, the old woman carried a small basket. The man held a stick about three feet long with a point on it. He used the pole to pick up leaves to put in the basket. I asked what they were collecting and she told me tea. They didn't speak English so I left it at that and moved on. I guess there's a certain type of leaf you can use to make tea.

Walking again through the farmland, I stopped at a pedestal monument with a cross on top at the edge of a field. At the base of the monument were many stones. Some of these stones were marked with loved ones' names and dates of death. You see these memorials throughout the Camino, piles of stones placed in the memory of loved ones. Some piles are massive, like the one at the Cruz de Ferro; some are just two or three stones at the base of a Camino marker stanchion.

Across a field is a tractor with a dump container behind it. The container is up in the dump position. I'm not a farmer. I guessed they were spreading fertilizer.

After this field, I went through another planted tree forest. Planted trees lined up in single file, row after row. The white bark made me think it was birch. I will assume that years from now these trees will be harvested for lumber.

A small surprise on today's walk was the dirt runway in a field just before Villamarco de las Matas. A wood four-foot by four-foot sign had a biplane painted logo for the Escuela de Ultralligeros, Ultralight School. Other information written in Spanish offered initiation flights, flight initiation courses, ULM pilot courses, and a cafeteria. I didn't see any buildings for a cafeteria. Maybe you had to fly there.

About twenty minutes later, another pedestal with two tiers for the base and a pillar with an iron cross on top, also had stones piled at the bottom.

Villamarco is small. In a short time, I am back in the countryside with about a two-hour walk to Mansilla de Las Mulas for our nightly stop.

The next town on my Camino is Reliegos, another community with crumbling adobe buildings. I am in and out of Reliegos quickly.

Eventually, I arrive at Mansilla de Las Mulas. The town derived its name from its history as a livestock market, primarily mules. I checked in to the Albergue de Gaia, a typical albergue with three bunkbeds per room, a public shower with three stalls, and a small kitchen area. There were three other pilgrims sharing the room with us. After getting settled in, Dave went out to check out the town, when he came back he told me he saw a farmacia where I might buy some knee wraps. He went with me to the farmacia and bought the elastic knee supports for both legs. Not far from the farmacia was the Esla River and part of the wall that once fortified Mansilla. We did some more exploring of the side streets until we found a cafe and grabbed a table outside. After about twenty minutes we did some more exploring.

Like most of the medieval towns we visited, there was a central square, the Plaza Mayor. Near the plaza is the Iglesia de Santa María from the eighteenth century, according to the sign in front, built over the sight of a church from the twelfth century. Outside the church is a monument to Saint James with a staff and gourd, used to carry water. Inside is an eighteenth-century Baroque altarpiece, statues, and artworks from the original church. Unfortunately, the church had just closed when I arrived.

I went down the street beside the church to see what I could discover. It was one of the arches in the ancient wall that surrounded the town. Known as Puerta del Castillo (Castle Gate), it dates back to the 7th century and Fernando II.

Not far from the Iglesia de Santa Maria is the Ermita de la Virgen de Gracia, Hermitage of the Virgin of Grace. The Virgin of Grace is the patron saint of Mansilla. The church's rectangular building was constructed with red brick instead of stone. A walkway with a bench on each side leads to the arched wooden doors. This church also replaced an original church. Inside, in an inset behind the altar, is a beautifully detailed statue of the royal virgin wearing a golden robe and carrying the child Jesus.

When we went out to get dinner, we headed to a restaurant suggested by the hospitalero at the albergue. We passed a gas station cafe which was open, then another restaurant which looked nice with table cloths on the tables, but it was closed. When we arrived at the recommended restaurant, it too was closed. We walked around some more and none of the restaurants were open. We finally asked a local walking by where we may find someplace to eat. That is when we found out that on Wednesdays all the restaurants in the town close for a day off. Maybe we could get a meal at an albergue with a bar, he suggested. We couldn't get a consensus between the three of us on what we should do next. This happened every once in a while. It can be difficult to find a consensus. We went off on our own to find something to eat. Rick and I made our way back to a local mercado to buy something to bring back to the Hostel. I thought it was a better idea than walking around all night looking for an open albergue bar and restaurant. The Hostel had a kitchen area with china, utensils, and a microwave. We bought a stuffed pizza and a baguette. I also bought a chocolate bar, pastries, fruit, and yogurt for tomorrow morning's breakfast and to take on my walk. Dave decided to go back to the bar we visited that afternoon. He discovered they had a dining area inside open for pilgrims.

CHAPTER THIRTY-THREE

10/7/2021
Mansilla de las Mulas - Leon

Getting dressed this morning, I put on the elastic knee wraps I bought at a farmacia yesterday. Hopefully, they will help make the walk easier.

It's 43°. Cool, but it's a beautiful day. I anticipate it will get about 10° cooler once we head into the Galicia mountains. I think about buying warmer clothes in Leon, maybe some thermal underwear. For some, this may seem silly, but I have lived in central Florida for over forty years. I consider anything under 50 degrees to be chilly.

Leaving Mansilla de las Mulas we crossed the Puente sobre el rio Esla (Bridge over the Esla River). On each side of the bridge is a small section of a 12th Century ancient stone wall that once surrounded the city. When constructed, the highest part was fourteen meters high, about forty-five feet. At some points, the wall was thirty feet thick. Medieval communities often needed to surround their towns with walls to protect them from invaders.

Another beautiful sunrise this morning. Leaving before dawn most days gave us an opportunity to see this wonder often. I managed to capture some nice sunrise photos and some nice morning photos of the corn fields with the Cordillera Cantabrica mountain range in the distance.

Another photographic opportunity came along when I passed a little yard with a goat, sheep, and chickens lazing and grazing. Took a few pictures, then went back on my way to Leon.

The walk to Leon is mostly flat and I pass through several villages. I walked on an asphalt road into the small town of Villamoros de Mansilla. The streets were empty. The town looked abandoned. The buildings of the town deteriorating like many I have passed in the last several days. I later learned that many of the buildings deteriorate due to the poor building materials that were available in this part of Spain. I also consider that many are left in a deteriorating condition on purpose to preserve the ancient atmosphere of the Camino.

I stop to photograph the Church of San Esteban (Saint Stephen). It is a rectangular building made of stone with a red tiled roof. A square bell tower in front with the bells seen through two arched openings on each side. Atop the bell tower is a massive stork's nest built around the cross. Since storks have moved south for the winter, nests are empty this time of year. I have seen many nests in bell towers along the way. It became apparent that a bell tower is a stork's favorite nesting site.

I continued quietly along the road through Villamoros de Mansilla until I heard the clicking of walking sticks behind me and turned around. I'm glad I did. I would have gone in the wrong direction had I not seen these pilgrims. Lost in my thoughts, I missed a yellow arrow or scallop shell telling me to turn right onto another street through the small community. It is amazing how easy it is to get lost going through a village with only a couple of roads. But, taking the wrong road out of town and heading in the wrong direction can put you kilometers and hours out of the way. I will learn the hard way in a couple of days.

Continuing my way along the correct road, I passed a pile of donkey poop in the middle of the road. Confirmation I was on the right path. A few days back I spotted a donkey tied to a tree outside a cafe. Rick later told me the donkey belonged to a pilgrim he met wearing a kilt. I didn't see the donkey again and did not meet its owner, but found piles of donkey poop many times on my walk. I wondered what he did with the donkey going through the cities. Did he walk his donkey through the city or take a path around the city? I suspect there could be issues if you walk a donkey through a busy city.

While walking through Villamoros de Mansilla, an older man riding his bicycle approaches smiling and wishing Buen Camino to me and the other pilgrims as he passes. It gives you a warm feeling when a happy local wishes you a Buen Camino. In this area, they are very friendly and welcoming to peregrinos. The livelihood of small hamlets depends on pilgrims passing through for their survival. Pilgrims passing through are appreciated.

After leaving Villamoros de Mansilla, I came upon a choice of paths to Puente Villarente. The *Tramo Recomendado* - Historic Route to the left is 2 km. The sign pointing right said, *Precaucion Tramo Comun con N-601* - Dangerous Route Road N-601 with a distance of 1.7 km to Puente Villarente. I take the Camino trail keeping me off highway N-601 leading me through a wooded recreational area and onto a wooden pedestrian bridge over the rio Porma, a tributary of the Esla River that I crossed when leaving Mansilla de las Mulas. Of course, I stopped a few times to photograph the park, the river, and another ancient arched stone bridge over the river.

I am greeted at Puente Villarente with a stone cross monument. The crucified Jesus hangs on one side of the cross, and on the other side is the blessed mother with the baby Jesus in her arms. This is the first time I noticed this style of a cross. I see many more in the coming days. I am interested in learning the history and symbolism of this style of cross.

In Puente Villarente I stopped at a covered rest area. Under the pavilion are a couple of picnic tables, a fountain that emptied into a narrow eight-foot-long cement trough, and a water fountain. According to a sign, the water in the cement fountain is not potable, not drinkable. The other fountain offered potable water. I top off my water bottle and then take pictures of the fountains. On top of the potable fountain is a sculpture of a pineapple. I remember from my days in the hospitality industry that the pineapple represents hospitality. Annually the Central Florida Hotel & Lodging Association presents the Golden Pineapple Award to the front-line employees in the lodging industry that exemplifies quality in Orlando hospitality.

Eventually, I leave the beautiful landscape of Spanish farmland and small hamlets, moving into the less attractive suburbs of Leon. I passed car dealerships and other businesses. Across the highway, I see a *Brico Depôt*, a big box hardware store similar to Home Depot or Lowes in the United States. I cross highway N-601, a four-lane highway with a grass medium, on a large pedestrian bridge with bright blue painted railings. On the other side, I walk along a cliff about thirty feet above the highway, a fence on my right protects pilgrims from a fall. Sticks and twigs are again weaved into the fence to make crosses.

Once over the highway, the Camino takes me to Avenue Madrid, leading me through the Leon suburb of Puente Castro linked to the city by a bridge of the same name over the Torio River.

On my route is the Hospital Santa Isabel, a healthcare complex of the University of Leon.

Walking along the street, I spotted an old woman with white hair wearing a blouse with red stars watching me from a third-story apartment window. I wave at her but am ignored. She just continues watching with a blank stare. I felt a different vibe than I felt from the old man riding his bicycle in Villamoros de Mansilla wishing everyone a Buen Camino. Maybe she didn't see me wave.

Crossing the Torio on a stone footbridge I stopped to view the Parque del Torio, a green area landscape lining the Torio River. I see the Campo de Futbol de Puente Castro, a soccer field, to my right.

The initial walk into Leon was a letdown from the walk through the beautiful Spanish countryside. Leon is a big city with high rise buildings, stores, and more traffic than I have encountered so far on this adventure. I even walked by a Kentucky Fried Chicken restaurant. You don't see many American chain restaurants on the Camino. Old high-rise buildings replaced the scenic farmland. The Parque del Torio was a pleasant but short respite from congestion. I appreciated this green area of the city.

I made my way through the streets of Leon to the Hostal Orejas, our accommodations for the next two nights. We are having a rest day in Leon. The room is nice having three single beds, instead of the usual bunk beds we often encounter at a hostal. No need to choose who gets the top bunk. The hostal is not too far from the city's historic district and there are many restaurants and shops within easy walking distance.

Once checked in, showered, and with a fresh change of clothes, we made our way to a laundromat for our daily wash. Traveling light, laundry is usually done daily. Sometimes the service is provided by the hostal for a fee or they provide laundry machines. Sometimes we need to find a laundromat. A couple of times, we hand washed our clothes and hung them on a line to dry which didn't always work if we arrived too late for enough time in the sun to dry.

Washing clothes at the laundromat in Leon became a little mini-adventure when trying to get the machines working. It took our money, but nothing happened. So, what did we do? We put more money in. It still didn't work. An old woman tried to help us, explaining in Spanish what we needed to do. She pointed towards the change machine, but that wasn't the problem. Then, there was a sign on the wall with a phone number above the change machine. That is where she was pointing. Seeing our confusion, she kindly called the number for us. In a short time, someone came in with a key for the machine, returned the extra money we put in, and got the washer going. Life was back in balance.

While we did the laundry, Rick told me he bought a long sleeve nylon shirt on the way into Leon for an extra layer to keep him warm. He said they were warmer than the cotton shirts. Since it was getting a little cool, it sounded like a good idea to buy a long sleeve nylon sports tee-shirt that would keep me warmer. I had a cotton one but wanted a backup. The cotton one also took a long time to dry and was cold to wear when it got wet. I used the free internet available at the laundromat to find a nearby sports clothing store. It was just a few blocks away and opened at 4:30. After the laundry was done, Rick, Dave, and I went there but found the prices too high compared to a similar shirt Rick bought earlier. I decided to try somewhere else tomorrow for a better price. A warm shirt will be nice to have in the next few days when we start walking through the Leon Mountains and then the Galicia Mountains.

That afternoon, when I found a few moments, I emailed Laura to see how her walk was going and that I was in Leon for a couple of nights. She replied that she was getting to Leon tomorrow. That cheered me up. I looked forward to seeing her again. She would let me know when she arrived.

That evening we went out to find a place to eat and found the Los

Alamos Restaurant. The menu was varied and I enjoyed my meal. Ordered a hamburger. I was surprised when it arrived with a fried egg on top of the burger. The usual side dish of papas fritas, fried potatoes, came with my meal. Everywhere we went, the usual side dish is papas fritas. I tried to order rice one night when I saw it on a menu but was told they were out of rice and got the papas fritas again. I like fried potatoes, but also like variety. I wanted to enjoy the local cuisine along the Camino. I guess potatoes are available around the world and they are generally inexpensive. The two typically "American" foods I had often on the Camino were French fried potatoes and pizza. I ate more fried potatoes and pizzas on the Camino than I have in the last two years or more at home.

CHAPTER THIRTY-FOUR

10/8/2021
Leon

Slept in this morning. Didn't get up until about 9 AM. For breakfast, we went back to the Los Alamos Restaurant, the same place we had dinner. We had a choice to sit outside, inside at a table to the left, or at the breakfast bar on the right. We grabbed a table inside. I had bacon, eggs, orange juice, and café con leche. I found bacon and eggs are rare on the Camino. A continental breakfast with café con leche, pastries, and toasted French bread with jam and butter is more common. If you were lucky, they had orange juice.

After breakfast, Rick and I went to find a sports store to get a long sleeve shirt I can wear for another layer in the cold weather coming up. K-2 Planet was a little over a kilometer away, about 15 - 20 minute walk. Dave stayed back to explore the historic district.

Following the GPS, we made our way through the city towards the Plaza de Guzmán El Bueno, an oval-shaped traffic plaza at the bridge across the Bernesga River. The centerpiece of the plaza is a landscaped fountain with a sculpture of Guzmán el Bueno.[xl] Alfonso Pérez de Guzmán or Guzmán the Good was a Leonese military man loyal to King Sancho IV. He protected the Plaza de Tarifa from the king's brother, Infante Don Juan, who was an ally of the Muslims. Infante

Don Juan even kidnapped Guzmán's son and threatened to kill him if Guzmán did not turn over the land. He refused to surrender and sacrificed his son.

Across the street from the Plaza de Guzmán is the Momumento a los Reyes de León, the Monument to the Kings of Leon, with a flower box about 36 feet long and 4 feet wide filled with white gravel and grass forming the day's date. Each day the date is changed. After this, we passed a statue of a lion on a pedestal. We walked the Avenue Condesa de Sangasta and crossed the river near the Plaza de San Marcos. We then passed the Parque de Quevedo which is named after the street it is near. The street is named after Francisco de Quevedo y Villegas, a Spanish poet and writer. On the way back, we strolled through this nicely landscaped park, past fountains and ponds and joining many other people enjoying the day. Watching ducks swimming in the ponds and peacocks strutting their stuff made the walk even more enjoyable.

As I crossed the bridge back over the rio Bernesga, I heard an accordion and immediately grabbed my phone to start recording a street performer. A man with short gray hair wearing gray sweat pants and a darker gray sweatshirt sat on a small simple rolling desk chair with extra pillows, one red and one green. A blue surgical mask covered his mouth but not his nose. Beside the accordion player was an open old leather case for the accordion and an old music box in a leather case playing a female French vocalist singing a romantic song as he played along on the accordion.

Street performers along the Camino are a treat and deserving of a euro or two for a few minutes of pleasure. They add charm to the day.

At the Plaza San Marcos is the Convento de San Marcos, a 16th-century Gothic church. A wide open plaza allows a full view of the intricate plateresque facade. Candlestick columns, gargoyles, floral designs, and other configurations, as well as medallions of Greek, Roman, and Spanish heroes, ornamented the entire front of the building which is several blocks long. Above the arch of an entrance is a relief of Saint James Matamoros riding his horse, sword raised in the air in combat, a small figure fleeing, others lying at the horse's hoofs. There is a tower above this entrance with a rose window above a coat of arms. A statue sits on top.

Originally built as a hospital for pilgrims part of the Convento de San Marcos[xli] now serves as a luxury parador hotel. This is the luxury parador depicted in the movie, *The Way*, with Martin Sheen when they decided to treat themselves for a night. The complex also contains a church and a museum. At one time, during the Spanish Civil War, from 1936 to 1940, the complex served as a prison.

On the steps of a concrete pedestal in the plaza, a bronze bearded robed pilgrim sits at the base of a cross looking contemplatively towards the sky, his hands folded on his lap. Sandals rest by his bare feet. The author of the statue is José Maria Acuña.

Heading back towards the Cathedral de Leon to meet Dave for lunch, I passed a retail store, Gnomos Regalos. In the storefront windows are jewelry and leather handbags. Out front on the sidewalk, under the plaque with the store name, was a life-size statue of Elvis Presley wearing a gold studded white jumpsuit, a belt with American eagles, gold stars, and red rhinestones. A microphone in hand with knees bend suggests he sings with gyrating hips. The influence of American Rock & Roll hits all corners of the world. I realized then that throughout my Camino, in both cities and hamlets, the predominant music played in the cafes and restaurants was English language 1960s, 70s, and 80s rock music. I was expecting to find more music reflecting the cultural history of the area. I was walking a historical pilgrimage, but the modern world moves in, as I suppose it should. It is important to remember and maintain culture and heritage, but equally important to move forward, blending history with modern technology that improves your life. For instance, it is nice to have Internet access in our albergue while enjoying traditional pilgrim meals.

The spires of the Cathedral de Leon filled the sky at the end of the narrow street. The street opened onto the *Plaza de Regla* or the cathedral plaza. Before us stood the impressive French Gothic Santa Maria Cathedral de Leon with carved portals and two towers flanking a large rose window. The Cathedral de Leon is one of the iconic cathedrals on the Camino Frances. The others are in Pamplona, Burgos, Astorga, and, of course, Santiago. The cathedral is also known as *Pulchra Leonina* or House of Light with 125 exquisite stained glass windows illuminating the interior. The construction of the cathedral built over the ruins of 2nd century roman baths started in the 13th century, and wasn't completed until the 19th century. Many problems over the centuries, such as the poor foundation from building over the ruins to poor quality limestone rock subject to deterioration from atmospheric conditions, required many modifications and additions over the centuries to maintain stability and to satisfy current taste in architecture.

When we caught up to Dave for lunch, it was a pleasure to see Les sitting with him. It gave us a chance to share updates on our Camino experiences. After lunch, Rick and I went to the cathedral to get our credentials stamped, but the office was closed until 4 PM.

Back at the hostal, Rick spent a couple of hours booking rooms for the remainder of our walk. We now have accommodations all the way to Santiago. This took some stress away from Dave and Rick. They were sharing the chore of finding a place to stay each night. As I said earlier, I went along with their choices. It was a lot easier.

I went to a bakery across the street from the Hostal and bought two dozen assorted cookies to share on tomorrow's walk. Dave bought some pastries, as well. He then went to the *farmacia* to get new inserts for his shoes. The old ones were worn out and causing blisters on the bottom of his feet.

Just made it back to the cathedral in time to get a credential stamp. It was 6:59 and they were pulling the door closed. They were gracious, however, and allowed Rick and me to get our stamp. Dave got his earlier when Rick and I headed to the sports store. After getting our stamps we started exploring the streets of Leon for a good place to eat.

The streets were busy on Friday night with many young adults, not just us old Camino folks. It was good to see. Dave had commented several times during our walk about the lack of young people in the villages. There were never any children around. In fact, in many cases, the lack of people altogether except for fellow peregrinos. We often walked through small villages with no one in sight, abandoned, except for the cafe staff or albergue staff. Rarely, we may see an old man or woman sitting in front of their home or working in a garden, but never any young families or children. It appeared that only elderly people lived in the hamlets and villages of the Camino, our age group. We wondered where the young people were. I guessed they were in the cities.

It was good to see young people in the streets of Leon tonight. The busy streets were alive with young adults. It is Friday night. The pubs and restaurants were packed. There was an area with vendors set up under tents. One vendor was making something with a hot fire, medieval style.

We roamed up and down the narrow streets, weaving through the people to find a place to eat that served steak. We all agreed on steak for tonight. Looking at the menus posted at the different restaurants, we eventually found a bar and restaurant with steak on the menu. We walked in, not sure if we needed to be seated. No one approached so we made our way past the bar to an open table towards the back. When we asked for a dinner menu, we found out we were in the wrong section. The area we were in only served hors d'oeuvre or tapas. The hostess brought us to another section towards the back of the restaurant where we had a wonderful meal.

CHAPTER THIRTY-FIVE

10/9/2021
Leon - Murias de Rechivaldo

We leave Leon today and head for Villadangos del Paramo, about a four-hour walk. At least, that is where I thought I was going. It turned out a lot different and gave me a good story to tell.

We started the day with a continental breakfast at the Hostal Orejas consisting of coffee, orange juice, toast with butter and jelly, and a mini muffin for 3 EU.

Before leaving I checked my email since the hostel had internet access. I was happy to see an email from Laura. I had hoped we might get together again yesterday, but her email explained that she was "shattered" from her walk and spent most of her time yesterday recovering. I know from the days we walked together that she was having challenges and understood the need to rest and recuperate. I also wondered, due to my insecurities, if she was avoiding me. I guessed telling her in Burgos that I cared about her might have been a little too much.

It was about 8:30 when we started. For the most part, the streets were empty in contrast to the busy evening and the crowds from the fair last night. It was also Saturday morning. Perhaps people were sleeping in.

I took a picture of the neo-gothic Casa Botine with the tips of its corner spires lit by the rising sun with wispy clouds in the backdrop. The rectangular building is another masterpiece by Antonio Guidi with construction started in 1892. Tomorrow I will see the Episcopal Palace of Astorga which he started in 1889 but left that project due to a dispute about changes requested by the Diocese of Astorga.

I would like to say, although I was a little disappointed with the aesthetics during part of my walk into Leon, I succumbed to its charm while I was there and hope to return one day to visit parts of the city I missed. There were many historical sites, museums, and gardens to explore. There were many restaurants with delicious food to enjoy.

As we made our way out of town, a woman walking in front of us was talking loudly on her cell phone. A man walked beside her. I recognized the woman's voice and looked at Rick. He thought it was Marta, as did I. Marta was the exuberant singer from Italy that sang for us at a communal dinner and breakfast a couple of days ago. I recognized her Italian accent. When we caught up, we saw that it was Marta. It was so good to see her again and immediately I felt her positive upbeat vibes. She greeted us with her usual enthusiasm and thanked both of us for posting our videos of her performance at breakfast which both Rick and I recorded. She told us joyously that the videos we posted on Facebook were circulating around the world. She thanked us again. I told her we wanted to make her famous worldwide.

On the bridge over the rio Bernesga, just past the Plaza de San Marcos, we stopped and asked another pilgrim to take our picture. Actually, she took several, using each of our phones for a group shot with Rick, Dave, Marta, her friend, and myself. Marta smiled broadly and made a heart symbol with her hands.

Once out of the historic and downtown area, the walk was more mundane. The street ran parallel to railroad tracks for a while. We entered a residential area with high-rise apartment buildings of five or six stories with little shops on the ground level. Passing one apartment building I looked up to see a woman shaking a carpet, a small throw rug, out her third-story window. I quickly grab my phone to get a picture. I like to get pictures that tell a story. This photo showed an old-fashioned simple urban lifestyle. I had seen people shaking carpets out their windows several times, but this is the first time I was able to capture it in a photograph.

As I said, the walk out of Leon was similar to the walk into Leon. Once out of the historic district and into the suburbs, it was pretty hum-drum. What makes the walk interesting is the people you meet. I caught up to a young lady from Majorca in her early twenties maybe, just starting her Camino today out of Leon. She was short, probably under 5 feet, and wide, very heavy. Her down jacket made her seem heavier. Her backpack looked very heavy, too. Her face was red and beads of sweat dripped down her round cheeks. It was cool this morning when we left, but the temperature was rising. Seeing how uncomfortable she was, I suggested shipping her bags ahead to make her walk easier if it was within her budget. I explained how it made my walks much more enjoyable, all I needed to carry was water and snacks. As much as she was struggling, I wondered if she would make it to Santiago if she continued to trudge along like she was today. I hoped she would.

On the bank of a small pond in Valverde de la Virgen was a metal silhouette about three feet high of a medieval pilgrim wearing a robe, wide hat, and a scallop shell on a chain. He carried a staff with a gourd tied to the top. Below, it said "*Fuente el Canin*," Fountain of the Dog. Beyond the pond, across about forty yards of grass was a stone and brick building built into the hill, the arched entrance protected with an iron gate. To the right was a red brick wall with another gated entrance into the earth. It made me think of the bodegas built in the hills of Moratinos. I wondered what was stored behind the gates of these underground rooms.

A man and a woman were taking pictures of each other at the sign with their cell phones. I offered to take a photo with both of them together, but they declined. I wondered why they declined.

Later, going through a tunnel under a highway, I saw graffiti on the concrete wall. It said, THE WORLD IS OUR ALTAMIRAS CAVE. There was a crude drawing of an animal, a bison or a bull. When I got to this part of the manuscript, I looked up Altamira Cave and found that The Cave of Altamira is in northern Spain in the Cantabria province, near the town of Santillana del Mar. The cave complex is famous for prehistoric parietal cave art, drawings that may be over 30,000 years old. The cave was discovered in the 1880s and became a popular tourists attraction once the drawings were authenticated. Unfortunately, the carbon dioxide and water vapor exhaled from the many tourist damaged the paintings and the caves were closed to visitors. A replica of the caves is at a nearby museum. A trial program was later started to allow five random visitors per week wearing special clothing to visit the caves. Due to the pandemic, the museum and cave tour was closed again. I understand that the museum has reopened and the limited public tours of the cave resumed. The Cave to Altamira is accessible if you are walking the Camino del Norte.

Just outside of La Virgen del Camino, I came upon a choice of Camino trails. The sign told me the path to the left was the scenic route. Straight ahead was the main route for the Camino Francés, a walk along a busy highway. According to the sign, the scenic route would add 3 kilometers and an hour to my walk so I decided to stay on the highway route. There was a map of the area on the sign, but I didn't look at it beyond a glance. I knew which way to go. I would take the highway route for two reasons: I didn't want to walk the three extra kilometers and the reviews on the wise pilgrim app also commented that the scenic route offered little shade and only a few places to stop for drinks.

I walked along the road looking for my next marker. I went around a curve and still didn't see a marker. I had not seen one for a while and wondered if I missed a turn.

I needed to stop for a moment to relieve myself so I went around a building and into a vacant lot. Across the lot, I saw pilgrims walking along a dirt path. I was pretty sure now that I missed an arrow, so instead of going back to the road, I walked across the lot towards the backpacks to follow them to Santiago. I followed along and soon came up to a road. Now I was sure I made the right choice for the highway route. I crossed the highway and followed the arrow back onto another dirt trail. I thought this was the correct trail and I was on my way to Villadangos and the Hostel Libertad.

I walked for a while through cornfields, many kilometers of cornfields. I took pictures of the scenery. Distracted by my thoughts and my photography, I forgot I should be walking near a road.

Eventually, I came up on the little hamlet of Oncina de la Valdocina. I stopped at a cafe, ordered a café con leche, and brought it back outside to sit. This seemed like a good time to enjoy the cookies I bought in Leon yesterday. Filled with the Camino spirit of sharing I offered cookies to the five fellow pilgrims relaxing at the table next to me. After a few minutes of chatting, I was back on my way, still in good spirits and pretty confident that all was well.

If I had looked at my GPS here, I may have saved myself some worry and extra walking. I could have taken a road to San Miguel del

Camino to put me back on the highway route. I didn't look at my GPS and didn't take the road to the highway route. Instead, I continued following the arrows of the scenic route believing it would take me to Villadangos.

The next town of Chozas de Abajo had its share of crumbling buildings, warped timber and interesting doors for me to photograph. I stopped at the Bar El Camino for lunch. It was almost 1:30 and I was getting hungry. The cookies I had earlier weren't enough to keep me going.

Linda from Holland was at the cafe and informed me that the food was excellent. I set my things on the table near hers and went inside to order. I looked at the menu board and chose a Nestea and a *salada mixta*. The attendant told me she would bring the food to me when it was completed so I went back outside. Just as I sat down, Linda got up to leave and wished me a Buen Camino. I didn't have a chance to talk with her. Linda, I had learned, was a fast walker, impatient to be on her way. The salad, by the way, was excellent with crispy greens, asparagus, and tuna.

Once back in the cornfields, I received a text from Rick with the room number at the albergue. Rick and Dave were already there. I turned on my GPS to check the time left to my destination and texted back that I was about an hour away. I didn't look at the map, just the time left to my destination. They had pulled ahead quite a bit, I thought. Usually, I was about twenty to thirty minutes behind. I turned off the GPS to conserve power on the phone and continued on my way. After walking for about another thirty minutes, I checked the GPS again to see how much further I had to go. It now told me I was one hour and twenty minutes away. Somehow I was now further away. It was then that I realized I was on the wrong route, the scenic route.

I missed the turn needed to take me to Villadangos. I was on a route that took me around the town of Villadangos. The scenic route went around Villadangos, connecting with the highway route at *Puente de Orbigo*. It was over an hour's walk backward to get to the Hostel Libertad. I wasn't sure what to do. I didn't want to backtrack an hour and a half.

I looked around. There was hardly anyone walking in view. This section of the Camino was sparse of pilgrims. The last person I spoke to was an old woman that peeled off the road to a little albergue on the edge of the cornfield. This is as far as I can go today, she said, Buen Camino.

I felt lost and unsure until I finally saw another pilgrim from Germany that told me the next town was Villavante and I could stay there. Looking at the GPS, I saw Villavante was about forty minutes away. Back to Villadangos was about an hour and twenty minutes. I didn't like the idea of going backward. Generally, my philosophy in life is to move forward and not look back. I decided to move on to Villavante. I texted Rick that I would catch up with them tomorrow. He suggested taking a taxi back. I decided not to do this. I would continue to Villavante.

I walked almost an extra two hours and I was tired. A four-hour walk had turned into over a six-hour walk, most of it under bright sun and no shade. Thank God the walk was flat.

I was happy to arrive in Villavante. It was getting late and I looked forward to finding a place to stay. It had turned to night and the town was quiet, deserted, in fact. No one around. I didn't see a soul. It felt surreal walking through the dimly lit streets of this ancient crumbling medieval village. I came upon the Albergue Santa Lucia, an old stone monastery I presumed. It was dark and foreboding. Like the monastery in Roncesvilles, it felt like I was again entering into a Frankenstein movie. Why are old monasteries at night always foreboding? I remembered my first sight of the monastery in Roncesvilles. It looked ominous as well. I walked up to a pair of old wooden doors with small windows protected by rod iron bars. The entry was barely lit, but enough to read the sign on the door that said "Closed." I pulled on the doors anyway. They were locked. My heart sank. Will I be sleeping in the streets of this ghost town?

What now? I thought. I checked the wise pilgrim app and saw that there was one other option for housing in Villavante, the Casa Rural Molino Galochas. I plugged the address into the GPS. It was fifteen minutes, on the outskirts of the village. I continued through the village, not sure where I was going. Soon, the buildings were gone and the path was rural again. GPS said I was close, but I didn't see any buildings. A farmer came around a curve and down the road towards me. I tried to ask him where to find Casa Rural Molino Galochas. He didn't understand. After a couple more tries I showed him the app. He then understood and pointed up ahead. He was telling me it was up ahead around the curve. And, it was.

I went up and around the curve. I saw a large two-story farmhouse house at the end of a long dirt driveway. The house and yard were lit up. A small outbuilding stood in the back right corner across a large yard from the house. I believe this is where the pilgrims stayed. Adirondack chairs scattered about the yard held pilgrims chatting and relaxing in the evening. It looked comfortable.

A woman about fifty came out of the house as I came down the driveway. I asked if she had a bed available. Apologetically, she told me no. I nearly came to tears. I was so exhausted from the long walk under the blazing sun. Don't you even have space on a floor I could use, I pleaded? I don't need a bed just someplace I can lay down.

She apologized again and said that was not possible, but told me to sit down and relax for a while. Take some time to figure things out. She offered me something to drink, a Coke or water. I drank the Coke while looking through the Wise Pilgrim app for another option.

Now, I still could have taken a taxi back to Villadangos and stayed with Rick and Dave at the Hostel Libertad, but I was being stubborn about going backward. I don't like going backward. For me, life is about today and tomorrow. I rarely dwell on the past. (Says a person writing a memoir about a past experience.) In a way, I also looked forward to a night on my own. Having a night that was separate from the others, my own Camino, my own unique experience. After all, I had thought about splitting off from them before I learned to just relax and walk at my own pace. I guess I did split off, but this wasn't intentional.

When I looked through the Wise Pilgrim app I saw that Hospital de Orbigo was between me and our next overnight stay in Astorga, so I looked for housing there. I clicked on the button to "reserve a bed in Hospital de Orbigo." The link took me to booking.com. Only a couple of options popped up. Two were sold out and one had one room available. I booked the one room available at the Albergue Casa Flor. I entered my credit card to make the non-refundable reservation.

Once the reservation was confirmed, I went up the steps to the front door. I knock and walked in, calling out "excuse me." The host came out from around the corner. I told her I found a place to stay and asked if she could call a taxi for me. I showed her the confirmation on my phone. "Oh, no," she said when she saw where I booked. "That's past Astorga. Too far. Are you sure you want to stay there?" I told her yes. At this point, I didn't think I had a choice. I had made a non-refundable reservation. If I knew it was past Astorga, I would have booked a room in Astorga. Maybe even the hotel we already had reserved for the following night, but that wasn't how my day was going. I had booked a room in Murias de Rechivaldo on the other side of Astorga.

I followed her back around the corner to the kitchen. On the stove was a frying pan with simmering chicken that smelt delicious. I secretly hoped she might invite me for dinner, but she didn't. Instead, she did as I asked and called a taxi service for me. "I have called a friend with a taxi," she told me when she hung up. "He will be here in about 30 minutes."

"Thank you."

I went back outside to sit and wait.

The taxi arrived on a path from the back side of the property. I didn't even know there was a road there. I was looking down the driveway in the opposite direction. The hostess of the albergue came out when the taxi arrived and explained to him where I needed to go. She wanted to make sure he understood where I was going since I didn't speak Spanish. I could tell she was looking out for me as best she could. I thanked her and got in the front seat offered by the driver.

I finally felt relaxed on the ride to the Albergue Casa Flor and tried to watch the night landscape on the way. When we arrived, I thanked the driver and paid the 35 EU fee.

The host of the albergue looked confused when I walked in and immediately told me they were sold out. Did you make a reservation? The list in his hand showed that everyone was checked in. I told him I made the reservation online. He nodded and looked back at his list. Okay, follow me. He leads me through the building and out the back door to a set of stairs to the second floor. When we entered, he patted a bed and said, this bed is yours. Before he left, he asked if I wanted the communal dinner. I told him, yes, I wanted the communal dinner. I didn't understand that I was supposed to pay and confirm with someone else. I had to track someone down. I thought telling him was sufficient.

There wasn't time to shower before dinner. I freshened up as best I could and went back downstairs to the dining room. There was one long table with a dozen or so chairs. A couple from Holland I met at the communal dinner in Hornillos del Camino was there. They asked how I was doing and where my friends were. I explained my missteps of the day and how my backpack was in Villadangos with my clothes and my charger for the phone. I did say I was glad to have a place to stay. They offered to lend me a charger for the phone and I was able to charge it while we ate dinner.

There was some confusion because I did not let that someone know I wanted dinner. She did tell me though that they had enough food and asked if I wanted to have steak, seafood, or pork. Of course, I selected the steak.

Others moseyed into the room and took a seat around the table. Linda from Holland was there and she sat at a chair across from me. A man named Matthew sat to my right. He was a talkative fellow and I learned a lot about him in a short period of time. I told him about my plans to write a memoir of my Camino experience. He said he was a videographer posting clips about his walk. This brought about a discussion on the importance of art and how we need to promote art in our schools and encourage people to pursue art. I also learned he was married and living in Melbourne, Florida which is on the east coast of Florida about an hour from my home in Orlando. He also admitted to being a recovering alcoholic for the last 27 years. I am glad that he is successfully conquering that disease. I have seen alcoholism ruin so many lives.

Matthew mentioned he was walking in memory of his deceased father and believed his father was walking with him. This belief was strengthened when he met a man on the Camino with a striking resemblance to his father, so much so that it brought him to tears while talking with the man.

I told him that I had lost my parents when I was young, my mom when I was only eight years old. Yet, even at that young age, she was a great influence on how I thought. I related a story I rarely tell about a day when I was angry at a friend or one of my brothers. I don't remember who it was, but I was so angry that I said "I wish you were dead." Mom overheard me and immediately scolded me. "What if someone said that about me?" It made me think and feel really bad. It was but a few months later that my mom died from Ovarian Cancer. To this day, I have never repeated those words and have tried to keep hate from my heart replacing it with love and understanding. I don't have hate in my heart and wish no ill will on anyone. It is not for me to judge.

Changing the subject, Linda asked if any of us heard of the ghost of Santiago. Supposedly, at night behind the cathedral a shadow of a pilgrim can be seen on the wall with no one around to cast the shadow. I was not aware of this myth but planned to look for the shadow when in Santiago.

As we talked amongst ourselves, the hostess asked what we ordered then brought out our meal. She placed the steak on the table before me and then asked Matthew what he ordered. He told her he ordered the steak, too. She apologized and told him they were out of steak, but had chicken or salmon. I ordered the steak he said. He seemed to be upset. She apologized again and he decided on the salmon. It was then that I realized, as I put a fork with steak in my mouth, that I was eating Matthew's steak. I was the one that had not ordered ahead of time and, in doing that, upset the apple cart. I felt bad but did not volunteer that I was the cause of the confusion. The steak wasn't even that good, a thin breakfast steak with little flavor.

Today was just one of those days for getting lost. After dinner, I tried to make my way back to my room. I was tired and wanted to shower and sleep. I didn't have time to shower before dinner service. I went out the side door, walked towards the back, and then up the stairs. It looked a little different, but I knew I was in the last room on the left. I opened the door, but there were other people in the room. I apologized and closed the door quickly. Confused once again, I went back downstairs to find the proprietor. He led me in the right direction to another set of back stairs.

This time, when I opened the door I was surprised to see someone preparing for bed. There was a motorcycle helmet on a chair by the foot of the bed. I thought I had rented a single room, a private room, but apparently not. I didn't mind, it was just something else added to today's confusion. I said hello, but he didn't speak any English. He just nodded. It looked like he had a long ride and was bedding down for the night.

I headed to the bathroom to shower. Undressing from the only clothes I had and setting them aside where they wouldn't get any dirtier. I will need to wear them tomorrow. After my shower, I put my boxer briefs back on and carried my clothes to the other room. I set them on the bedside table, crawled under the covers, and tried to sleep, but I was restless. Eventually, I fell asleep.

CHAPTER THIRTY-SIX

10/10/2021
Murias de Rechivaldo - Astorga

Had a hard time getting to sleep last night. I was tired but still wired from my adventure of the day. The building also creaked and popped throughout the night like an old haunted house. I was sharing a room, fortunately, he did not snore.

I was up a 7 AM. Breakfast was served from 7:30 until 8:30. My roommate for the night was sleeping, so I tried being quiet as I dressed in the same clothes I wore yesterday. They were dry but the black long sleeve tee shirt was streaked with white sweat stains. Yesterday, I layered clothes for the cool morning temperature. It started at 43 degrees then got up over 70 and I began to sweat. I had taken off my jacket, but not the long sleeve tee-shirt and the short sleeve tee-shirt I wore over that. I could have washed the tee-shirt last night, but it is 100% cotton and would not have dried by morning. Wearing a wet shirt in cold weather is uncomfortable and could also cause me to get sick. Today, it is 39 degrees at 8 AM with a forecasted high of 66 for Astorga.

I left the Albergue Casa Flor at about 9 AM. The hostess knew my story and told me I could stay and relax for a while before walking to Astorga. I thanked her for the offer, but saw no reason to hang around.

Might as well make my way back to Astorga and see what the city had to offer.

Although it is cool this morning, the blessing is I only have about an hour's walk to Astorga. I strolled casually along the red brick path through the small community taking the time to photograph the local church with a giant stork nest on top of the bell tower and a pink and blue morning sky in the background.

I stayed off the highway, taking a gravel path through plowed hay fields with rolls of hay scattered about the fields. The familiar sound of crunching gravel accompanied me and comforted me. I was in no hurry since the walk to Astorga was short. I arrived about 10 AM and found my way to the Albergue for tonight, Imprenta Musical Alojamiento. I knew I could not check in that early but I rang the bell on the counter with the hope they might make an exception. The elevator door opened and an older man stepped out and went behind the counter. By pointing to the sign on the counter, he told me that check-in time was 2 PM. He twisted his hand a little bit and said "*Uno y media*" meaning I might be able to get to our room at about 1:30.

I asked if I could sit in the small lobby for a bit to rest. He nodded un the affirmative and then got back in the elevator.

I pulled up Google Maps to find an open restaurant. There was one just a few blocks away. When I arrived, there was a line out the door so I moved on to find another restaurant. I didn't feel like standing in a line. What I didn't realize was that it was Sunday and most cafes opened later on Sundays, hence the long line. It is easy to lose track of the days when walking the Camino. The day of the week has no bearing on your daily journey.

When I turned a corner, I saw the fabulous Palacia de Gaudi. It looked like a fairy tale castle with terraces, battlements, and several towers and spires reaching for the morning sky. Antonio Gaudi, a famous architect in Spain, started building the castle for the Episcopal Church in 1890 but left the project over a dispute with the diocese regarding changes to the design they wanted. Other architects finally completed the project in 1910. The Astorga Episcopal Palace currently houses the Museo de los Caminos (Museum of the Ways) occupying four floors of the building with a collection of Renaissance and baroque sculptures.

While circling the building and looking for angles of the church to photograph, I spotted the Cafe Gaudi across from the palace adjacent to the Gaudi Hotel. I went in and ordered a café con leche and a chocolate pastry to enjoy. I sat at a table and made some notes on my phone to use later for this memoir. I noticed the cafe had a second floor, so I went up the stairs to explore and was able to photograph the Episcopal Palace from a higher angle.

After my coffee, I went back to the plaza outside the Episcopal Palace and had the pleasure of filming a bearded man playing guitar and singing a beautiful Spanish song. After that, I spent time photographing the Gaudi Palace and Astorga's Santa Maria Cathedral next door. It took a couple of centuries to complete the construction of the Astorga Cathedral, so it represents a blend of late Gothic, Renaissance, Baroque and Neoclassic architecture. It was started in the 15th-century and completed in the 18th-century. The Renaissance main facade of the Astorga Cathedral has three towers, a central tower flanked by two taller towers. You may notice the stone on one tower is different from the other due to the time it took to build the cathedral with different quarries used to provide stone.

After photographing the Palace and the Cathedral, I walked through the Plaza España towards the Ayuntamiento de Astorga, the Astorga Town Hall. The construction of this predominately Baroque building began in 1683 and features two towers and a belfry. The towers include the coat-of-arms of the Marquis of Astorga and the coat-of-arms of the city. The tops of the towers are adorned with gargoyles, balustrades, and other sculptures. The belfry's center bell is a working clock. El Reloj de los Maragatos, the clock of the Maragatos, uses original mechanisms to move the human figures, the left side a nun and the right side a priest, to swing a rod to ring the bell. They moved like figures on a wind-up toy.

About one o'clock, I head back to the Hostal to check in. I was inside at the counter when Rick and Dave arrived. They were exhausted after a six-hour walk with several climbs along the way. For a change, I was the one refreshed. Usually, I'm the last one there and tired. Today was an easy one-hour walk to town and an easy stroll around town exploring.

Dave and Rick departing Molinaseca predawn 10/13/2021

They were also very hungry. Apparently, there weren't any open cafes on the route they followed since it was Sunday. We went next door for a good meal and just in time. They had just opened and were packed within a few moments, people out for a meal after Sunday services, I thought.

Afterward, Rick went to a nearby laundromat while Dave and I took a short nap.

Later, I went back to the cathedral for a tour of the inside. The ticket cost was 4.50 EU for peregrinos. The cathedral contains amazing artwork, exquisite statues, paintings, and a lot of gold plating. The dome of the main chapel's nave must be fifty feet high with Christ on the Crucifix about three-quarters up. Bas relief sculptures cover the reredos, the wall behind the altar. Throughout the cathedral, ornate stained-glass windows help light the interior. Aside from the main chapel, the Astorga Cathedral also has fifteen small chapels in honor of Christ, the Virgin Mary, and several saints, including Saint James the Pilgrim, Saint John the Baptist, Saint Joesph, and Saint Jerome.

For dinner tonight we had pizza. We have that often. It is the one thing we can usually understand on the menus and is Dave's favorite. I think it is a New Jersey thing growing up on New York-style pizzas. I can relate.

CHAPTER THIRTY-SEVEN

10/11/2021
Astorga - Rabanal del Camino

Walking through the lamplit cobbled streets of Astorga at 8 AM, the sun gradually lightens the sky between the buildings. The days are getting shorter approaching fall. At eight o'clock it is still pretty dark. The sun is just thinking about rising. A headlamp may be needed in the days to come if we start our walks any earlier, before the twilight hour.

On the road out of Astorga, I passed the Iglesia de San Pedro de Rectivia with an impressive steep angled modern a-frame cantilever over the entrance. The modern construction was unexpected. We passed so many gothic and romanesque churches over the past several weeks it was unusual to see a church built in the 1970s[xlii] with a contemporary architectural style. Yet, the exquisitely detailed Religious Mosaic artwork adorning the facade around wooden entrance doors called your attention.

About two kilometers outside Astorga, on the corner of a highway intersection through the fields near Valdeviejas, a hamlet of Astorga, is the Hermitage of Ecco Homo, a simple traditional stone-built church. This is the style I am used to seeing, a rectangular shape with a belfry and a single bell. The portico of this church welcomes the tired pilgrim with a stone wall to sit on for a rest.

Next, I walk through Murias de Rechivaldo, my residence of last night. The community is small and I passed through quickly. The next small community is Santa Catalina de Somoza. I followed the dirt path into the village towards their simple stone church, the parish church of Santa Maria. This one has two bells in the belfry. The church contains the relics of San Blas, the patron saint of the town.[xliii] As I approached I saw the giant stork nest on a ledge of the belfry tower.

There are several curiosities discovered on my walk. A pilgrim mannequin, for instance, with long white hair leaning on a wall in the courtyard of a pub wearing a wide-brim brown hat with a scallop shell attached and an embroidered yellow arrow. He also wore a brown jacket matching the hat, a plaid button-down shirt, and a blue surgical mask over his mouth and nose as a subtle reminder of the world we live in today.

Santa Catalina de Somoza offered several building ruins to photograph. One appeared to be under renovation. A two-story structure attached to another taller two-story building already renovated with a car parked in front. The wall on the east side of the second floor of the smaller building was missing and the splintered warped timber of the trusses was visible. Pieces of stucco hung from the upper timber. On the street level, fencing and barricade sections blocked access to the deteriorated area. Maybe they were tearing it down, not reconstructing it. I think sometimes the deteriorating buildings are left on purpose due to their historical significance or for the pilgrims and tourists to enjoy and photograph, as I do.

Another ruin consisted of just one stone wall with a timber-framed open entrance. Behind the wall stood a block chimney twice as high as the wall. Across from this were a couple of other mounds that may have been separate buildings. This area had five or six homes that have crumbled back to mounds of rubble.

In El Ganso is another church with a stork nest built on the bell tower. Stone buildings line the street, some with colorful blue or green wooden doors or windows. I became fascinated with the colorful historic doors and windows on my Camino through Spain and took many photographs of them. El Ganso is small, as are many of the towns I pass through on the Way of Saint James. There aren't any monuments in El Ganso, but there is the Mesón Cowboy, a wild west style bar that was featured in the French film *Peregrinos*.

On the way out of El Ganso, a red metal Templar cross is mounted on a boulder, a rock, in the center of the dirt path that runs along the road. A couple of minutes later is a rest area with a stone picnic table and another Templar cross of stone on a pedestal on a six-foot square column.

Walking through El Ganso, I meet Roy and Patricia from Northern California. Before California, Roy told me, they lived in New Jersey when he worked for AT&T. Of course, I let them know I grew up in New Jersey and added that I now lived in Florida. As we walked, I learned they became interested in the Camino de Santiago when they did a planned tour of Spain's wine country a few years ago. Part of the wine tour was to walk a short distance on the Camino. Through the vineyards, I presumed. With that short walk, they were hooked, and here they are, walking all the way to Santiago.

It came up that we would reach the Cruz de Ferro the next day. At the Cruz de Ferro, pilgrims toss a stone they bring from home to rid themselves of a burden. I joked the only burden I had is the damn rock I'd been carrying for the last couple hundred miles. Roy said I'm right there with you. He mentioned that Patricia's rock had actually been stolen and she had to find another one. Rocks and stones aren't hard to find on the Camino, but the one to place at the Cruz de Ferro is carried with you from home and represents your burdens of life. Pilgrims walk rocky paths daily and can pick up a stone almost any time to place at the base of the cross, but do these last-minute stones carry the same spiritual value? I wondered why someone would steal Patricia's stone since the stone is so personal. Perhaps her stone was just misplaced or lost somehow.

As usual, after a few moments of walking together, we put some distance between us, wishing Buen Camino before splitting off.

I get a text from Rick. It is a picture of Dave relaxing in a white plastic yard chair holding up a mug of beer as in a toast to their arrival to Rabanal del Camino, another daily trek completed.

The Camino markers turned me towards the right onto a narrow dirt path with a slight climb into the oak woods. A fence on my right lined the dirt path. Weaved into the fence were crosses made from twigs, a common addition to fences on the Camino. So much of the Camino is about memorials to loved ones lost.

The wooded path was an easy walk with just a gradual incline, so I walked lackadaisically until I tripped over a tree root sticking up in the path, a reminder to walk carefully. Eventually, the path declined and opened onto a road. I saw a two-wheeled green wagon across the road. Set back from the road was La Condela Albergue, our residence for the night in the mountain village of Rabanal del Camino. Always a good feeling to come up on your albergue at the end of a day's walk. Regardless of whether the walk was easy or hard, it's nice to reach the end and have time to relax. I shall toast myself to the end of a day's walk.

When I arrived, Dave and Rick were relaxing at a table on the patio outside the cafe, already showered and refreshed. I set my poles to the side and sat down. Dave went in for a beer. He came back with his beer and a Nestea for me. He also ordered a ham and cheese sandwich for me. I can get it when I go inside to present my passport and get my credential stamped, he told me.

I came back out to enjoy my sandwich and Nestea. Sandwiches in Spain are made with a French bread, a baguette. Only once on the entire Camino did I see regular white bread. Even toast in the morning is done with the baguette sliced diagonally.

After eating I went in to shower. I also rinsed out the shirt and underwear I wore that day while taking my shower then hung them on a line out back to dry. I went and sat with Rick. He was enjoying a pork dish. He told me he was sitting there and could smell the food that was cooking. He had asked the hostess what they were cooking. Based on his sense of smell, he ordered the dish for lunch.

La Condela is at the entrance to the village of Rabanal del Camino on highway LE 6304. To the east is a beautiful view of the countryside. To the west is the road into town. Dave and I decide to walk into town to explore. We follow the highway past the Ermita de la Vera Cruz and the Cemeterio de Rabanal del Camino. Then, we take a slight right off the highway and onto Calle Real, the street that runs through the center of town. The town is only five or six blocks long and it doesn't take long to reach the other end. On the way, we pass the Ermita de San Jose on the right. Up a bit and to the left is the Iglesia de Nuestra de la Asunción. Behind the church is the Monasterio de San Salvador del Monte Irago with the monks doing vespers (chanting) each morning and evening in the church. Following monastic tradition, the daily liturgy in the church is celebrated with Gregorian Chants. Unfortunately, I missed the vespers since it conflicted with the dinner schedule. It was important to get nourishment for a long walk and climb tomorrow.

I stepped through the old wooden doors of the chapel to see what it looked like inside. The interior, dimly lit by three small windows in the semicircular vaulted apse, presented a mystic monastic aura. A single light on the Crucifix hanging on the wall behind the podium put a special emphasis on the suffering Christ figure. A solitary man kneels at a pew praying. I took a photograph of the Crucifix, then left. I didn't want to disturb the man's prayers.

Finally, near the west end of town is another church, the Iglesia de Santa Maria.

Rabanal del Camino with several more albergue and several bars, as well as a small mercado, depends on pilgrims passing through to survive. This small community of about 60 people, like many along our walk, needs the pilgrimage to Santiago. I imagine life was extremely hard over the last year or so when everything was shut down due to the Covid pandemic.

Heading back to the albergue, we stopped at the mercado to buy fruit and snacks for tomorrow. It is always good to have a few snacks to enjoy when walking long hours.

I decided to take a path behind the Ermita de la Vera Cruz to visit the Cemeterio de Rabanal del Camino instead of staying on the paved road. There is something about these old Spanish cemeteries that draws my attention. I visit for a while then continue past the back of a house with children playing in the yard towards the albergue. When the children see me, an old bearded americano, they go running towards the house to let the adults know I was there. No adults came out of the house, but I guess I surprised the kids.

I recommend the food at La Condela. Rick, Dave, and I had a wonderful meal before retiring for the night.

CHAPTER THIRTY-EIGHT

10/12/2021
Rabanal del Camino - Molinaseca

A strip of orange, a strip of yellow, then shades of blue lit the sky to signal the sun will soon break the horizon to start the new day. It is a blessing each morning to experience the sunrise over the landscapes of Spain.

Leaving Rabanal del Camino, I see an opportunity to photograph the church bell tower with the now orange sky as a backdrop to create wonderful silhouettes.

Once through Rabanal del Camino and back into the countryside, I make my way to Molinaseca, excited about another day of walking. I programmed the address of the hostal in the GPS, Tr.ª Manuel Fraga, 6, 24413 Molinaseca, León, Spain. All I need to do now is stay on the trail, follow the arrows, follow the scallop shells and follow the GPS when I get to Molinaseca. If it were only that simple.

I turned back towards town for another look. Since we walk west, I try to do this often in the morning to watch the sunrise. I spotted the sun shining through a tree with the bell tower of the church dominating the landscape view of the town in the background. I also take a few selfies with the sun behind me. Golden sunbeams create a star pattern in the photograph at the edge of my hat.

I turned back to continue my way. A little hungry, I reached into my jacket for a prepackaged coffee cake I bought yesterday at the mercado when I suddenly get really dizzy. I started stumbling and feeling queasy. For a moment everything went white. I thought I was passing out. I was falling towards a narrow ditch on the side of the path when I managed to regain some balance. If I had stepped into the ditch, I may have broken or twisted something in the fall. I lifted my head and saw a sign on a pair of four-by-four posts about ten or twelve feet from me and make my way there. I held onto the post for a good five or six minutes, until my head cleared a little. No one passes while I am there. I see no one in front of me or behind me. I wondered how long it would have been for someone to find me if I did pass out. Still feeling uneasy and a little dizzy, I begin walking across the asphalt road, highway LE-142, and back onto the dirt trail to continue through the fields. I am in the middle of nowhere and can't just stop. I extended my poles to have them ready for balance. I had not used them in the last couple days since the journey was mostly over flat land. Now, I know it is important to have them ready in case I get dizzy again. Within a few minutes, the fogginess in my head cleared. Several thoughts crossed my mind as to the cause: a change of blood pressure due to the elevation, a change in sugar, or maybe it was just staring into the sun for my photographs that caused my disorientation. I hoped it was over and did not reoccur.

As I made my way up Monte Irago towards the Cruz de Ferro, the gravel path takes me through a forest with hillsides colored with ferns changing to amber, orange and brown in the cooling fall weather. Although the rise in elevation from Rabanal del Camino to the Cruz de Ferro, considered the highest point on the Camino Frances, is about 400 meters, it was not a particularly hard walk for me.

About an hour and a half from Rabanal is Foncebadón. At the entrance to Foncebadón, a wooden cross stands on a flagstone pedestal in the center of the road. The once abandoned village, or ghost town, is returning to life with the resurgence of the Camino in the last twenty years as a few entrepreneurs opened albergue and cafes to cater to pilgrims. The colorful La Taberna de Gaia, a medieval-style restaurant, is one example I passed.

An older gentleman with long white hair and a white beard wearing a faded green hooded sweatshirt sweeps the cobblestone path to the El Albergue de Peregrinos Domas Dei. A marble plaque on the wall tells me the albergue was rehabilitated with the financial help of the American Pilgrims on the Camino Organization.

This may be a town to consider for an overnight on my next Camino Frances. The village is charming.

Out of Foncebadon, the gravel path began to rise and curve to the left. From this elevated view, I saw cows grazing in a penned area in the valley. Beyond the cows were ruins that may have been a church. A tower stood with a window opening that may have held the bell. A three-foot rectangular stone wall, once the exterior walls of the building, and rubble were all that was left.

Around the curve on the right side of the path is an eight-foot simple wood cross. A few feet ahead on the left side is a Camino marker sign with both a yellow arrow and a scallop shell symbol. I sometimes wondered about the placement of the Camino markers. The only road out of Foncebadon is the one I am on. I could not get lost. Perhaps I should not say that since I have proven I could. In this case though, there were not any choices of paths to take. Although I do have to say, if you don't see a sign for a while you can begin to get nervous. They can be comforting to see and put you at ease if you have been walking for a while.

I cross over highway LE-142 again and turn left to stay on the path running parallel to the road until I reach the Cruz de Ferro (Iron Cross).

When I arrived at the Cruz de Ferro, a long line of pilgrims wait their turn to leave their stones, to leave their burdens. One by one, or a couple together, climbed to the top of the stone mound to drop a stone and say a prayer.

A tour bus parked across the path to the left detracted from the special spirituality of this sacred location. But, I suppose, everyone has the right to visit the site in any way they can. Walking there is not the only option. The German group from the bus stood under the portico of the Ermita de Santiago Apostol, a short distance from the cross. They were joined for services and just finishing a hymn. Unfortunately, I didn't get a chance to video the singing. Their pastor went on with the service. I waited for a while to see if they might start singing again, but they did not. They remained there for a while and I became disappointed I couldn't get up close to the chapel without disrupting their services. Impatient, I moved on after taking photos from a distance.

The Cruz de Ferro sits at the top of a five-meter pole on a mound of stones, known as "humilladeros."[xliv] The Cruz de Ferro is believed by some to be a marker for pilgrims traveling during the winter months when everything else is covered by snow. Others believe the marker was put there by the Romans to distinguish a territorial border. A popular belief is that the cross was put there by Saint James. The myth is that he came across a pagan priest performing human sacrifice. With "righteous anger"[xlv] he threw a stone at the pagan altar. The altar shattered into thousands of pieces and Saint James put the cross in its place to signify the power of the almighty God.

Today, pilgrims passing by the cross say a prayer and then place a stone or rock they brought from home at the base of the cross, a symbol of leaving their burdens behind them.

I climbed to the top of the pile and tossed my stone towards the base of the pole. Since I don't believe I have any great burdens, I asked God to rid the burdens of my family and friends. Back at the bottom of the mound, I retrieved my phone from a female pilgrim that was behind me in the line of pilgrims. She had offered to take my photo when she saw that I traveled alone.

I didn't feel that great spiritual uplifting many describe about their time at the Cruz de Ferro. It was nice, peaceful, and spiritual, but many have described their experience as overwhelmingly spiritual and overwhelmingly emotional. I did not feel that but felt that I should. Sometimes I think that I may be too stoic.

From the Cruz de Ferro, the Camino begins to descend. I walk on the shoulder of LE-142 until I come upon an establishment adorned with dozens of flags from around the world. Pilgrims standing on the road sang joyously as they watched a man raising their flag. As I passed this colorful establishment I heard a dog barking and spotted him at the edge of the building behind a stone and timber wall. He was growling and barking towards the singing pilgrims, protecting his turf I suppose. Even though he was bearing his teeth, I approached. He stopped barking and sniffed my fisted hand through the fencing then allowed me to scratch his head. He was a sweet dog with sharp teeth.

After passing this establishment of flags, I walked for about an hour descending, passing cows in small pastures on the hillside. Then the trail brought me to a rocky river ravine. I needed to be careful on this descent since the slabs of rocks were smooth and somewhat slippery. I am happy it was not raining. I believe these rocks would be more slippery than the ravine rocks encountered descending into

Zubiri which feels like ages ago. The small to medium river rocks near Zubiri, although uneven, allowed ledges for foot placement. These rocks were larger, longer, and wider. I placed the points of my poles in cracks or crevices in the slabs for leverage and to absorb some of my weight and made it to the bottom without falling or twisting a knee or ankle. My biggest worry on this walk is twisting a knee. I can deal with stiffness and throbbing at times, but a twisted knee could put me down for days and be really inconvenient.

Once through this treacherous descent and back to a gravel trail, I see in the valley below the two bell belfry of the local church peaking over the rooftops of El Acebo de San Miguel. The rooftops, I noticed, were dark, covered with slate instead of red tile. Walking through this village, I also notice many of the block buildings had wood staircases and wood balconies, deteriorating and warped timbers, of course. More photographic fodder for my recorded journey.

Walking through El Acebo de San Miguel, even taking time for my photography, only takes about fifteen minutes. Then, I am back on the country trail.

About an hour later, I passed through the tiny village of Riego de Ambros. It takes maybe ten minutes to walk. I stopped for a moment to photograph a detailed relief above a residential entrance of the Blessed Mother with the baby Jesus. The bust of Mother and Child is set in a scallop shell.

Following Riego de Ambros is another slippery treacherous descent over loose slabs of rock grooved with centuries of running water. Again, I am glad it is not raining.

After the rocky descent and back onto a dirt trail, I step over the Arroyo de Prado del Mango, the Mango Meadow Stream, which is no more than a muddy trickle. The next hour is an easy walk.

At the base of the mountain on the road into Molinaseca is the Ermita de Nuestra Señora de las Angustias, Our Lady of Sorrows.. A curiosity about this church is that in the past its doors were covered with iron plates since the faithful would often pull a splinter or chip from the door as a relic.

There is a certain joy or satisfaction when you finally arrive at your destination. Although the walk is enjoyable (or not), it is nice to reach the end. I arrived at Molinaseca and according to the GPS, the casa was just ahead. "You have arrived at your destination," my phone announced. I looked at the house. It was a small quaint pink building with the front yard encircled by a rod iron fence. When I went to push through the gate I saw the padlock and immediately knew that somehow I had screwed up again.

I thought I had it down pat. With GPS how could I possibly get lost? It will take me right to my albergue for the night. Wrong. It only works if you put in the correct address. It seems that I left out some information. My GPS brought me to La Casa del Reloj, not to the Hotel La Casa del Reloj.

A bench up ahead gave me a place to sit for a moment and call Rick to bail me out again. I was on a walkway on a Roman bridge overlooking the playa fluvial, the river beach, on the rio Meruelo. I read many pilgrims soak their feet in the cool river water to soothe their aching feet.

From the bridge, on the opposite shore, I saw a vibrant bustling group of people sitting at umbrella tables enjoying the day and beverages from the cafes and bars at the beach. From the description of my view, Rick told me to make a left at the second bridge across the river and continue on that street for several blocks. He would meet me outside the building.

Rick told me he and Dave had a hard time finding the place, too, because it wasn't well marked. The entrance was a large wooden door that opened in two sections, like a stable door. To get in you unlocked the upper section, swung it open, and then reach in to get the bottom open.

Hotel La Casa del Reloj, a comfortable country home, was charming. Inside, a fireplace stood in the center of a large room on the first floor. A living area with comfortable seating was inviting. On the side wall was a buffet for food service and a few tables for dining. At the far end of the room was a wood desk used for check-in. The entire area was decorated with old farm equipment on walls and shelves. The sleeping rooms were upstairs. The second floor also had a comfortable sitting area outside the guest rooms that included a television and a library of books on shelves built into the walls. The beds in our room were comfortable and the room spacious.

CHAPTER THIRTY-NINE

10/13/2021
Molinaseca - Villafranco del Bierzo

As usual, we left Molinaseca in the predawn, walking through narrow deserted streets dimly lit by an occasional street lamp attached to the front of a stone building. We walked in search of a morning café con leche.

About an hour later, I crossed the bridge over the rio Boeza and saw one of the three neo-gothic towers of the Castillo de San Blas[xlvi] through the trees. The Castillo is located in Campo, a suburb of Ponferrada. When I first saw the tower I thought it might be the Knights Templar Castle that I heard about, but it is actually a castle built in the late 19th century by Paciano Ucieda, an owner of a large part of Campo. Based on a dream, he built the castle at the base of the rio Boeaz styled after the Knights Templar Castle in Ponferrada. Unfortunately, the fairy tale castle he envisioned has deteriorated and suffered from vandalism. The grounds are open, but the building is abandoned and closed to the public.

On the way into Ponferrada, I walked past another abandoned building in ruins. These crumbling buildings fascinated me and I enjoyed photographing them. They are part of Spain's history and culture. Looking through photographs of these buildings to refresh my memory while writing this memoir, I thought about the new ruins being made today in Ukraine, another country rich in culture. Instant ruins, I thought. Brought on by the invasion of another country, not unlike the invasions in Spain over the centuries by both Christians and Muslims. I find it disheartening that these invasions still occur. Centuries ago it was about religion, so we are taught, but it is really about land and control over the land, as it is today in Ukraine.

Walking into Ponferrada, we joined up with Randall from Costa Rica. I first met Randall in Carrión de Los Condes during dinner at the Hostal la Corte. Randall is the fellow from Costa Rica that lost his passport. I learned from him a few weeks later that the policia found his passport and shipped it to his next albergue to pick up when he arrived there. Randall was making his way to the Knights Templar Castle when we ran into him. When we asked, he agreed to join us for breakfast when we came upon a restaurant. It was time for a break and we were ready for breakfast and a café con leche.

It was a good restaurant with a varied menu for breakfast, more than just toasted baguette and fruit. They had a full breakfast menu, including eggs and pancakes. Randall was very helpful when we ordered since he spoke fluent Spanish. I ordered eggs and pancakes, along with café con leche and orange juice. The breakfast was good, but you could tell the pancakes were not freshly made by the uniform small size, probably frozen pancakes warmed up. They weren't as fluffy as freshly made. They were good, but I was expecting a high stack of pancakes. Instead, I got three mini-pancakes. I thought about how Americans are spoiled by the serving size we get here in the states. Everything is jumbo size, unless you are in a fancy gourmet restaurant. In that case, the servings are small and served on large plates making the meal seem even smaller with the price still huge.

After breakfast, we walked by the Castillo de Los Templarios, the

Knights Templar Castle. The structure is a massive and imposing medieval fortress built on the rio Sil in the late 1100s by Ferdinand II to protect the town and the pilgrims walking to Santiago. The Knights Templar took possession of the Castle in the early 1200s when Ponferrada was given to them by King Alfonso IX. The Templars then continued to expand the fortification of the castle fortification. The walls of the polygonal structure include varying size towers with double and triple battlements. The entrance to the castle requires crossing a draw bridge over a moat. Two flags proudly fly over the castle, the flag of Spain and the flag of Castile and Leon. Currently, the castle is a museum and houses the Knights Templars 'Library.

At the foot of the castle is the Baroque Iglesia de San Andres from the 17th century.

Not long after passing the Knights Templars 'Castle I fell back from Rick and Dave and continued on my own. I followed the Camino markers up and down cement stairs through Ponferrada. Eventually, I crossed the rio Sil to walk along the Parque de la Concordia, a scenic route along the river. The path passes the Light Factory, Museo de la Energía, an old coal power station converted to a museum that depicts how electricity was produced from coal. The factory operated from 1920 to 1971. A curiosity of the museum was the wooden sculptures on the front lawn, bare butt naked male human couples. It is unclear what they represented or how the sculptures fit in with the Light Factory. Did they represent the plant workers? Were they naked because of the high heat of the energy plant? The plant used coal to heat water from the Sil River to create steam energy. Or, was it just artistic license?

After the Light Factory, the Camino turns to the left away from the River Sil taking me past the Iglesia de Santa María de Compostela, a small quaint church in a residential area of cottage homes on tree-lined streets. I followed the arrows to walk the sidewalk beside the church. At the back of the church was a small statue of the Blessed Mother. I took a photo of the statue with the church in the background. The sun was just peaking over the roof of the church which created a glorious sunbeam to reach out and touch the Blessed Mother Mary.

While walking through Columbrianos, I took pictures of some purple flowers in the aster family (symphyotrichum) and yellow flowers (Jerusalem artichoke) in a flowerbed built on top of a three-foot high wall. I followed the wall around the corner to the Iglesia de San Esteban de Columbrianos, a parish church built in 1778 with a belfry that had to be rebuilt in 1948 after being hit by lightning.

Continuing on my way, I met Erik from Tennessee. He commented that I had a good eye for photography because he saw me taking flower photos. Eric is originally from the Netherlands but moved to the United States and works in the IT business. He told me he just turned fifty the week earlier. He is also having some knee issues and said he may have to have knee surgery when he returns home. When the doctors did a scan of his leg, they found a hole in the cartilage of his knee. Before we separated I gave him my information and we became friends on Facebook. Once home, I checked out his profile and learned he is a "priest-in-charge" at Saint Mark's Episcopal Church. I also learned that at the end of May 2022, Erik became an American citizen. Congratulations, Erik.

While walking with Barbara, another wonderful woman I met on this section of my Camino, we discussed the challenges many pilgrims have on their pilgrimage. She went on to tell me about a fellow pilgrim she met with brain cancer. Due to the brain cancer, he has no feeling in his legs and needs to walk with forearm crutches. Since he cannot feel his steps, he has trained his eyes to tell his legs where to go. In other words, he has to look at each individual step for the proper placement of his foot.

On another day I came upon a professional film crew with shoulder cameras and a pole mic. I slid by trying not to interrupt their production. Many people have made films about the Camino so I didn't think this group was particularly unusual until I found out later that the person they documented was blind. Another example of someone determined to walk their pilgrimage.

I cannot imagine trying to walk this difficult endeavor without sight or without feeling in my legs. The Camino brings out the true spirit of a person. These pilgrims are an example to stop worrying about little problems in life and to walk with faith and determination.

A good portion of the path from Ponferrada to Villafranca del Bierzo goes through vineyards and quaint villages like Fuentesnuevas and Cacabelos.

In Fuentesnuevas I photograph the entrance to Madame Tatouage Body Art, a tattoo parlor. Above the old wooden doors is a balcony designed to look like a cart with wagon wheels on each end of the balcony and an oil lantern to light the way. Small flower boxes add color to the scene.

The Church of Nuestra Señora de la Asunción in Fuentesnuevas is an 18th-century parish church with a two-bell belfry and the now-expected stork nest. Also, I noticed a hangout for dozens of pigeons.

Outside of Fuentesnuevas red and black cows graze in small pastures. The trail takes me by vineyards and over a small stream, then past a section of birch forest.

It is hard to describe the many villages I pass through without being repetitive. Cacabelos has narrow cobbled streets, old stone buildings with old wooden doors, albergue, and an old church, the Iglesia de Santa Maria. There is a museum, Museo Arqueológico de Cacabelos, with exhibits from archeological sites on the banks of the rio Cúa in an area settled as far back as the Paleolithic era. The museum has exhibits from the Castro Ventosa and La Edrada archeological sites, as well. I walked through town without stopping.

About halfway between Cacabelos and Villafranca del Bierzo I find the Estudio de Escultura A Nogueira. Looking through the gate I spot a variety of cement statues - a pair of horse heads, nude male and female figures, and an odd-looking sculpture with three columns and antenna-looking appendages on top. Small colorful ceramic tile designs decorated parts of the columns. Another sculpture was a hand holding a mallet and a chisel.

Entering Villafranca del Bierzo I pass the Romanesque Iglesia de Santiago with the Puerta del Perdon, the door of pardon. The northern doorway of the church, for those unable to make it to Santiago, offers pilgrims a chance to have all their sins forgiven if they enter through this door on a Holy Year, a year in which the Saint James holiday on July 25 falls on a Sunday, and take communion.

After the Iglesia de Santiago, I pass the Villafranca del Bierzo castle, a small privately owned castle built in the 1500s.

There are many other things to see in Villafranca del Bierzo. The Calle del Agua is lined with monuments and mansions and has earned the heritage status of Property of Cultural Interest to preserve Spain's cultural history in art and architecture.

There is another old Roman bridge over the Burbia River. The Puente Medieval de Villafranca is made with thick stone walls and three large semicircular arches. At the entrance of the bridge is a statue of a pilgrim with his staff with a hanging pumpkin, a hat with a shell and a cross on his chest.

In the warmer weather, you can enjoy the cool waters of the Playa Fluvial de Toral de los Vado, the beach park along the Burbia River, or stroll along the walking trails.

I follow the GPS down a steep hill to the Hostal Burbia on the banks of the Burbia River. After settling in and resting for a bit, Rick, Dave, and I head out to explore and find someplace for dinner. We end up at the El Casino Bar Restaurant. On the way to dinner, I took some exterior shots of the Collegiate Church of Santa Maria built in the 16th century on the site of a Cluniac monastery from the 11th century.

CHAPTER FORTY

10/14/2021
Villafranco del Bierzo - Laguna de Castilla

Leaving Villafranca del Bierzo, there are three options for the Camino. The main route is through the valley along the rio Valcare. Another option is the Ruta Pradela to the north with a tough 400-meter climb and descent offering views of the valley. A good climb for those looking for a workout. The Ruta Pradela ends at Trabadelo to join the main route. The other is the Ruta Dragonte to the south, a scenic route through mountain roads, country trails, and tiny hamlets with steep ridges up and down. Great for the more adventurous. These alternate routes are more scenic, but also longer and slower. These routes developed in medieval times when the nobles of the area demanded a toll from those wishing to enter Galicia. This is one reason why medieval pilgrims often took the Dragonte or Pradela routes, to avoid the tolls. In the early eighteenth century, Alfonso VI abolished the toll.

Due to time and the easier walk, I took the highway route that ran along a river, the rio Valcare. The route proved more scenic than I expected with the river running alongside the road for several kilometers. Today's walk gave me an opportunity for many river photos. The road on my right didn't bother me. I pointed my view left whenever possible. I made the assumption that the mountain route was more scenic, forgetting that there is beauty everywhere if you decide to see it.

Unexpectedly, while walking on the dirt path between the road and the river, I start feeling a bit lightheaded and foggy again. I think about when I nearly fell from a dizzy spell walking from Rabanal del Camino to Molinaseca and hope this passes. I need to keep moving. This is no place to stop. I continue forward and eventually, the feeling goes away.

I stopped at a cafe in the small community of Trabadelo to warm up with a café con leche. It was still pretty chilly for me. At just a little after 10 AM, the day had not warmed up much.

When I stepped into the cafe, I was happy to see Rick and Dave. With a smile, I said, " Hey, what's up." They didn't respond. They didn't say a word. Not the reaction I expected. Usually, I get some kind of ribbing about my pace or have a comment about the day's walk. I thought the silence was strange. I left my pack near the table and used the bathroom. When I returned, I ordered my café con leche and a pastry. I sat down just as Rick and Dave were getting up to leave. Rick gave me a couple of pats on the back when he left but didn't say anything. I wondered what that was about. I stayed to finish my coffee, considering that sometimes people get a little moody on the Camino. They don't want to talk or be social. No different from regular life. We all get to a point where we just get tired of it and it starts to show. Life is frustrating. People are frustrating. The Camino can be frustrating. The environment around you, as awesome as it is, can also be cruel. The heat, the cold, the rain, the strain of the climb, the pounding descent, uncomfortable beds, and more can bring you down. Sometimes you just want to go home, go back to the way it was. Maybe feel sorry for yourself for a while. But, there is no reverse. Instead, look around. See what you have. See where you are. See the good around you. Go forward. Move along on your Camino to find the wonders ahead. I try to remember this as I walk.

On the way into Trabadelo I had passed stacks of logs and stacks of lumber. On the way out, I found out why all the wood was there. An old-fashioned sawmill making lumber out of logs. In an open-air building, I saw a middle-aged man in a blue jumpsuit feeding logs into a saw, cutting them down to the right size. Saw dust flew about him, like flurries of snow, coating his jumpsuit.

This small ancient community, like many we passed, looks like it is falling apart. A roadside building had a roof caved-in in several areas and the balcony that ran along the front of the building held up with rotted timber, dropped off at the end with a missing railing. An ancient stone chapel I passed leaving Trabadelo was a wonderful historic site, yet sad. The stone tower had a balcony with its bell hanging on the street side of the balcony. The tower and balcony sagged dangerously

Ancient Roman Ruins outside Castromaior 10/18/21

with old warped timber.

Out of Trabadelo, I walked again along the rio Valcare, enjoying the stroll and watching grazing cows in small shaded pastures along the river. In about an hour though, I am back on an asphalt road and entering La Portela de Valcarce. On the roadside is a cement statue of the pilgrim Santiago with staff, water gourd, robe, and a wide brim hat. The hat and robe are adorned with scallop shells. Across the road is a gasoline station. The Camino doesn't pass many gas stations, no need for them on a walking trail.

While walking through town I saw about twenty huge pumpkins stacked in front of a stone building partially blocking the wooden door. Each pumpkin was so large it would fill the wheelbarrow that stood next to the building. I wondered if the Spanish people carved pumpkins for Halloween as we do in America. If they did, these would make monstrous Jack O'Lanterns.

I moved on and came upon the Iglesia de San Juan Bautista, a small Baroque-style stone chapel dedicated to Saint John the Baptist. It had the unstable look of many ancient buildings on the Camino. Built on the side of a hill, the entrance was four steps down off the road making the chapel subject to flooding, I thought. When I went inside to look around I expected a well-worn interior, as well. Surprisingly, the inside was pristine. The nave of the church consisted of eight polished wooden pews butted up to the side walls, four on each side of a center aisle. The pews were about six feet long to seat a tight three people or two comfortably. What really amazed me though was the reredos, the wall behind the altar, with its magnificent intricate artwork, adorned with gilded gold. Two stories high was the crucified Christ on the cross at the center top, on each side a statue dressed in the robes of monks. The one on the left had a brown robe; the one on the right had a white robe. Below the cross was a statue I believed to be Saint John the

Baptist. To the left of him was Mother Mary with the slain Christ in her lap. On the right, the Mother Mary in royal dress held the baby Jesus. Throughout the Camino, the splendor of these churches contrasted sharply with the conditions in the surrounding community. Seeing the smallest and seemingly poorest churches with deteriorating exteriors yet resplendent alters and artifacts made me wonder about the use of money in the Catholic Church in the past. I do realize that many of these churches were built by patrons hundreds of years ago and helped pilgrims on their way to Santiago, but also think about how many more poor could be fed by the money used to build the church. God's house does not need to be adorned with gold and silver. A simple structure for the faithful to gather and worship works just as well.

When I entered, there were two people in the church. In the front pew on the right sat a woman wearing an off-white blouse and off-white wide-brim hat. A man with a forest green polo shirt and tan Khaki pants sat behind her in the second row at the left end. Together, they were praying the rosary. The man said one part and the woman followed with the ending, the response. Repeating ten times for the Hail Mary then one Our Father before returning to the Hail Mary. Rosary beads are used to count contemplative meditative prayers to bring people closer to Jesus through His Mother Mary. I wanted to get more detailed photos of the interior, but I felt like I was intruding, so I backed out to leave these pilgrims to complete their rosary.

I leave the church and return to my walk along the river and pastures with grazing cows until I reached a stone bridge and cross over the river into Las Herrerias. I come upon a building with riding saddles hanging on a wooden rod suspended under a balcony. On a wooden sign attached to the balcony is painted "horses," above that is a stenciled phone number on another wood plaque. Next, I came to a small rest area on the rio das Lamas river bank. The stream's waters bubble over the river rocks creating a soothing melody. There are a couple of picnic tables under a pavilion and an exercise machine made with pipes. The scene is very peaceful, a nice place to rest or exercise. I take some photos and move on.

Once through Las Herrerias and back on a dirt path, I start the steep climb towards O'Cebreira, stopping at Laguna de Castilla for my accommodations for the night at Bar Albergue La Escuela. We wanted to stay in O'Cebreira, but rooms were not available.

I entered Laguna de Castilla, greeted by a horse parade, a rider on horseback followed by five other horses with saddles, but no riders. Later that evening, I would encounter a cow parade passing the albergue as I enjoyed a Nestea sitting at a table in the albergue bar with Rick. Unfortunately, my cellphone was charging in the room so I couldn't make a video of the parade. Rick was putting together his daily video of photos taken so far that day. He quickly saved his work and managed to record part of the parade. It was fun to watch the farmer leading the herd back to the barn with the aid of a small Shepherd. One cow missed the turn into the barnyard gate, nonchalantly plodding up the hill instead. The farmer's wife followed to retrieve the cow. With the assistance of the dog and a stick to lightly swat the cow's rump, she turned it around and brought her home for the night.

Shortly after the cow parade, a group of young pilgrims arrived to town. Five young adults in their early twenties. It was fun to watch their camaraderie, laughing and joking with each other. They were right outside the window by our table freshening up at a faucet. One took the time to kick a soccer ball around with the albergue owner's young boy. Each tried to show off their moves to the other.

The Bar Albergue La Escuela was nice. The food served in the restaurant was excellent. The staff was very friendly. The bunk beds in the room were adequate. The thin mattresses, however, were well-worn and a little uncomfortable. The bed was a bit short for me, I kept hitting the frame of the bed with my feet. Yet, somehow, I slept well that night. Walking for six hours a day will do that to you.

CHAPTER FORTY-ONE

10/15/2021
Laguna de Castilla / Triacastela

Our original plans were to stay in O'Cebreiro last night. Unable to find accommodations there, we stayed in Laguna de Castilla instead. This turned out to be a blessing for a couple of reasons. For one, the climb into O'Cebreiro is steep. We split this steep climb into two days. The real blessing, however, came when we arrived at O'Cebreioro. As usual, we left early, starting our climb predawn, and arrived just as the sun began to rise.

Along the road at the entrance to the village is a stone wall with a spectacular view of the landscape we walked through in the last week or so, a beautiful valley below and the mountains beyond. I looked down into a deep undulating valley and then to the grey silhouette of mountains on the distant horizon. Beside me, on a stone platform in the wall, is a bronze female statue, legs crossed at her ankles and hands folded in her lap. She sits meditatively facing the village of O'Cebreiro, a pilgrim at peace.

To my right stood a dozen or more fellow pilgrims that came to watch the sunrise. Among them were our Camino friends, Phil and Muriel. As usual, Phil's greeting was warm and cheerful and Muriel offered a peaceful pleasant smile. I am so impressed at how happy this man seems to be. I always feel the goodwill in his heart and the true spirit of the Camino in his soul.

We stood at the wall and watched the dark skies get lighter as the twilight changed to dawn. The sun traced the mountain rim with gold gilding as she peeked over the top on her ascent into the sky. An orange glow began to fill the skies on the horizon. A few cumulus clouds take on the orange tint. The sun's golden fingertips of light reach into the sky to create the splendid pastel dawn of a new day. Somehow this just felt right. It was going to be a good day.

After being blessed with this wondrous sunrise, the pilgrims gathered backpacks and started the daily walk toward Santiago.

Before moving on, Phil asked me if I had visited the church, the Church of Santa Maria la Real (Saint Mary the Royal). I explained that Rick, Dave, and I stayed in Laguna de Castilla last night and just arrived. He told me the church doors open at 9 AM and suggested I stay and look around. "You know a miracle took place here," he said.

The "Miracle of the Eucharist"[xlvii] occurred when Juan Santin, a farmer from Barxamaior, trudged his way up the mountain through the ice and snow of a severe winter storm to hear Mass and receive Communion. A priest, who was having some doubts about his faith, was preparing for the Mass, not expecting anyone to attend due to the severe storm. When the farmer arrived, the priest laughed and chided him for traveling through the storm for a little bread and wine.

The priest hurriedly went through the ceremony of Mass until he spoke the words of the Consecration when the host in his hands actually turned into flesh, blood dripping through his fingers to stain the corporal, the small white linen cloth on which the chalice is placed. The wine in the chalice changed to blood. The monk fell to his knees praising God with his faith restored.

Some people believe the Chalice at O'Cebreiro is the Holy Grail, the cup used by Jesus Christ at the last supper and used by Joseph of Arimathea to collect his blood at the Crucifixion.

While waiting for the doors to open, I walked around the property. Outside the church is a grass courtyard nestled between the buildings. At the front of this yard is a bust on a block pedestal of Don Elias Valiña Sampedro. Six memorial plaques are set on the ground around the bust. As a reminder for people to respect the area, three colored chains are strung between marble stanchions about 18 inches high. The two end chains were white, the center chain blue. Beneath the chains were colorfully painted smooth rounded river stones. Some were painted with great detail - a ladybug, a bumblebee, or a bird. Others were more childish in design but not less heartfelt. Cartoonish characters, crude drawings of animals, or splotches of different colored paints decorated the stones. A few had words, written in Spanish, of love or Memoriam for loved ones.

I learned that Sampedro served as the parish priest from 1959 to 1989 and was instrumental in restoring the church and the ancient hospital, which is now a hostel.

Sampedro, who wrote a thesis on the Camino's history while at university, was a strong supporter and promotor of the walk. When he took his own Camino in the early 1980s, he noted that many of the original trails had disappeared and he had a difficult time finding the way. On his next Camino in 1984, using leftover highway paint, he started marking the trail with yellow arrows to steer pilgrims in the right direction. I found these arrows painted on roads, houses, stone walls, fences, guardrails, and trees. They were everywhere and helped immensely. It is unimaginable how difficult walking the Camino would be without these markers.

At 9 AM, the church opened for visitors. When I pulled open the sturdy wood door and stepped inside, I was awed by the simplicity of the sanctuary. A simple stone block wall with three narrow windows for light. Jesus Christ hung on a wooden cross in the center. The lighting created two shadows of the Crucifix on the rear stone wall, one on each side of the wooden cross. I wondered if it was done intentionally with the shadows representing the crosses of the two thieves at Calvary with Jesus. An altar draped with an embroidered white cloth, a podium in the center, and chairs to the side completed the setup. To me, this simple design was more inspiring than the ornate gilded gold sanctuaries of the other churches I had visited.

At a side altar is a mausoleum with the remains of the monk and Juan Santin. At a small altar to the right is a sealed reliquary lined with red velvet to display the Chalice and paten used in the Mass and a tabernacle with the stained cloth.

A carved wood statue of Saint James sits on a shelf on a side wall. He holds a book in his left hand and his staff with a gourd in his right, scallop shells on his cloak. At the base of the shelf is an arrangement of yellow flowers shaped like an arrow.

On another shelf is the splendid Royal Blessed Mother wearing a crown and holding the toddler Jesus in her lap. A bouquet of flowers rests at her feet.

There is another intricately carved statue of Saint Francisco de Assísi (1182 - 1226) wearing a monk robe tied with a rope, holding a cross, and a child at his left leg clings to his robe.

Before leaving I lit a candle asking God, as I did at the Cruz de Ferro, to lift the burdens from my family and friends allowing them to live the rest of their lives happy and healthy.

While I was walking around the building taking photographs of the ancient slate stone church and churchyard, I met a pilgrim named Steve. We chatted for a while and he tells me he is Catholic. He mentions he has a daughter living in Florida. And I believe he said he was from New Jersey. He asked if I was Catholic. I told him I was raised Catholic through grammar school and high school, but I wasn't a practicing Catholic at this time. I then said that this experience may bring me back. He smiled and said, welcome back.

After visiting the church, I made my way through O'Cebreiro following Sampedro's yellow arrows past hobbit-like homes, thatched roofed stone buildings known as *pallozas*. A *palloza* usually has two sections, a lower room for animals and an upper room for the family. The family area will have a private room for the parents. Everyone else shares the common area. In the center of the common area is a fire pit for cooking. Around the fire pit are benches used for sleeping. There are nine surviving *pallozas* in O'Cebreiro, three available for pilgrims to visit and learn about the simple lifestyle of villagers sharing their homes with livestock.

I should have stayed longer to visit a *palloza* and enjoy a café con leche. I did walk around a bit and take some pictures but not many. Knowing you have many hours of walking ahead, makes you want to keep moving. Or you won't get anywhere, Barry had said to me a few days ago.

I leave O'Cebreiro along a dirt and stone path through the forest. After just a few minutes of walking, I suddenly felt a welling of emotions, and my eyes filled with tears. Where did this come from, I thought. Perhaps God is speaking to me in some way, trying to bring me back into the fold. Welcome back. Is this the spiritual uplifting many pilgrims tell about?

I am glad that I walk alone so I can process these emotions.

Along this stretch of the Camino is the Monument to the Pilgrim, a bronze statue of a pilgrim fighting against the wind, leaning forward and pushing off on his walking stick for a steep climb. I am at the Alto de San Roque at altitude of 1270 meters.

I trudge up an extremely steep climb on a cobbled road. Even the youngest and fit struggled with this climb.

It was on this climb that I met Lars and Chloe. I passed Chloe who was carrying a very heavy backpack. I knew it was heavy by its size, but also by how she walked, leaning forward to maintain her balance on this steep angle of ascent. Just ahead was Lars, also with a heavy pack, including a tent. He had stopped to pet a German Shepherd lying in the middle of the road. A black and white border collie stood beside the Shepherd watching Lars.

I walked up, put out my fist to let the collie take a sniff, and then started scratching the collie's head. Most dogs like their heads scratched and this dog seemed to be enjoying it until it suddenly swung its head around to bite my hand. I was quick enough to avoid the bite. I stood up and nicely admonished the dog. "What did you do that for?" I asked. "I am just trying to be nice." I put my hand out for the dog to sniff again, but it backed away. I left it at that.

I found out Lars was from Belgium and the girl carrying the heavy pack was his older sister. Lars is 21 and Chloe is 23.

At the top of this climb is the O Tear - Bar Restaurante in Hospital Lugo. After the extremely tough climb, many pilgrims stopped at this bar for a beverage and a rest.

I dropped my day pack on a chair and went inside to use the

bathroom and get something to eat and drink. I sat at the table and watched a German Shepherd that would head into the road barking, as if calling to the pilgrims, a warning or a welcome, I am not sure. There was another large dog, a large overweight yellow Lab mix. His job was to lay lazily around for pilgrim petting.

As I sat enjoying the break, the group of college age friends I saw last night at Laguna de Castilla finished the climb, one by one. As each arrived at the top of the climb, the cafe crowd cheered and clapped for each one, congratulating them for making the extremely steep climb. I wished my friends were there to cheer me on.

That is what I had envisioned for my Camino, traveling together with friends encouraging each other, cheering each other on. I suppose that is the Hollywood version.

In the Village of Padornelo, a small town with maybe a dozen buildings, I passed the parish church of San Juan. I take a few photos of the church and move on.

I walked along the road through Fonfria watching the cattle grazing on the hillside of the valley below. I passed the Albergue Reboleira. A round palloza building with a thatched roof served as the hostel's restaurant. Although it has the charm of an ancient building, it was constructed in 1999.

Making my way on the dirt path beside a stone wall protecting a pasture, I see cows making their way toward me. It is another cow parade. I start the video, filming about twenty-five to thirty cows guided by a German Shepherd and a herder with a stick. I back into a crevice in the wall to avoid being knocked over by a passing cow. They are just a few feet from me. I could reach out and grab one of the horns if I wanted to. The herder was the last in line, tapping the cow in front of him with his stick to keep it moving. I wished him a Buen Camino when he passed and received an annoyed look in return. I don't believe he liked me filming him and his cow parade.

I was walking along another stone wall when a horse came out through a break in the wall and headed up the road. There was no saddle, but I did see the reins hanging from his head. A moment later, I saw the head of a sheep peek out through the break in the wall and look in my direction as if checking for traffic. It then entered the road with three other sheep behind it. They scurried to catch up to the horse. There was no shepherd or farmer in sight. They were heading out on their own.

Today was a fortunate day, I had the pleasure of seeing two parades, a cow parade and a sheep parade.

About a kilometer from Triacastela, in the Village of Ramil, is the 800-year-old centennial chestnut tree of Ramil. A young tree when the *Codex Calixtinus* was written, now nearly nine meters in diameter with twisted, almost artistic, irregularities in the trunk offering a wonderful background for a portrait of yourself and friends on the Camino. Its gnarly nooks and crannies in the trunk and thick branches make this one of the most photographed places on the Camino.

I entered Triacastela, which gets its name from three castles that once stood there. Unfortunately, none exist today. I followed the main road to the right to the Pension Albergue Lemos. The facilities are modern, clean, and comfortable. On the back side of the building is a large terrace with fantastic views of Mount Oribio and the town of Triacastela.

After we settle in, Rick, Dave, and I head out to explore and find a place to eat.

CHAPTER FORTY-TWO

10/16/2021
Triacastela - Sarria

We headed out today with overcast skies which soon changed to drizzling rain. The rain can make the trail muddy and the rocks slippery. I tried to make sure I had a well-planted foot before taking the next step forward.

Although this stage of the Camino from Tricastela to Sarria is among the shortest, there is a degree of difficulty due to an ascent to reach the peak of Riocabo during the first part of the walk.

Out of Triacastela I walked peacefully through the woods. Before reaching San XIL, I spot a large, sculptured scallop shell, maybe five feet in height and painted green and white, built into a flagstone wall on the side of the hill. A stone u-shaped path circles around a stone pool of water to the fountain beneath the shell. There is a stone bench on each side of the shell, a resting place for pilgrims. I take a few photos and then continue on my way.

I just finished taking pictures of a small church and cemetery and was about to turn right following the arrows back into the woods when I saw someone hurrying up the road towards me. As this person approached, I realized it was Rick. I waited a few seconds for him to get closer before asking what happened. He walked with me for just a minute or two, just long enough to tell me he missed the turn and had stayed on the road. Then he hurried past me, like the Brer Rabbit in Alice Through the Looking Glass. "I'm late, I'm late." Rick seems to always walk like he is in a hurry. He could have stayed on the road since this was the bicycle route for the Camino, but he wanted to stay on the pedestrian way. I lost sight of him within a few seconds.

I turned another corner and came upon a small house with a stone wall enclosing the yard of the Terra de Luz. On top of the wall were Camino and Spanish memorabilia, old boots, and small farm tools. The owner of the property had also set up a Donativo stand under an open-sided stone building in the yard. The homeowner offered fruit, snacks, and drinks for weary pilgrims, only requesting donations. The open-sided shed had a small couch and cushioned chairs around a coffee table like a living room. A guitar hung on the back wall. There were old walking sticks and other Camino memorabilia. The yard between the house and shed was nicely landscaped with lawn furniture and empty wire spools for tables. On the wall in the yard were a few stones painted with quotes. One said, "Your Soul is the 1 thing you can't compromise Judith Holanda." Another said, "The importance to put great love in the small things (Mother Teresa)." The word love was represented with a red heart.

The owner, a nice man with a goatee, probably about 30 to 35 years old, asked if I wanted a coffee. I declined the coffee but did take a banana for the road, dropping a euro in a wicker basket. Of course, I took some pictures of the cool-looking Donativo to preserve these memories.

Just a few minutes past the Donativo was the Laberinto de Samos. The wooden sign, painted with white lettering in both Spanish and English, said "Welcome to the Samos Labyrinth. This is a sacred place for you to enjoy, connect, pray, meditate & receive guidance for your Way." Beyond the sign was a spiral created with large stones or boulders circling through half a dozen trees.

A few minutes later, I passed half a dozen white cows and one red cow munching on hay in a rack under a plexiglass cover. About twenty yards away was a stone barn and an old tractor.

A little later, I had the pleasure of filming another cow parade making its way through a small hamlet. Patrons sat at tables outside a cafe watching. Who wouldn't want a cow parade passing by when having lunch with their special aroma added to the meal? Cows are marched through the cobble-stoned streets to barns or other pastures by a herder with a stick and a dog to keep the cows moving in the right direction. This is the third time I've watched a cow parade. I continued my walk through town sidestepping the patties left by the cows.

I walked for an hour or so through an oak forest, enjoying the solitude.

On the outskirts of Sarria, I met Roberto and walked with him for a while. Roberto is from Madrid but told me he is originally from Sarria. He started his Camino in Leon. Roberto was recently laid off from the banking industry. His job was eliminated by the digitizing of the industry. He was with BBVA, a multinational financial service company based in Madrid. He was walking the Camino based on a suggestion from one of his three daughters that did the walk last year.

As usual, when meeting people on the Camino, we exchanged our stories. I told him I was from Orlando, Florida and retired from the hotel business. He replied that part of his honeymoon was in Miami and they drove four hours one day to go to Disney World. Another part of his honeymoon was in California.

At one point he changed the subject to political history. Of special interest to him is the period after WWII. He believed the United Kingdom and France kept their eyes closed to communism, giving in to the communist following the war. During World War II, the government of Spain under Francisco Franco was officially neutral but maintained political and economic ties to Germany.

Roberto told me he liked the Germans because they fought against communism. He believed Franco, however, trying to recover from the war, did not support the fight against communism. Franco believed the young people needed to stay at home to rebuild Spain.

We separated when Roberto decided to stop for something to eat.

Sarria, located about 114 kilometers from Santiago, is the last town where you can start the Camino and meet the minimum distance to get the Compostela. It is also the point where the Camino Frances connects with the Camino del Norte (North Way).

Sarria is a municipality in the province of Lugo in the autonomous region of Galicia. It is one of the largest towns in the province. With buildings from the 19th and 20th centuries, it is not a quaint medieval village like many of the towns we visited during our journey.

The town was founded by King Alfonso IX towards the end of the 12th century. Coincidentally, he died in Sarria from an illness on a pilgrimage to Santiago to give thanks for the Reconquest of Mérida.

On the way to my albergue, I passed the Church of Santa Mariña de Sarria with a Roman numeral clock at the top of the front facade below the belfry. Outside the church was another double-sided cross with the crucified Christ on one side and the Blessed Mother holding the baby Jesus on the other side.

Just past the church, I spot Dave standing at a corner outside a bar talking with Linda from Holland. I join them to walk together for a while until Linda splits off to go her own way. Dave and I make our way towards the Pension Aqua Rooms located in Sarria's historic district just minutes from the church.

The Pension Aqua Rooms is a nice small establishment with only three rooms, each with a private bath. We are greeted warmly by the hostess originally from the Boston area, if I remember correctly. There is a refrigerator stocked with beers, sodas, and water in the front room across from her desk. There is a price list on the door and a basket to leave payment. Much of the Camino is on the honor system. We have a room with four beds and an adjoining room with a dining table. An oddity to this establishment is that the building is old and the floors are uneven. The tilt of the floor made it feel like I was going to roll off the bed when I laid down to rest.

After settling in, we went out to find a mercado. We stocked up with cold cuts, bread, snacks, and pastries for dinner and tomorrow's breakfast. It was nice to sit around the dining table enjoying sandwiches and recounting our day's walk.

CHAPTER FORTY-THREE

10/17/2021
Sarria - Portomarin

Leaving Sarria, I descended the steep narrow lamp-lit predawn streets past stone buildings centuries old. The skies between the buildings showed the black of night. The street was empty except for Dave and Rick up ahead. We left Sarria in the dark for our next night in Portomarin.

The stone-paved street led me past the 12th-century Albergue Monasterio de La Magdalena, a former monastery. We crossed the rio Pequeno then out of town and into the Spanish countryside.

Back in the woods, I heard birds greeting the new day with cheerful songs. Leaving the woods, I noticed the morning fog hanging low over a green grassy field like a layer of soft fluffy cotton. The golden leaves of the trees in the distance are illuminated by the rising sun. Eventually, the fog burns off. I continued walking along the grassy field. About a hundred yards beyond the grass field is a corn field. Beyond the corn field are bright blue skies and a few low-hanging clouds, remnants of the morning fog.

Up until this point Dave walked with me, but pulled further ahead each time I stopped to take photos. I didn't expect him to wait every time I stopped to take a photograph. Rick was already well ahead.

I came across a small lone building, maybe 18 x 18. Inside was a small altar covered with notes, photos, scallop shells, small stones, little medals, a few pieces of fruit, and some coins. Above the altar was a bust of a woman wearing the black and white head covering of the sisters of a religious order. The bust was enclosed in a frame covered and protected by intricately designed iron bars.

From the top of a rise, I saw the village of Ferreiros, which means blacksmith, and the Iglesia de Santa Maria de Ferreiros, a Romanesque church built in the 12th century, with its adjoining cemetery.

As I approached, an intricately designed small building caught my attention with spires, battlements, and a cross peeking over the wall that surrounded the cemetery's sacred grounds. In my ignorance, I did not realize this was a mausoleum until I went around the church to the cemetery. A cement bowl, I assumed to be a holy water font, sat on the ground at the start of a flagstone path lined with mausoleums. At the end of the path, a mausoleum built as magnificently as a Gaudi castle held seven chambers for the departed. The dates of the departure ranged from 1948 to 2008 and there was one empty crypt. Although the church is from the 12th century, I noted that all the occupants of the crypts were from the 20th century.

There are many small hamlets between Sarria and Portomarin. Walking through one of these small hamlets, I passed a barn just as a farmer, with the help of three dogs, led his four cows out of the barn and down the road. The dogs ran alongside nipping at hooves and snouts to let the cows know they were in charge. Another cow parade, small, but just as delightful to watch as the others.

Attached to the rod iron bars covering a window in another hamlet I noticed a replica of a witch riding a straw broom, perhaps in homage to Maria Soliña, a Galician witch from the 17th century[xlviii] that managed to live through the witch burnings of the Inquisition. Galicia is known as the land of witches and magic. The magic is often felt while passing through the fairy tale forests of Spain.

In another tiny community, I spotted my first hórreo. A hórreo is a traditional structure commonly found in Galicia used to store grain. They are rectangular ventilated buildings of varying sizes made of stone or wood raised from the ground by pillars with staddle stones. Staddle stones are bowl-shaped and placed upside down on the pillars to curtail access by rodents. This hórreo was about five feet wide and twelve feet long. The ends were block and the sides were red brick. Each brick had seventeen small holes for ventilation. A narrow wood door hanging on rusted hinges allowed access to the corn, root vegetables, or grains stored inside.

Approaching Portomarin, I followed a road leading to the banks of the rio Miño and a long bridge crossing high above the river to the new town of Portomarin. The original town was flooded in the 1960s when the river was dammed to build the Belesar Reservoir. Monuments and buildings of historical value, including the 12th century San Xoân de Portomarin (Church of Saint John) and the Capela de San Pedro (Saint Peter Chapel), were moved piece by piece to their new location. The original town of Portomarin now lies underwater below the new bridge.

The bridge is pretty high up. If you suffer from acrophobia (fear of heights), don't look down. Since I grew up around New York City and its many skyscrapers, I am accustomed to looking down from great heights. When I looked over the railing, I saw brown hair atop a boy's head. He wore a red sweatshirt, blue jeans, and a yellow nylon day pack similar to my blue one. He stood patiently on the old bridge with his line in the water waiting for his catch.

Since the waters were low, I also saw some stone-building rooftops taken over by the river's vegetation to form small islands in the wide river. I didn't realize these were the old buildings from the original Portomarin until I learned about the town's history. I also learned that these ancient buildings and the old bridge from which the boy was fishing were underwater when the waters are high. They disappear from sight, a lost city from antiquity.

Across the river, I saw the new town rising up the mountainside. At the peak was the Church of San Xoán built as a church and a castle. It is a Romanesque rectangular building with crenelated battlement crowns on defense towers at each corner. These tower crowns and a large medieval rose-shaped window above the main arched entrance capture your attention from a distance.

At the end of the bridge were an unwanted 45 steps up to the town's stone arch gateway. The steps offered a challenge after several hours of walking. I trudged up the stairs using my poles to assist in the climb. I walked through the stone arch to enter town only to find another steep climb on a cobblestone road. At the top of this climb, the suffering Jesus hung on a cross. The grieving mother Mary clung to the base.

Glad I took the scenic route into town. I learned later from Rick and Dave that the highway route included a steep dangerous difficult decline of 45 - 50 degrees.

That night when we went out to dinner, we found a nice little restaurant off the town square. We sat inside and looked through the menu options. The three of us decided to order steak. When we ordered three steaks, the waitress gave us a quizzical look and then asked, "Are you sure you want three steaks?" We returned with our quizzical looks. "Hold on," she said. She came back with a raw steak that was huge, almost two pounds. We cut the order to two steaks to split between us. Even then we had steak left over.

CHAPTER FORTY-FOUR

10/18/2021
Portomarin - Palas de Rei

Our next overnight is in Palas de Rei.

We leave about 8 AM. It is still dark. Once out of Portomarin, we walked on a gravel path alongside the road. The sky is getting lighter and the fog is lifting. I see many pilgrims ahead of me. Since leaving Sarria, I noticed many more pilgrims walking to Santiago. Not unexpected since Sarria is just over the 100-kilometer minimum needed to qualify for a Compostela Certificate when you arrive at the cathedral in Santiago.

I crossed the road, turned right, and walked a gravel path along the front of a fertilizer plant. The pungent odor is much stronger than the more subtle odor experienced when walking through farmland. To some, the odor may be annoying or gross, but to me, it is a natural organic smell and much better than the stench of the pollution and the toxic fumes of a city.

Once past the plant, I turned left onto a path with tall hedges on each side to block the view of the fertilizer plant on my left and the road on my right. I emerge from the hedge row to see a field on my left and the road on my right. Ahead, on my left is another hórreo on a rectangular pedestal of flagstone about five feet high. Wood slats on the sides allow ventilation.

Just a little more than an hour out of Portomarin, I am back into a patch of woods with a thick carpet of browning ferns. The monotone view looked like a sepia-tone photograph of the forest.

Out of the woods and on a road with a slight incline, I passed an old man walking slowly, slightly hunched, and using his walking stick to support his weight. It is obvious the walk is taking a toll on him. He sees me and begins to moan as if on cue, repeating several times, "coffeeeee. So tired. I need coffeeeee!" That is all the English he seemed to know. Fortunately, we came up on the Hosteria de Gonzar. I went around back to the bathrooms. The old man went inside to get his coffeeeee.

After taking care of business, I went into the restaurant and ordered breakfast at the counter, including coffeeeee, cafe con leche. They took my name and would call out when my food was ready. I thought about joining the old man, but he spoke no English, so I just nodded at him and sat at another table to enjoy my break. I felt for the old man but really didn't want to hear him whining anymore. Maybe if he spoke English, I could have helped soothe his pain. I don't know, maybe I should have tried. I think he just needed to rest for a while and get his thoughts turned around to feel better going forward.

I followed the road through Gonzar and am back in the countryside within a few minutes. In this section of my Camino, I meet Chris and Richard. Chris, born in Spain, now lives in England. Richard is British. I hope to remember his name by thinking of Richard the Lionhearted. I often forget the names of the people I meet. It is a fault I have had forever. If I don't deal with someone on a regular basis I will forget their name.

Passing by a home in Castromaior, Chris points out a small decorative wicker corn crib or hórreo about two feet square. It stands about five feet high with a thatched roof. It is different than the others, a miniature decorative version made for the home with a couple of dozen corn cobs strung on the outside. It looks like a birdcage. At the base of the pedestals are colorful potted plants and small wood garden sculptures. Taller wood sculptures, about three feet high, one of a pilgrim, the other an upright figure with the face of a hog, stood in the yard. A wood carving of a locomotive and two rail cars used as flower boxes was parked at the curb near the corn crib. Other examples of the artist's talent decorated the yard.

Chris reminds me of the ancient pre-Roman ruins in the area, telling me that we need to keep our eyes open since the ruins are not very well marked. On the outskirts of Castromaior, she spots the informational sign for the Castro de Castromaior. The sign sits about twenty yards off the path and is easily missed if not actively looking for it. I am glad that Chris reminded me of this wonderful archaeological site. Without her help, I may have walked right past since the fort is hidden behind a hill of dirt around the perimeter of the site, a result of the dig.

The Castro de Castromaior is an archaeological site of a Celtic culture living in the Iberian Peninsula over 2000 years ago. Archaeological finds date back to 4 BC. The site is about 5 hectares or a little over 12 acres. According to the signboard, the original fort was abandoned when the Romans arrived.

From where I stood, all I could see was a ten-foot high mound of dirt. I climbed a path up the mound. From the top I saw the remnants of an intricate stone fort complex comprised of many rooms. I spend about a half hour walking around the complex, first taking photos from the mound that surrounded the site, then walking through the hallway maze. I think about how life might have been 2000 years ago before the birth of Christ.

When I was done taking photos I saw that I could follow another path out of the site to the Camino trail, a shortcut to save a few steps.

Walking through the small community of O Hospital, I passed a barn stuffed with rolls of hay. A side room contained baling equipment that is pulled behind a tractor.

I passed a sign for Hospital da Cruz Hostal and Mesón Labrador Restaurante. Beneath are two rusted and faded aqua blue arrow-shaped signs pointing down a path to the left. One read "Ice Cold Beer, Enjoy Your Time" with a rendition of a foaming beer mug at the tail end of the arrow. The other said," Coffee, Always Fresh Brewed" with a rendition of a steaming cup of coffee. I was tempted to take a break and enjoy a cup of cafe con leche. I decided otherwise since I had spent some time at the Castro de Castromaior.

Just outside O Hospital is an irregular-shaped stone monolith with a plaque that reads *xunta de galicia conselleria de politica territorial obras publicas e vivenda* (Regional Government of Galicia Ministry of Territorial Policy Public Works and Housing) and informs me I am 78.1 Km from Santiago. I am almost there. Three more days and I will be in Santiago de Compostela. It is hard to believe I have walked through Spain for a month. It seems so long ago that I started and, yet, it seems like it was yesterday. I have seen so much. Experienced so much. Although I was upset a few times with the guys pulling ahead every day, I don't regret for a moment that I have taken this journey. Especially, once I got beyond those negative thoughts.

The community of Ventas de Narón is the site of a battle between Muslims and Christians in the year 820 during the reign of the Asturian King Alfonso II. Leaving Ventas de Narón, I passed the Capilla de la

Magdalena, a simple structure once used as a hospital for pilgrims. The wooden door of the chapel is decorated with symbols of chalices, a pilgrim shell, and a cross.

From here, I travel along an asphalt path with a beautiful panoramic view of the Spanish countryside.

Walking through another village, I see an old woman sweeping her property. A German Shepherd lays nearby watching me pass. Next, I pass pastures and longhorn cows grazing or eating out of a feeder.

In Ligonde, an old man sits on a log outside a building entrance, both hands cupping the handle of a cane between his legs, and beside him is a broom and dustpan with a long handle. I think about how clean the proud Spanish people leave their communities, even the big cities. A few times, when leaving predawn, I saw the street cleaners at work.

I peeked through the window of a building to see a line of black and white cows, heads protruding through bars, waiting to be fed. Sheep graze in a field nearby.

There is a rough patch with an incline through a boulder-filled ravine. Not bad, compared to some I have traversed. The worst was the rainy decline into Zubiri. The boulders on this incline are useful steps, but I still need to be careful to keep from tripping.

Near Portos is the Albergue a Paso de Formiga which caught my attention with a wonderful courtyard decorated with giant sculptures of ants five or six feet high. Of course, I took some photos of the massive insects.

After the albergue, I passed pastures littered with cows and a beautiful stretch through a wooded area, the path strewn with brown fallen leaves. Yet, the trees still held enough green to provide comfortable shade. This opened up to a less densely wooded area with mowed grassy areas. Circular cement tables and benches set back about twenty yards under a canopy of trees provided an area for pilgrims to relax.

When I arrived in Plas de Rei it was 71 degrees and sunny, a beautiful day. It felt like I was back in Florida.

I checked in to the Pension Pardellas, a nice place with three single beds in the room. Covering the wall behind the headboards is a landscape photo, giving the rooms a more spacious feeling. After settling in we head out to do our daily laundry. The laundromat is a couple of blocks away.

There is a bar/cafe next to the laundromat and Linda is sitting outside. We join her and chat about our day while enjoying a beer (Nestea for me). A woman approached me babbling about something. It appeared she wanted to use my phone to make a call. I let her dial a number, which she did, then handed it back to me. It was hard to understand her but it seemed she was asking me to put in a bank number. The guide booked warned us to be aware of scams the closer we got to Santiago. People trying to take advantage of pilgrims. Walking through Spain on a spiritual journey, becoming one with nature, with yourself, and with God, it is easy to forget that not everyone has the Camino spirit. She moved on mumbling when she realized she would not get anywhere with me.

CHAPTER FORTY-FIVE

10/19/2021
Palas de Rei - Ribadiso

When I left Palas de Rei, I passed a small church with a carpet of fog hanging over the adjoining cemetery. The rising sun casts a pinkish glow on the fog creating an eerie ghostly scene. I took a few photos and then went on my way.

Later, I came across a girl at a water fountain with a bloody nose and bloody tissue hanging out of her nose. I asked if she was OK. She said, "Yeah, yeah, yeah. It is what it is." She appeared to be dealing with a familiar problem. If not, I would have tried to help. But my help wasn't needed, so no chance for chivalry today. I moved on.

I walked through mostly forested areas today. Very peaceful with the now familiar rises and declines of the trail.

When walking on dirt and stone along a corn field, the path veered around a corner to the left. I spotted a man about fifty years old, staring across the cut field to the horizon, deep in thought. A girl in her young twenties stood about 6 feet behind him facing the other direction. She appeared impatient, pacing, shifting her weight, wanting to move on. Based on the difference in age, I believed they were father and daughter.

The contrasting actions, made me think about how the Camino affects different people, especially the difference between the young and the old. Older folks have much more life experiences to reflect upon. They have experienced more joys and losses. On the Camino many walk to ponder their losses, reflect on their lives, to grieve. Others, between jobs, walk to consider their next opportunity, the next direction to take in their life. I think most younger people are more carefree about their Camino, walking more for the adventure than the spiritual experience. I noticed the attitude difference several times. The young seem more playful and jovial about their walk. Older folks are having a good time, but often seem more serious and contemplative about why they walk.

In another small farm community, I heard squawking and then saw an old woman at a barn entrance holding two chickens by their legs, stuffing the live chickens into a canvas bag. Was this tonight's dinner? People live a simple life in rural Spain without large supermarkets at every corner. Throughout our travels through villages and hamlets, the mercados (stores) were often no larger than my living room. Even in the bigger cities of Burgos, Leon and others, I did not see the large supermarkets familiar in the United States.

About an hour outside of Palas de Rei, I came up on the Albergue Casa Domingo near Campaño. I stopped to photograph a huge twelve-foot high scallop shell sculpture. I'm sure many pilgrims have had their pictures taken near this shell.

In O Leboreiro is the Casa de los Somoza. A life-size detail sculpture of Saint James stood out front on the sidewalk, complete with staff, water gourd, and scallop shell on his wide-brimmed hat.

Next, I passed the gothic Iglesia de Santa Maria de Leboreiro. A wicker corn crib or hórreo with a thatched roof, a little larger than the one I saw in Castromaior, stood on the corner of the church property near their sign. A stone wall surrounded the church with a picket gate to the courtyard and church entrance. The Virgin Mother holding baby Jesus in both arms is sculpted in the relief on the tympanum above the entrance

I waited momentarily before crossing a single arched stone bridge over the rio Ulla as a young man took photos of his girlfriend.

I entered Melide, a bustling, but not very attractive city, complete with traffic congestion. I lost track of the signs but followed a young girl wearing a backpack, obviously a pilgrim. On the main road, we made a left walking past shops and cafes. She hesitated at a busy street corner, both of us looking for the Camino marker. I finally spotted it on the corner diagonally across the street. I pointed toward it to let her know. She did not speak English so this is how I communicated. She smiled and nodded. We waited for the traffic light to change. Crossed the street and waited for the signal to change to cross again to the other corner.

It was an unusual walk through town with markers bringing us down narrow back allies between the buildings. In many cities, I would hesitate to enter an ally, but I felt safe on the Camino.

On the way out of Melide, I spotted through the cypress trees the belfry and steeple of the Romanesque Iglesia de Santa Maria de Melide, a rectangular building with a semicircular apse at the end. Unlike most other churches, the tympanum under the entrance arch above forest green wood doors is completely smooth, void of any sculptured relief or painting.

I continued along a sidewalk when I saw a woman with dark hair running up the hill of a side street by a twelve-foot stone wall and mumbling to herself. Obviously upset about something and in a hurry.

She wore a loose-fitting sleeveless off-white dress that buttoned up the front, black sneakers, and white socks. Once again I thought of the Brer Rabbit, "I'm late, I'm late."

I was back in the countryside when I walked by a long building with twenty-two windows on the side and two large metal cylindrical containers in front. I assume the containers are for holding grain.

I turn left at the end of the building and walk a dirt path and soon entered another forested area. I crossed the rio Catasol stepping on six large boulders with gaps between them to allow the water to flow.

I crossed another small stream and a rest area on the right. A sign states "Parroquia de Boente (Santiago)," parish of Boente. The rest area is pleasant with a couple of shaded picnic tables. I continue by since I am not tired and have no need to rest.

In A Peroxa is a sign with a map showing the location of a couple of churches and a of couple albergue. It also had phone numbers for the Policia, Gardia Civil, Centro de Saude (health center), Parque de Bombieros (fire station), and other services. What caught my attention, however, was the graffiti that said "Trump is Dumb, Trumpist R Dummer, Qanon = Madness." Sometimes it is hard to get away from the divisive partisan politics in the United States.

Entering Ribadiso required a slight detour due to construction work on the small bridge over the rio Iso with a path along the left side of the road. Construction equipment was repaving the road and bridge. Once I crossed the bridge I noticed a sign on the side of a building for the Pension Ribadiso and walked in thinking this was the right place even though the GPS on the phone said I had a few more kilometers to go. I went inside to double-check and was kindly informed that it was up the street. I had put Albergue Los Caminantes in my phone. I also became confused because of two places with similar names. One was the Pension Albergue Los Caminantes and the other was Albergue Los Caminantes. The second one was actually in Azora, a kilometer or so down the road, the one programmed in my phone. Fortunately, Rick and Dave were walking down the street towards a cafe and set me straight. After checking in to the Pension Albergue Los Caminantes in Ribadiso, I joined Dave and Rick at the Meson Ribadiso across the street for lunch. It was a nice place with outside seating and wonderful food.

That evening we went back to the Meson Rebadiso for dinner, sitting at an outside table towards the back. I remember enjoying a delicious bowl of soup as a starter to my meal, sitting back, and watching fellow pilgrims enjoying the evening.

We went to bed that evening with just two more days of walking, about eight hours, four hours each day, and just one more overnight in O Pedrouzo. It is exciting to know that my journey will soon be over, but also, it is a strange feeling. What is next? Is this the experience I wanted? Then I realized, like the young woman with the bloody nose said, "it is what it is."

CHAPTER FORTY-SIX

10/20/2021
Ribadiso - O Pedrouzo

I start off on a beautiful day knowing I am soon coming to the end of this journey or rather, this part of the journey; for reaching Santiago is not the end, but just a section of the continuing journey through life. I can now continue my journey with the new knowledge picked up while walking the Way of Saint James.

The walk is slightly downhill on a stony terrain passing by fields and through woods. I walked for about forty-five minutes before reaching a road crossing.

Occasionally, the Camino trail crosses over roadways, then back into the woods. Coming up on one of these crossings near A Calzada, I saw the path partially blocked by a black van with a maroon car parked beside it. A group of nine people huddled together near the van. As I got closer, I noticed a few people with 35mm SLR cameras and others with cell phones. One person held a mic on a long pole over the group. I didn't think much about this. Many people like to record their experiences walking the Camino de Santiago. You can see many of these on YouTube and a few make it to major streaming platforms. I have a few videos and over five thousand still photos on my cellphone as a recording of my journey. Other pilgrims, like myself, also share their experiences through the written word. The scene was interesting so I did snap a few photos.

I found out later in the day from Rick that this group was recording the pilgrimage of a blind person and there was another blind pilgrim ahead of this one. When I learned this, I looked back at my photos of the group. After looking closely at the photo, I believe the blind pilgrim to be a young dark-haired girl in her twenties. The others in the photo were looking at their cameras or cell phones, while this young lady stood with her head tilted down and towards the right. Her eyes appeared closed and her expression one of deep thought. In another photo her head is tilted down and to the left. Now, knowing this may be the blind pilgrim, I consider she may be listening, trying to hear the sounds around her, the voices of the other pilgrims, and the words leading to her contemplative thoughts. This young lady exemplifies the challenges pilgrims overcome making their way to Santiago. My own problems seem insignificant. Overcoming the issue I have with an arthritic knee is minor compared to walking blind. I am blessed to only have a few minor problems on my Camino and in life.

Next, the Camino took me through a rock formation about twelve feet high. Trees formed a canopy over the path making a tunnel effect. Several trees grew out of the rock formation, possibly from a seed that made its way into a crack many decades ago. Vines draped the rock wall. I stopped at an inset in the rock formation with a dozen crosses carved into the rock, another memorial on the Camino. On a boulder at the base were dozens of family photos and dozens of memorial prayer cards with renditions of the Royal Mary, the suffering Jesus, or Jesus with his Sacred Heart. The memorial also included a pile of stones, ribbons, and several country flags.

I walked through the small community of Ferreiros on narrow cobbled streets. Once through Ferreiros, there is a wide Y or a T in the road. A Camino arrow told me to turn left. As I approached, the unusual Tia Dolores Bier Garten came into view. The first thing I noticed was a five foot diameter tree stump with brown beer bottles placed over spikes to cover the sides and top. The bottom of the bottles had pilgrims 'names, a few had names on the sides.

I saw this as an opportunity for a video and pulled out my phone. First, I focused on the tree stump, then followed the bottles up the side of the entrance arch, along the top, then back down the other side. Through the arch, I saw a garden area with trees, bushes, and sections of the building sides covered with bottles. Thousands of bottles decorated the establishment. A dozen small tables and chairs provide seating for patrons.

I followed the courtyard wall, the top covered with beer bottles, to the end of the building then turned right.

Back in the woods I noticed a patch of Eucalyptus trees with peeling bark. I saw bright green moss growing on the side of another tree, possibly oak. I start seeing the husk of chestnuts littering the path. I look ahead to see tree shadow lines crossing the path with the regular pattern of railroad ties.

An interesting, artistic-looking piece of farm equipment sat on the side of the road at the edge of a small field. The side arms swung up had rakes with long tines, I assume for loosening the soil.

The GPS brings me into O Pedrouzo. A charcuterie (delicatessen) with a white two-wheel food cart on the sidewalk in front of the window gave me a quaint small-town feeling. The top shelf of the cart held a flat of nectarines and a flat of potatoes. On the bottom shelf were several large assorted colored round squash and a wicker basket with dried corn cobs. A yellow and white striped canopy protected the produce from the sun and weather.

Just past the deli I saw the sign for the hostel, one vertical above the horizontal: Pension PR and Pedrouzo.

I contacted Rick to find out where they were. He told me they were at a table outside a bar waiting for me to walk past, but since I followed my GPS into O Pedrouzo and not the yellow Camino arrows, I came into town a different way. Rick told me to head back a couple of blocks and then walk up the hill. I found them two blocks up the hill. I went inside to order a sandwich and Nestea before sitting down with them to enjoy good company. The hostess brought out my ham and cheese sandwich. I had to keep an eye on my napkin while I ate to keep it from flying away.

Back at the hostel Rick booked his covid test for the flight home and showed Dave and me how to sign up, too. We were fortunate to book times close together.

When we went out to discover a place to eat, we saw Linda and her friends outside a cafe. They were discussing dinner plans, as well. Matthew from Melbourne was also there. We had talked about finding a place for a good steak. We went in a different direction than Linda and her friends but ended up together having pizza.

Matthew sat with Rick, Dave, and me at one table. Linda and her friends sat at the table behind us.

This was our last dinner on the Camino. Tomorrow we will be in Santiago.

CHAPTER FORTY-SEVEN

10/21/2021
O Pedrouzo - Santiago de Compostela

We head out for our final day of walking the Camino de Santiago. It is a shorter walking day, about 18 km and about four hours. Usually, we walked twenty to twenty-five kilometers or more for five hours or more. We discussed heading right to the pilgrim's Office to schedule our Compostela appointment. According to my research, you schedule an appointment and return at the designated time to get your Compostela Certificate.

It is dark when we leave O Pedrouzo so we wear our headlamps. Yesterday, I had problems with my headlamp because the batteries were low and I had not packed extras. Fortunately, Dave had spare AA batteries and I replaced two of the three batteries in my lamp. It seemed to work fine.

A full moon helped guide us out O Pedrouzo until we entered a densely grown forest and the moonlight disappeared. Huge oaks and other trees formed a canopy that blocked the full moon's light. Rick and Dave pulled ahead and I watched their lights disappear into the darkness. With only two of three batteries, my lamp was not very bright. I could only see five or six feet in front of me. I tread carefully on the uneven path.

Unexpectedly, my headlamp started to flicker and then went out completely and I temporarily freaked out. I was in near total blackness. I could barely see my hand. How could I possibly make it through this forest without a headlamp? I could wait for another pilgrim and hope he would walk with me at my pace until the forest lightened. I could use my cell phone flashlight, but how long would that last? If the phone died, then I would not have GPS or be able to call for help. How did the medieval pilgrims make it all the way to Santiago under these conditions?

I reached up, grabbed my headlamp, and gave it a gentle shaking. It came back to life. Relieved, but still anxious, I continued through the dense forest. Would this happen again? Three pilgrims passed wishing me a Buen Camino. I tried to keep up. Tried to keep the headlamps in sight. Eventually, their lights disappeared. I could not keep up. Why is everyone in such a hurry?

My lamp flickered two more times, filling me with apprehension each time. Finally, out of the forest and with the full moon's light, I walked without the assistance of the headlamp.

I reached a highway overpass and hesitated, looking for a marker to tell me which way to go. Do I cross the overpass or turn left? I looked around trying to find a yellow arrow. I looked at the guard rails, the road surface, and other surfaces that may be painted with an arrow, but it was still dark and I didn't see any. I heard someone coming up from behind. A girl was walking quickly and with a purpose. She wishes me Buen Camino but moves on telling me she is in a hurry. She wanted to get to Santiago for the noon Mass at the cathedral.

The pilgrim's Mass is important for many pilgrims. Many wish to see the botafuneiro. During Mass, the botafuneiro, an enormous incense burner, swings across the length of the church nave dispensing smoke. Botafumeiro is a Galician word meaning "smoke expeller." The thurible or censer is a container suspended by a chain and used during Christian liturgy for burning incense. [xlix] The swinging of the botafuneiro during the ceremony of the holy Mass is impressive and a sight pilgrims want to see. A priest pushes the botafuneiro to start the swinging, then eight men in red robes, known as tiraboleiros, pull on ropes attached to a complicated pulley system to build momentum until the botafuneiro reaches a height of nearly seventy feet, almost to the roof of the transept and reaching speeds up to 50 miles per hour. I've heard two theories about this ceremony. One, the smoke symbolizes the pilgrim's prayers rising to heaven and the heart of God; the other, the smoke was used to mask the bad odor of unwashed weary pilgrims. I believe the first is the original purpose and the second, a side benefit of the practice.

As the sky lightened, I went by the Church of Saint Pelagius in Lavacolla, Sabugueiro. The sun just above the horizon in a cloudy overcast sky peaked through a tree on the right side of the church and cast a bright spot on the building's gray stone. The scene offered an opportunity to take an ethereal photograph. Converting the photo from color to black and white with a warm sepia tone gave the photograph an aged appearance.

On the way into Santiago, I passed a statue labeled "El Templario Peregrino," a figure with a helmet, cape, a Templar cross on the front of his garment and atop a staff he held in his right hand. He stood on a pedestal with a sword in his left hand and his shield at his feet leaning on his left leg. The shield also displayed the Templar cross.

I came upon a colorful sign with "Santiago de Compostela" in red lettering on a wire frame rack in front of a high hedge. Fading stickers of all types of advertising, flags, logos, fraternal lodges, etc. covered the letters. It was a good feeling to see this sign. I entered Santiago and will soon have my Certificate of Completion, the Compostela.

I used the GPS to continue my way to the Hostal Mexico PR. When I arrived, I took the elevator to the registration desk on the second floor and was surprised that Rick and Dave were not yet there. The room wasn't ready, so I sat on a comfortable chair in a room to the left of the registration desk to wait for the guys. I texted Rick to let him know I was at the hotel. He replied that they were still twenty minutes out. Somehow, I had beaten them to Santiago. This gave me a certain satisfaction since this was the first time I arrived at a destination before them, not counting my walk from Murias de Rechivaldo to Astorga the morning after I took the wrong path. For over thirty days Rick and Dave beat me to our daily destination, but today I had the satisfaction of beating them. I had won the race to Santiago. The tortoise beat the hare. I know I said it is not a race to Santiago, but a pilgrimage, nonetheless, it made me feel good about myself. I later learned they got lost following a school group through a park and needed to backtrack a bit. I remembered walking by the park near a school complex. There were people walking through the park when I passed and I could understand the temptation to follow them for a more scenic walk, but I stayed on the road. I also remembered my experience from a few days earlier following the wrong people and ending up on the wrong path. I did learn it is okay to occasionally take the wrong path, as long as you learn from the experience and get back on track as best you can. After all, we all make mistakes sometimes. I learned not to carelessly follow someone else's Camino. I needed to walk my own Camino.

Since our room was not ready, the clerk told me I could store my day pack in a room adjoining the sitting area and asked if needed anything or if I wanted a coffee or a soda. I thought that was nice of him and I told him a cafe con leche would be nice. Later, when I started to leave he asked me if I wanted to pay for the coffee or put the charge on the room. For some reason I thought he was offering me a free coffee. He was very gracious when he offered. I paid in cash.

After waiting about thirty minutes, I received a text from Rick wanting to know where I was. They were at the Pilgrim's Office waiting on their certificate. I had forgotten that we discussed going directly to the pilgrim's office to make the appointment for a certificate. Even though I beat them to Santiago they beat me to the Pilgrim's Office for the Compostela. Following the GPS, I had gone directly to the hotel. The Hostal Mexico PR was about a twenty-minute walk to the cathedral. My satisfaction with beating them to Santiago was replaced by the disappointment that we did not arrive at the Pilgrim's Office together as a symbol of our successful journey. I guess I am too romantic in my thinking. I walked alone most of the journey. It is more in line with the Camino I walked that I also went alone for my certificate.

On the way to the Pilgrim's Office, I came up on Rick and Dave at a table outside a cafe. Dave raised a beer to my arrival, a huge beer. Must have been in a thirty-two ounce mug. Rick later told me when ordered, he asked for the largest beer they had for Dave. The beer looked welcoming, but I will have my usual Nestea when I get back with my certificate. Rick pointed up the street to the pilgrim's office with a couple people out front talking to the attendant.

Outside the office entrance stood a collapsable menu board with a QR Code and basic instructions for registering for the Compostela. I scanned the QR Code but could not get connected to the site to register due to a bad internet connection. After several tries, the door attendant told me to go inside to another person for manual registration. I filled out the form and gave it back. She then assigned my number and I went to the back to wait in line.

There was a long hallway lined with backpacks leading to the doorway into the registration counter with service windows like ones found at a bank. The electronic board above the entrance let me know there were over thirty people ahead of me. With that many people waiting for their Compostela, I decided to walk around. I would keep an eye on the electric sign.

First, I walked out back to a beautifully landscaped garden area with another two-sided cross on a six-foot high column. Several pilgrims milling about were also waiting their turn. More backpacks were leaning against a wall.

I went back inside and entered a small chapel. Sitting in a pew, I took a few moments to reflect on my journey while I waited my turn. I thanked God for giving me the ability to make this journey and to see the wonders he created for Spain.

I thought about why Rick, Dave, and I each walked our Camino. For Rick, it seems to be about pushing to his limits. He is like that, always wanting to go one more step or one more push-up. He also walked in memory of his two sons that passed on way too early. Rick was very spiritual and emotional during moments in his walk. Much more than I was. At times I felt I should have had more spiritual moments, but my stoicism usually won over. Did I miss something? Did I miss an opportunity to truly get in touch with myself, to get in touch with God?

Dave told me he walked to reflect on his life and as an example for his kids, to show them they can accomplish their goals. I also believe he just enjoyed getting out to see more of the world.

My walk was about the wonder of the world around me; the

beautiful landscape, the architecture, the people. For me, I walked to have a story to tell. A story that might have a message or a lesson to offer others to learn from. Through words and pictures, I hoped to tell a story that may inspire others to reach for their dreams and their goals. I wish I had more spiritual moments to share, those special miracles. But, maybe the miracle is all around me every day, not just on the Camino. It is the beautiful world all around us. The miracle is there every day. We just need to learn how to see it. It is the wonder that is all around us, the wonder of the world, the universe, the people.

I did talk to God throughout my Camino, but it was pretty much one way. I thanked him for my arthritis which slowed my pace allowing me to see this wondrous world. I placed a stone at the Cruz de Ferro, asking God to relieve the burdens from my family and friends. I thanked God for keeping me from falling into the ditch when I had my dizzy spell. There are many times I find myself thanking God, not just on the Camino de Santiago. Whenever I have a close call, I thank God for getting me through. So far, he has kept a pretty good eye on me and saved me from many mishaps.

After receiving my Compostela and Certificate of Distance, I returned to the cafe to get my Nestea and a bite to eat. Afterward, we headed to the cathedral. Passing through a passage, I spotted an old covered single horse-drawn carriage in an open-sided room. The black carriage had a grey upholstered seat covered with a canopy for the driver and an enclosed compartment for the passengers. There were yellow wheels and yellow bars to attach the horse. This carriage was built for a dignitary. I'm sure it is used for special events.

The passage opened to the Plaza del Obradoiro in front of the Santiago Cathedral. The plaza teemed with pilgrims of all ages hugging each other with jubilation, celebrating their arrival. Many took selfies with the huge intricately designed baroque facade of the cathedral as the backdrop. We were no different, taking photos to record our arrival. We also saw several pilgrims we had befriended on our journey. California was among them and he offered to take a photo with the three of us together.

Other important buildings surround the plaza. The Rajoy Palace across the plaza facing the cathedral serves as the town hall and the parliament building for the Xunta, Galicia's regional government. The ground level of the neo-classical palace has an arched walkway running the entire length. Atop the central triangular feature of the building is a depiction of "Saint James, the Moor-slayer" on horseback, sword draw against the Moors at the battle at Clavijo in 844 C.E.

The Reyes Catolicos Hotel, a state-run 5-star parador, was on the left. This luxurious hotel was built around 1500 as a hospital to accommodate pilgrims. It is considered the world's oldest hotel. The hotel offers elegant rooms and upscale dining in two restaurants. Room rates may be up to $400 per night in peak season. Inside, the Parador is like a museum in its splendor. Four beautiful garden cloisters offer a comfortable area for guests to rest. Perhaps on my next Camino, I will splurge for a few special nights.

While hanging out in the plaza, taking photos of the cathedral, and watching the people, I heard the unique sound of a bagpipe, an unexpected sound, reverberating from a corridor to the left of the cathedral. A street performer stood in the passage, the sound of his pipes echoing through the passage as a homage to Galicia's Celtic roots. I recorded his performance, then drop a few Euros into his case. When we returned to the cathedral that evening to attend Mass, he was still there, this time accompanied by another man with a single drum hanging at his waist, keeping time for the bagpipes.

Since 2021 was a Holy Year, I looked for the Holy Door and found it on the back side of the cathedral. A friendly security guard stood at the open iron gate that protects the oak door. The door was narrow, only wide enough for one at a time. Rick, Dave, and I took turns going through, entering into a dimly lit room. I felt this was a special moment.

During a Holy Year, a year when the Saint James holiday, July 25, falls on a Sunday, the Holy Door, also known as the Door of Forgiveness, is open. When passing through the Holy Door accompanied by confession, prayer, Mass, and communion, your sins are washed away. The church grants a plenary indulgence, the total forgiveness of all sins. Your soul is cleansed and you skip purgatory and go directly to heaven. I'm not sure how long this blessing last. Is it only good until my next sin when I start accumulating points against me again? Was I supposed to find a confessional to confess my sins to a priest? There was an altar and area for one to confess to a priest. A woman was speaking with the priest while I was there. I made my brief confession directly to God. Hope this counts.

The concept of the Holy Door, the Door of Forgiveness, comes from the words of Christ who said in the gospel of John 10:9, "I am the door: by me if any man enter in, he shall be saved, and shall go in and out, and find pasture." [1]

Due to the Covid pandemic, this Holy Year was extended through 2022 by a decree from the Pope to accommodate the faithful that could not travel to Santiago.

I remember going to confession as a kid in grade school. I remember it was somewhat frightening. I went to Queen of Peace Catholic Grammar School taught by the Sisters of Saint Joseph. As a class, we marched from the school to the church next door. Then, one by one, we entered a confessional to speak with the priest inside. I would push past a curtain, closing the curtain behind me. Kneeling

Santiago Cathedral 10/22/21

inside, I started the process, "Bless me Father for I have sinned. It has been two weeks since my last confession." This was followed by a litany of sins which were sometimes made up because I felt I needed to say something. How badly can a nine-year-old sin? I really didn't know how many times I talked back to my dad or didn't do what I was told, so I would make up a number. "Father, I lied three times and I said dirty words, six times." The priest sat behind a yellowed plexiglass window with holes drilled through so that we could hear each other. You couldn't see who it was, but sometimes you knew by the voice. Sometimes you knew the priest if you were there when he entered the confessional. There were several confessionals to choose from. If you knew a priest gave a harsh penance, you avoided that confessional box. At the end of your confession, the priest issued his penance. "Say five 'Our Fathers 'and ten 'Hail Marys 'he would say, or something to that effect. He ordered more prayers if you were particularly bad. From the confessional at the back of the church, I would make my way to the front to kneel at the railing in front of the altar to say my prayers and ask for forgiveness. I didn't do that in Santiago. My confessions and

request for forgiveness are made directly to God now.

Once through the door, my eyes needed to adjust to the dimly lit room. Attached to the wall on each side of the door were ornately decorated bowls for holy water. In front of me was a statue of Saint James. To my left, red glass candle holders on an iron stand were ready to light. I lit one of the candles for the sisters at the Ermita de Nuestra Señora del Monasterio in Rabé de Las Calzadas that gave me the string chain with a tiny medallion of the Blessed Mother. I asked again for the Lord to relieve my family and friends of their burdens, just as I did at the Cruz de Ferro. When I finished, I dropped a two Euro coin in the box beneath the candles.

I looked back towards the door to see a faithful woman passing through the doorway on her knees in the Catholic tradition of humility and suffering for the forgiveness of one's sins. I am not that traditional.

I turned back the other way and entered a small opening, going down about five concrete steps, and through a narrow block passageway in the substructure of the church below the cathedral's main altar. About five feet in on the right was an inset in the wall with a glass window in the stone for viewing of a silver reliquary box containing the remains of Saint James, Santiago. There was a kneeler for those that wished to pray. In front of the reliquary was a small table covered with a white cloth. A silver Crucifix stood in the center of the table with a Peace Lily arrangement on each side. The relief on the front of the table featured two doves drinking from a chalice.

I exited this darkened corridor at the other end and went up another set of stairs to enter the splendor of the Cathedral of Saint James.

The spacious interior of the cathedral is impressive with a large gothic vaulted dome. Columns support the interior and also serve to separate various parts. Sculptures of Saint James, Jesus, the Blessed Mother, Apostles, kings, angels and cherubs, and other ornate carvings decorate every area of the interior.

Back outside, I walked around for a while to explore Santiago before we went back to the hotel to rest before going out again for dinner.

The Crypt of Saint James

CHAPTER FORTY-EIGHT

10/22/2021
Santiago de Compostela

Didn't get up until 8 this morning. It felt a little strange not setting out for our daily Camino walk. Instead, we casually made our way back to the Cathedral area to find someplace for breakfast.

During breakfast I checked my emails and I was happy to see one from Laura. It lifted my spirits immediately. I wanted to email her for the last several days but held back because I had expressed some of my feelings towards her when we last saw each other in Burgos. At that time, I thought I saw some discomfort in her reaction. I was wary of being pushy. Strangely, when I looked at my horoscope yesterday, it said to leave romance to chance for everything to fall in its place in time. It also said forcing the issue makes things worse in the long run. So, I didn't send an email. Foolish of me I suppose, but she did email me today. I usually just have a curious interest in what a horoscope says, but sometimes they seem to reflect some general truths.

I learned that Laura will arrive in Santiago tomorrow, but we are leaving tomorrow on a 2 PM flight for Barcelona. We will need to be at the airport about 11 AM. It seemed unlikely that I will be able to see her again. That saddens me immensely. Although, I still held the joy of hearing from her. I am tempted to change my plans for the trip home so that I may get to see her one last time.

It has been a long time since I felt attracted to someone. With Laura, I felt a connection, if only in my mind. Not a sexual connection like some might assume. Maybe a spiritual connection. Maybe it's the magic of the Camino and it will eventually fade away. I hope not. I think that she felt a connection, as well. I don't know if it is the same type, but I know we enjoyed each other's company when we walked together.

She stated in her email that she may continue on to Finisterre. In the hope of seeing her again, I suggested she could spend a few days in Barcelona. Or, that we may see each other again at the New Orleans Jazz Festival. She had been to a couple in the past. There will be a jazz festival in 2022, from April 29 to May 8. I hope she replies to my email.

Went to the Pilgrim's Mass at noon. It was spoken in Spanish, but I am familiar with the ceremony since I was raised as a Catholic. Unfortunately, the ceremony did not include the swinging of the botafumeiro. It hung from the ceiling in stillness. They don't do this ceremony at every service. I did hear there was one at the noon Mass yesterday. I realized then why the girl that passed me in the dark earlier was in such a hurry. She said she wanted to be in Santiago in time for the noon Mass. I didn't realize it was to see the Botafumeiro.

Attendance at mass was high and we needed to sit in pews to the right of the alter instead of directly in front. Although I am familiar with the ceremony of the Catholic Mass, there was one part I found surprising. A young priest stepped up to a raised podium and I expected a sermon, but instead, I was treated to a remarkable voice singing a hymn. His angelic voice carried throughout the cathedral. It was a joy to hear.

When Communion was offered I joined the line to complete the necessary requirement for the expulsion of my sins for passing through the Door of Forgiveness.

After Mass, we went to the Pilgrim House for information and assistance printing our covid form needed to get on our flight home. The pilgrim house is maintained by volunteers to serve pilgrim needs. They had a nice setup with a sitting area inside and one out back in a courtyard. The girl we spoke with was from Baltimore. Rick emailed her the covid form that she printed for us.

Afterward, we had lunch and walked around the Cathedral area as tourists visiting the gift shops. Rick bought a medallion for a staff he had at home already adorned with medallions from other countries he has visited and from the Grand Canyon. He also bought a gift for his wife Lisa. I bought a tee-shirt for my roommate and friend Joe. After that, we went back to the hotel to relax for awhile before exploring some more in the evening

We found a nice Italian restaurant for dinner. The staff at the Restaurante Italiano La Piccola in the Praza de Fonseca was wonderful and the meal was delicious. I saw Chloe and Lars and their friend at the Italian restaurant. When I last saw Chloe, she was struggling up a climb bearing a heavy backpack and I suggested she may want to ship it ahead. When I asked if she did that, I was told she did on a few occasions.

On our final evening in Santiago, I thought again about why I walked the Camino. Yes, I walked to have a book to write and photos to enjoy. Yet to this day, I don't really know why I walked. It just sounded like a good idea once I wrapped my mind around it.

Walking the Camino is very personal. We all share a common bond, yet, we all walk our own Camino. For each individual it is different. Each person has their own reasons and beliefs. Each experiences the input in different ways.

The thoughts while walking vary and it's impossible to really understand why each individual walks. Even when they try to explain you will only get a synopsis. There are usually a variety of reasons that cannot be distinctly described.

There is a lure about walking the Camino, some say a calling. Once you walk the Camino, you want to walk it again. Only those that have walked their own Camino may understand this obsession. It is difficult to describe to others.

The Camino is addictive. Why do we want to keep living the Camino life? The Camino is life, your own life taken step by step.

Eldad had said I was being a romantic and maybe that's part of it. The Camino is like a romance with the experience, with the people, with the country, the landscape and so much more. It becomes a romance story that never ends because it becomes part of you residing deep within you, within your soul.

That night, I started reading *Ethics* by Aristotle on my iPhone in which he states that a contemplative life is the highest and most satisfying form of life possible. A contemplative life is one filled with deep and serious thought. I thought about how well Aristotle's ideas apply to the many hours of walking alone on the Camino. Aristotle was talking about the life of a philosopher, but on the Camino, aren't we all philosophers? We walk in contemplation, free from the distractions and disturbances of our daily lives. Inseparable from practical life, these distractions seemed to disappear on the Camino. Your only concerns are to walking, eating, and sleeping. Along the way you make Camino friends walking on the same paths, but making their own journey. Everything else going on in the world is trivial. I found it a pleasure to be free of the constant bombardment of negative news, the bickering of opposing political parties, the ups and downs of the financial markets, traffic congestion, and the other annoyances of daily life. Life is simpler on the Camino.

So, the day ends. My official Camino has come to an end. Tomorrow we leave for a few days in Barcelona and then back to the United States.

I didn't go to Finisterre. Next time I will.
The Lighthouse at Finisterre, the end of the world.

CHAPTER FORTY-NINE

10/23/2021
Santiago de Compostela - Barcelona

With the official Camino de Santiago completed, we made our way to the airport for our flight to Barcelona to play tourist. We arranged for a taxi and head out for our flight. The flight is just under two hours.

During the flight, I had the pleasure of sitting next to Mercedes from Canada. We talked a little about our expectations of the Camino. Both agreed it was different than what we thought it would be. For Mercedes, it was all the different people she met. I referred to them as Camino friends and agreed they made the trip for me, as well.

We landed at Barcelona's El Prat Airport about 4 o'clock. After grabbing our backpacks at baggage claim, we went outside the airport's terminal to meet the driver Rick had reserved online yesterday. When he texted to find out where he was, he received a text from a different driver wanting to know where we were. We met him at the designated area. After we arrived at the Hotel Flora Parc, Rick received a text from the original driver to find out where we were. Some kind of mix-up with dispatch or drivers caused a moment of confusion. Or, maybe one driver took the ride from the other. Whether this was intentional or not, we made it to the hotel.

We had decided to stay near the airport since we needed to go back for our covid test. The Hotel Flora Parc is in the community of Castelldefels just 15 minutes from the airport. The hotel is nice. I have no complaints about the facilities, but the area is blah compared to the historic districts we encountered during our Camino. This area was more residential and lacked the charm of the quaint villages encountered on the Camino Frances. It reminded me of the boring residential area I walked through entering Leon. Am I a travel snob? Although booking a room near the airport had advantages, we were away from the historic district of Barcelona, so at first, I was somewhat disappointed about the location based on the number of people that told me Barcelona was a great city.

That evening, we ate at a small Italian restaurant so that Dave could get his Margarita pizza, his favorite meal. I ordered macaroni carbonara. Rick had the same with spaghetti. The food was good but the service was lacking. There was just one waiter and the cook in the back who I assume was the owner. The waiter was working hard but also took several breaks outside the front door for his cigarette. There was a priority for his need to smoke.

Dave was getting antsy to go home and mentioned going back on Monday to JFK. Rick and I wanted to stay until Tuesday as originally planned since the flight from JFK to Orlando is sold out on Monday. Since we are flying on standby, it would mean staying a night in New York. Rick looked at other options, such as flying through Atlanta instead of JFK. In the end, we all stayed as planned.

I think after walking through Spain for more than thirty plus days, all of us were ready to head home. Especially since we were not in the scenic area of Barcelona.

CHAPTER FIFTY

10/24/2021
Barcelona

Dave is still a little antsy about getting home and frustrated that he doesn't have control over that decision. I believe that he is more accustomed to making his own decisions. Many factors made the change to our reservations a little involved. We are flying on Delta Friends and Family tickets. A Covid test is required. Tickets could not be changed online.

We took a taxi back to the airport for our Covid test. We had scheduled our tests for around 1:30 PM, each of us about ten minutes apart. We found out when we arrived that the booking was for 1:30 AM, not 1:30 PM. When making the online reservation we did not realize that the website was using a twenty-four-hour clock. We should have booked 13:30 for our appointment. Fortunately, we were able to get in line for our test without much delay since they were not busy.

Not too far from the hotel is a mall. Dave and I walked there after returning from the airport. He wanted a bag he could use for his backpack so the straps didn't get caught up on the conveyors at the airport. We went through several shops in the mall looking for something that would work but we were unsuccessful. Rick had stayed back to take care of the laundry.

While we were gone, Rick found a seafood restaurant online that he wanted to try for dinner, so he and I walked several miles toward the beach. Since Dave is not a fan of seafood, he stayed back.

The Tibu Ron Beach Club was right on the beach and busy, with both inside and outside seating. The place was hopping with a lot of young people. Spanish pop music is played through the sound system. We were seated inside. After reviewing the menu for a few minutes, I decided on grilled scallops with Thai sauce as a starter and codfish as the main entree. Even though Galicia is noted for its seafood menus, we didn't take advantage of the seafood options while there.

After dinner, we went down to the beach to check out the view of the Mediterranean Sea. A sand artist had cordoned off a section of beach just off the wooden boardwalk to create an elaborate sand castle with amazing detail, it was hard to believe it was made from sand. Spiring towers, arched windows, gateways, and a small mote were just some of the intricate details. Two lights created shadows that added depth to the details.

Standing on the beach, we watched the sunset, then headed back to the hotel.

CHAPTER FIFTY-ONE

10/25/2021
Barcelona

I had a hard time getting to sleep last night. Kept thinking about Laura, another part of my journey coming to an end, a fond memory of my journey. I woke thinking about her. Will probably never see her again. Hard for me to understand why I was attracted to her. I am usually independent and like being alone. Yet, I felt good when we walked together. Somehow, she warmed my heart. Even a year later, as I write this story, I wish we kept in touch.

Got up at 7:30, took a shower, and went downstairs for breakfast. Rick came down a few minutes later. He said that he found a laundry about a block away and asked if I had any to add to his. All I had were the clothes from yesterday. I had clean clothes for tomorrow's trip home but added the dirty clothes to his anyway. Why not? I wouldn't need to wash them when I got home.

After laundry, we planned to take a taxi to the historic district of Barcelona. Since Dave has been to Barcelona, he decided to walk to the beach instead, about a mile and a half away, about 45 minutes. He left before Rick came back with the clean laundry. I waited for Rick's return.

The taxi took us to the Cathedral of the Holy Cross and Saint Eulalia, more commonly known as the Barcelona Cathedral. The gothic revival cathedral serves as the seat of the Archbishop of Barcelona, Catalonia, Spain. The architecture is amazing with towering spires, arches, crosses, stained glass windows, flowery designs, statues of saints, and gargoyles of assorted grotesque creatures along the roof. The church is named after Eulalia of Barcelona, a young virgin girl martyred at age thirteen by the Romans for not denying her Christian faith. Her body is entombed in the cathedral.

Rick and I sat outside a cafe opposite the Barcelona Cathedral for lunch and people-watching. Rick ordered an americano pepperoni pizza and I ordered a chicken Caesar salad. I was a little tired of pizza. I wanted something different. If there was a disappointment I want to point to on my Camino, it is the similarity of my meals, especially breakfast with toasted bread, butter and jam, and cafe con leche. While we ate, I took pictures of the cathedral from my table. Afterward, we walked around the cathedral for photos of the intricately designed building.

In the cathedral plaza, a man creating bubbles by dipping a pole with a string loop on the end into a bucket of soapy water entertained the young children. Pulling the pole from the water, he released dozens of bubbles for the children playing in the plaza, running and jumping to catch and pop a bubble. If I were a youngster, I would be right in there with them.

As we walked through Barcelona, many of the streets were bubbling with pedestrian traffic. The narrow streets were not made for cars. Unlike American cities, noted for automobile traffic, these streets flowed with people. Seldom did I see cars driving through the narrow streets of the old quarters in the Spanish cities I have visited. We joined the flow making our way towards the marina. Many photo opportunities of graffiti doors, shop windows, decorative street lamps, door knockers, and more were presented to me. It is a great joy for me to walk through new places to photograph. Preserving my experience to aid my memory. When looking back at old photos, memories are brought forth. Usually good memories, occasionally sad.

There were streets with traffic once out of the old quarters. We waited for our opportunity to cross the main thoroughfare to the pedestrian walk along the water's edge. I took a photo of a copper-colored huge lobster sculpture atop a walkway with a slotted wood top for a semi-shade. We watched a yacht, maybe sixty or seventy feet, back up and maneuver into its slot between two other boats in one smooth move. I was impressed with how well the captain handled the craft. If you knew my reputation of backing into things with my pick-up truck, a land-based vehicle, you would have more understanding of my admiration for this captain's feat.

When we were ready to go back to the hotel, we stepped into a hotel and asked the desk clerk to call a taxi for us. He turned towards his terminal and asked for a room number. We said we didn't have one. He then informed us the service was for hotel guests only. The clerk pointed up the street when we asked where we could find a taxi. I found the hotel's rules lacked the hospitality I was accustomed to on the Camino Frances. The Hospitaliers were always willing to help the Camino pilgrims.

We pushed through the door and back into the street. Looked up the street in the direction the clerk had pointed. About two blocks away was a busy intersection and we walked in that direction. While walking there, I spotted taxis at the traffic signal. We crossed the intersection and flagged a taxi to bring us back to the Hotel Flora Parc.

Back at the hotel, we rested until, at seven o'clock, Rick suddenly jumped out of bed as if a fire alarm had just gone off. He hurriedly put on his shoes and jacket. I asked, are you going somewhere? Yes, to dinner. We need to get up early in the morning. I'll wait in the lobby. No hurry. Rick is a take-charge kind of guy, so there was little discussion. Outside, he headed up the street. I wasn't sure where he was headed, but that's where he was going to have dinner. There was little discussion with Dave or me about where to eat. We rushed to a street we passed yesterday several blocks long and lined with restaurants and shops, canopied tables and chairs all the way down the street. It did look like an interesting area to check out for dinner ideas. At the end of the street was the Church of Santa Maria de Castelldefels.

We walked along the Avinguda de Santa Maria and another side street checking out the different options. Many of the restaurants didn't appeal to me at the moment. Maybe because Dave had mentioned a steak restaurant he spotted on his walk. A good steak makes me look like my black labrador, drool dripping down my chin. I'm exaggerating, of course.

We chose the Efsane Istanbul Bar Restaurant Cafeteria, a Turkish menu restaurant. We sat at a table and the waitress soon took our order. I selected a combo platter with chicken, lamb, and beef. A salad came with the meal. In the end, it was good to try something different.

This was our last dinner in Spain. Tomorrow we fly back to the United States.

CHAPTER FIFTY-TWO

10/26/2021
Barcelona - United States

On our flight home, Dave, sitting in a seat behind me, tapped my shoulder and told me to take a look out the window. I'm glad he did for I got to see that beautiful mountainous landscape one last time.

Rick was upfront in first class. Dave and I were sitting in business class which was comfortable for the long flight with more room than standard class. We were flying on Rick's Delta retired employee friends and family program for a greatly reduced rate, but we were flying on standby, so there is some risk involved. Rick kept an eye on the flight. If it filled up, we would have to wait on the next flight. We booked our departure for a Tuesday because that is a less busy day. Everything looked good. Was even hoping to get moved up to first class, but found out later that only the Delta employee would be in first class. This was not available to friends and family. Didn't matter to me. We were heading home after a great experience in Spain.

It was a long flight from Barcelona to JFK Airport in New York. In New York, Dave leaves us for his home in New Jersey. Rick and I take a flight to Orlando. A short flight, compared to the first leg of our trip home.

After we landed in New York, I replaced the SIM card I purchased in Spain with my Boost Mobile SIM card. My phone was back in business. I texted Joe to let him know I landed and would be in Orlando just after 11 PM.

While waiting for our flight, we grabbed a bite to eat at the Brooklyn Beer Garden. I ordered a pastrami sandwich, fries, iced tea, and New York Cheese Cake for dessert. Rick ordered chicken wings. The bill came to $48.85. Welcome to New York prices and goodbye to the pilgrim dinners for $11-$13.

Lisa picked us up at the airport to bring us home. I was tired but still wired. Looking forward to getting home and into my own bed. I also wondered how the dogs would greet me. Would they jump with joy because I was gone for over a month? My ego hoped they would. As it turned out, they were pretty hum-dum. Both spent a few moments sniffing my clothes to find out where I had been. Then it was back to routine.

I found out from Joe that he discovered earlier that day that Sadie, the female mixed Lab, was taking advantage of my absence to sleep in my bed. He kindly washed the gritty sheets and comforter for me. It was truly appreciated. At this point, I was awake for close to twenty-four hours and was glad I didn't discover this when I decided to go to bed. I did stay up a couple more hours talking with Joe because I was wired and could just not go to sleep. When I did go to bed, I slept well.

CHAPTER FIFTY-THREE

Post Camino

For me, walking the Way of Saint James is a metaphor for the journey through life. Through a life's walk a person has many experiences of joy and sorrow, comfort and pain. We also meet many people along the way. People come and go throughout our life. If you are lucky, you walk the journey together for a while but eventually, they move on their own journey until they reach the end.

Life goes back to the old normal when you return home from walking a Camino. For some, this is tough and brings on what I call post-Camino blues. For thirty days or so, you have lived a different life, the life of a pilgrim. You walk daily in self-thought. You walk partly with new Camino friends. Some you may only know for the few minutes you walk together but they become your Camino friend nonetheless, sharing a common bond.

It is difficult to sum up in a few paragraphs, the experiences of such a journey. How have I changed? What have I learned?

I don't think I have changed too much. I'm still me. I still hold the same beliefs. I just had more time to think about them on my walk.

I did learn to walk at my own pace. I did learn that this was my own journey and not to worry about someone else's journey. The walk is what you make it. If you stress over the little things, it will be less enjoyable. If you learn to relax, it will be more enjoyable.

After returning home, I continued my walking campaign. Getting up each morning for my walk around the neighborhood. I do this to stay in shape and to stay healthy. I enjoy the walk, but it's not the same as my Camino. It's missing the sense of adventure and wonderments of the Spanish landscape and villages. The history of our neighborhood may be sixty years at most, not the thousands of years of the small hamlets in Spain. A neighbor I met one morning asked me how my walk was going. I told her it was a bit boring compared to the last month. "Ah," she said. "What can I do to make it better?" "You can build a massive medieval cathedral," I jokingly suggested. It wouldn't work here. It would bring more congestion, more traffic, and all the other things that growth brings to an area.

One change I noticed on my return home is the constant feeling of returning to Spain for another Camino. This seems to be a common feeling among pilgrims that may be hard to explain to those that have not enjoyed this special experience. It is something that gets into your soul, into your being. The Camino calls to you to come back and visit again. And, this I will do. Hopefully in the near future.

Writing this memoir of my trip kept me thinking about the Camino throughout the year. I started jotting down some of these thoughts. I include them below.

12/10/2021

Spoke to a friend, Steve, from high school that will be in town this Monday and meeting him for breakfast near his hotel in Titusville. Later that day, he drives to Palm Beach.

I am excited to see him for many reasons, particularly because he walked three days on the Camino with his wife and son a few years ago while he was in Spain for business. That was all the time he had. He started in Roncesville. I planned on teasing him for not starting in Saint Jean Pied de Port for the more challenging trek across the Pyrenees on the Napoleon route. I decided not to "tease" him, but did suggest he take that route should he walk the Camino again.

It is a post Camino contact with a fellow pilgrim that understands your feelings. You let it out like those at an AA meeting. People that have not walked a pilgrimage do not understand. What are the words - exuberance, solitude, wanting, a bonding, being one with yourself, one with God, and one with nature, being part of a family, and seeing the wondrous landscape? All of this. All the sensory receptors are alive during a pilgrimage if you open your eyes, your ears, your mind, and your heart.

1/22/2022

What has changed? The saying is that the Camino will change you. I keep thinking about how I have changed. I am still me. My basic thoughts and beliefs have not changed. I try to take life as it is. Like the walk across Spain, I try to go through life day by day, enjoying the moment and hoping for the best day. I try not to let the world news get to me or let people get to me. I tell myself that anger, worry, wants and other negative thoughts or reactions will drain me. Make me feel bad. So I avoid these attitudes. However, I am human and they do sneak in. They are there, but when I feel them, I try to move past the situation that put me there. This is how I live. Moving on the best I can. Walking my Camino.

So, what has changed? What has changed is that little needling thing in the back of my mind that says do it again. Walk another Camino de Santiago. Take the time to get away from today's world.

Take the time to go back to the old world to enjoy a new world. Take the time to dig deep into myself once again. Get out there once again to live. Change the scenery daily. Keep moving on the best I can.

1/30/2022

Learned by text today that Isla had passed on. Isla is the little girl that was the purpose of Les 'walk. She made it through Christmas but relapsed after the first of the year. So sad when a child leaves us, I have great empathy for the family and friends of this little girl. I wish for her peace in heaven and for her family and friends' peace on earth.

2/9/2022

I want to go back. Walk another Camino. But, this time, try to be more relaxed. It took me days to realize I didn't need to keep up with Rick and Dave. It was all I knew and at times I was a bit confused, especially pre-GPS. Several times, it was tough for me to find the albergue that was booked. It was tough getting out of Pamplona. But, that was all part of the experience that gave me some insights into myself.

Yet, I want to go back. To have another experience like no other.

2/10/2022

Rick and I give each other post-Camino support. Rehashing memories when we get together. It's like everything else in life is insignificant to the walk. Is this walk so holy that all else is insignificant? The daily life of our other world was left further behind each day we walked. Life on the Camino is day by day without a thought of the outside world unless you choose to introduce it. I found it best to leave it alone, trying to keep the worries of home and home politics out of my thoughts. I preferred to think about where I was, what I was doing, and what I was seeing. I tried to live in the moment worry-free. And, now home, I try to do the same thing. Live worry-free. I have the belief that all works out in the end.

5/31/2022

Lesson learned. What did I learn from walking the Camino de Santiago? Who knows? I guess I should know, but I don't know that I have changed all that much. I am still me, the ever-evolving me. But, how have I evolved? Maybe the change is too subtle for me to notice.

Rick, Dave, and I are planning to return to Europe to walk another Camino in April 2023. There is a calling felt to walk another Camino. That's new. But, why not? I have time. Yes, there are the usual apprehensions about leaving home for six weeks or more. Excuses that I can use. Not as many as the first time though. Yet, there are hassles such as following current requirements to enter a foreign country. At the time of this writing, Covid is still an issue. Money is always an issue. Arranging for bills to get paid on time. I expect with current inflationary pressures the cost of travel will be at least ten percent higher. There are other concerns. But, once I am on the flight out of Orlando, I expect, that the concerns will be left behind, just like they were the first time.

6/1/2022

Writing is a solitary act, like walking the Camino, when one comes to terms with their thoughts. Thoughts that are then placed on paper.

6/2/2022

I learned to walk the Camino once I learned it was not a competition. But even to the end, I felt the need to beat Rick and Dave to Santiago.

6/28/2022

I was surprised by my feelings towards Laura and realize how foolish this may appear to some, but emotions are real and intensified on the Camino. Camino magic perhaps. I don't want to appear like a stalker, but I may have unintentionally done so. I knew once the Camino was over, it would be difficult to keep up with any of my Camino family. I have a hard time keeping up with my own family and with friends living just a few blocks away. I did hear from Laura around Thanksgiving and Christmas, 2021, but that was it. I hope she is doing well and would like to hear from her again.

7/4/2022

This was my walk and it took me a while to realize that. I envy those that start alone because they know from the start that it is their walk and they will often walk alone. I thought at the beginning that I would be walking more often with the people on the journey with me. Walking your own Camino doesn't mean not sharing your Camino, your journey, with another.

8/10/2022

An aspect of the Camino I really enjoyed was the distance from the daily hum drum, living with usual stresses, or some unwanted stresses, and leaving them behind, if only momentarily. Sometimes it tries to follow you. During my Camino, I found out from Joe that the septic system backed up. I left a credit card to use for such an emergency. He ended up not using it, but called a friend that was a plumber to temporarily fix the problem. When I got home, I eventually replaced the system. It wasn't cheap and affected the dates for my next Camino. A planned September departure is changed to April. This may be good though with an opportunity to see Spain in the spring.

I believe walking the Camino is a life-changing event, or maybe, a life-revealing event. In so many ways, the effort is rewarded with beauty, knowledge, renewed self-awareness, kindness, new friendships, understanding, and much more. All this greatly outweighs any challenges that are encountered. In fact, it is getting through the challenges that are the most rewarding in the end.

I learned not to expect too much going in. Take the Camino as it comes to you. My expectations going in were based on books I read, and videos and movies I watched. How could I meet those expectations? The walk is different for each person. We all walk our own Camino and I needed to walk mine.

I hope everyone enjoys this story. I hope I have motivated people to walk their own Camino through Spain and through life.

Buen Camino!

Bibliography

Aristotle. *Ethics,* A Public Domain Book. Kindle Edition ASIN: B00847T3TU, Publication date: May 17, 2012.

Boers, Arthur Paul. *The Way Is Made By Walking: A Pilgrimage Along the Camino de Santiago.* Downers Grove, IL, 2007.

Brierley, John. A Pilgrim's Guide to the Camino de Santiago: Camino Francés St. Jean Pied de Port - Santiago de Compostela. Florres, Scotland: Camino Guides, 2019.

Chermside, Bradley. *The Only Way Is West: A Once in a Lifetime Adventure Walking 500 Miles on Spain's Camino de Santiago.* Self-published, 2019.

Codd, Kevin A. *To The Field of Stars: A Pilgrim's Journey to Santiago de Compostela.* Grand Rapids, Michigan: William B. Eerdmans Publishing Company, 2008.

Coelho, Paulo, and Alan R Clark. *The Pilgrimage.* New York: HarperCollins Publisher, 1995.

Dintaman, Anna and Landis, David. *Camino de Santiago, Camino Frances: St. Jean - Santiago - Finisterre.* Harrisonburg, VA: Village to Village Press, 2020.

Eanes, Russ. *The Walk of a Lifetime: 500 Miles On The Camino de Santiago.* The Walker Press, 2019.

Foskett, Keith. *The Journey in Between: A 1000-mile walk on El Camino de Santiago.* Self-published, CreateSpace, 2016.

Gitlitz, David M and Linda Kay Davidson. *The Pilgrimage Road to Santiago: The Complete Cultural Handbook*, New York: St. Martin's Press, 2000.

Melczer, William. *The Pilgrim's Guide to Santiago de Santiago*. New York: Italica Press, Inc., 1993.

Mitchell-Lanham, Jean. *The Lore of the Camino de Santiago: A Literary Pilgrimage*, Minneapolis, MN: Two Harbors Press, 2015.

Raju, Alison. *The Way of Saint James Vol 2: Pyrenees - Santiago - Finisterre*. Singapore: KHL Printing, 2013.

Rupp, Joyce. *Walk in a Relaxed Manner: Life Lessons From The Camino*. Maryknoll, New York: Orbis Books, 2007.

Tranchant, Claude. *Boots to Bliss: The intriguing story of a 21st century pilgrim who walked The Way of Saint James*. Self-published, printed by Clark & Mackay Rocklea Queensland, Australia, 2012.

Movies

The Walk. Directed by Emilio Estevez, FilmBuff, 2010.

Web Sites

Ancient Origins" Reconstructing the Story of Humanity's Past, https://www.ancient-origins.net

Architecture Courses, https://www.architecturecourses.org

Authentic Basque Country, https://www.authenticbasquecountry.com

Britannica, https://www.britannica.com

Catedral de Santiago, https://oficinadelpergrino.com

Catholic Herald, https://catholicherald.co.uk

Catholic Online, https://www.catholic.org

Centers for Disease Control and Prevention, https//www.cde.gov

Creative Travel, https://creativetravelcanada.com

El Camino con Correos, https://www.elcaminoconcorreos.com

El Camino of the Way, http://elcaminotheway.com/en

El Pais, https://english.elpais.com

Follow the Camino, http://www.followthecamino.com

Fundación Jacobea, https://www.fundacionjacobea.org

Galicia Guide: Your Guide to Everything Galicia,
    http://www.galiciaguide.com/

Hillwalk Tours: Self-Guided Hiking Tours,
    http://www.hillwalktours.com

Historia Medieval del Reyno de Navarra, www.lebrelblanco.com

King James Bible Online, https://www.kingjamesbibleonline.org

Knights Templar History, https://www.lordsandladies.org/knights-
    templar.htm

Oficina del Peregrino, Catedral de Santiago de Compostela,
    https://oficinadelperegrino.com/en/

Salt + Light Media, https://simedia.org

Sendtur, https://sendtur.com

St. James Cathedral Seatle, https://stjames-cathedral.org

Statista, https://www.statista.com

Stephen Morris, author, www.stephenmorrisauthor.com

The Bill Beaver Project, http://thebillbeaverproject.com

The Village News, https://www.thevintagenews.com

U.S. Energy Information Administration, https://www.eia.gov

Visit Leon, www.

Visit Navarra, https://www.visitnavarra.es/en

World History Encyclopedia, https://www.worldhistory.com

About the Author

Retired from the hospitality industry.

I've longed believed that I struck out on my own when I was eight years old to Walk My Own Camino. That was the year my mom died. That was the year I learned about self-reliance to move forward. There was my father and four brothers, one a twin, but still, the world changed for me. Then, when I was fifteen my dad died. I moved on to the next phase of my life, living with my older brother Ron and his new wife Lorraine. I went away to college. I dropped out and moved to Florida when I was twenty. Worked for Walt Disney World for three years. Then tried several other options - delivering potato chips, selling life insurance, commercial sheet metal ductwork. Finally ended up as a hotel convention service manager and moved into hotel group sales positions. Eventually, I retired.

That was the journey of my life, my personal Camino. The path I walked, like walking the Camino de Santiago, had many ups and downs, joys and sorrows, elation and depression. That is the path of living. We all experience these emotions or issues of life to different degrees. But, we move on. One foot in front of the other.

i "Camino de Santiago Routes," Follow the Camino, March 22, 2022, https://followthecamino.com/en/camino-de-santiago-routes/

ii " The Jacobean Route. (Part 1) The Primitive Way," iberinbound.com, Iberinbound | Incoming travel Agency, November 15, 2019, https://www.iberinbound.com/destination/the-jacobean-route-part-i-the-primitive-way/

iii "The Codex of Calixtinus - Way of Saint James in Galicia", Xunta de Galicia, Accessed August 2, 2020, https://www.caminodesantiago.gal/en/discover/origins-and-evolution/the-codex-of-calixtinus.

iv https://www.catholic.org/saints/saint.php?saint_id=59

v "The Symbolism of the Scallop Shell on the Camino," Hillwalk Tours Self-Guided Tours, Hillwalk Tours, https://www.hillwalktours.com/walking-hiking-blog/camino-scallop-shell-symbolism/

vi "St. James the Greater," St. James Cathedral, Seatle, https://www.stjames-cathedral.org/Prayer/jameslegend.aspx

vii Stephen Morris, "Saint. James the Moor-slayer - Stephen Morris, author," Stephen Morris, Author, Posted July 17, 2018, http://www.stephenmorrisauthor.com/Saint-james-moor-slayer/

viii " Knights Templar," lordsandladies.org, modified March 6, 2019, https://www.lordsandladies.org/knights-templar.htm

ix "The Powerful Curse of Jacques de Molay, the Last Grand Master of Templars," Ancient Origins: Reconstructing the Story of Humanity's Past, https://www.ancient-origins.net/history-famous-people/curse-jacques-de-molay-templars-005431

x " Knights Hospitaller," lordsandladies.org, modified Marc 6, 2019, https://www.lordsandladies.org/knights-hospitaller.htm

xi " Associations of Friends of the Way - Way of Saint James in Galicia: official web," accessed September 20, 2020, https://www.caminodesantiago.gal/en/discover/associations-of-the-way/associatons-of-friends-of-the-way

xii "Medieval Architecture History," ArchitectureCourses.org, https://www.architecturecourses.org/medieval-architecture-history

xiii " Vaccine Effectiveness: How Well Do the Flu Vaccines Work?" Centers for Disease Control and Prevention, updated January 3, 2020, https://www.cdc.gov/flu/vaccines-work/vaccineeffect.htm

xiv "What is the Compostela and how do I get one?" El Camino con Correos, https://www.elcaminoconcorreos.com/en/blog/what-is-the-compostela-and-how-do-i-get-one

xv "Pilgrims on the Camino de Santiago 2021," Statista, https://www.statista.com/statistics/772722/annual-number-of-pilgrims-who-walked-the-way-of-Saint-james-to-santiago-de-compostela-spain/

xvi "The Compostela accreditation of the Pilgrimage to Santiago," Catedral de Santiago de Compostela, https://oficinadelperegrino.com/en/pilgrimage/the-compostela/

xvii "The Citadel of St. Jean Pied-de-Port," The Bill Beaver Project, March 1, 2018, http://thebillbeaverproject.com/2012/03/02/citadel-Saint-jean-pied-de-port/

xviii "Peregrinos del Camino de Santiago," El Camino of the Way, http://elcaminotheway.com/en/the-way-news/other-componentsremaining-component-views/jacobean-tradition/61-the-camino-villages/237-camino-santiago-towns-villages-collegiate-church-maria-roncesvalles xix "The French Way: Roncesvalles and its Collegiate of Santa Maria," Foundation Jacobea, March 7, 2019, https://www.fundacionjacobea.org/en/ways-of-santiago/the-french-way-roncesvalles/

xx "Day 2: Roncesvvalles to Zubiri," Creative Travel, March 7, 2014, https://creativetravelcanada.com/camino-de-santiago/ways/the-1st-stage/day-2-roncesvalles-to-zubiri/

xxi The Abbey, https://www.facebook.com/theabbey.es/about/

xxii Carlos Ferreira, "San Fermin: The saint behind the running of the bulls," Salt + Light Media, July 10, 2012, https://slmedia.org/blog/san-fermin-the-saint-behind-the-running-of-the-bulls-2

xxiii "Plaza del Castillo: You Need to Get There," Authentic Basque Country, June 11, 2021, https://www.authenticbasquecountry.com/l/plaza-del-castillo/

xxiv "Wind farms: Green energy: When Spain had the wind in its sails," El Pais, June 2, 2017, https://english.elpais.com/elpais/2017/06/02/inenglish/1496410806_286113.html

xxv "Electricity in the U.S.," U.S. Energy Information Administration, https://www.eia.gov/energyexplained/electricity/electricity-in-the-us.php#:~:text=Wind%20energy%20was%20the%20source%20of%20about%208.4%25,1.4%25%20of%20total%20U.S.%20electricity%20generation%20in%202020

xxvi Larissa Harris, "Entire Abandoned Spanish Villages Are Being Sold Cheap to Rains Money," The Vintage News, September 28, 2019, https://www.thevintagenews.com/2019/04/25/spanish-villages/?firefox=1

xxvii The Lore of the Camino

xxviii "Organize your trip to Navarra," Visit Navarra - Official Website of the Navarre tourist Board, August 10, 2020, https://www.turismo.navarra.es/eng/organice-viaje/recurso/Localidad/2116/Estella.htm

xxix Carlos Sánchez-Marco, "Historia Medieval del Reyno de Navarra," Decembrer 25, 2012, http://www.lebrelblanco.com/anexos/a0280.htm#santosepulcrooo

xxx "Church of the Holy Sepulcher (Torres del Rio)," https://second.wiki/wiki/iglesia_del_santo_sepulcro_torres_del_rc3ado

xxxi "Toro de Osborne," Osborne, https://www.osborne.es/en/toro-de-osborne-across-the-world

xxxii "St. John of Acre Hospital," September 9, 2020, https://second.wiki/wiki/hospital_de_san_juan_de_acre

xxxiii "Legends of the Camino: The Battle of Roldán and the Giant Ferragut," Albergue Milpés, April 1, 2020, https://www.alberguemilpes.com/en/la-batalla-de-roldan-y-el-gigante-ferragut-historias-del-camino-de-santiago/

xxxiv "Azofra, La Rioja French Way," Sendtur.com Way of Saint James, https://www.senditur.com/en/population/azofra/

xxxv "Saint Bridget of Sweden Biography, Legacy, & Facts," Britannic, https://www.britannica.com/biography/Saint-Bridget-of-Sweden

xxxvi John Hogan, "St. Anthony's Fire," World History Encyclopedia, https://www.worldhistory.org/St_Anthony%27s_Fire/

xxxvii "San Nicolas de Puente Fitero," Fundación Jacobia, April 27, 2021, https://www.fundacionjacobea.org/en/ways-of-santiago/san-nicolas-de-puente-fitero/

xxxviii "Ultra - What Does This Camino Word Mean?" Caminoways.com, November 11, 2013, https://caminoways.com/what-does-ultreia-mean

xxxix" Terradillos de los Templarios | Camino de Santiago | Pilgrim," Pilgrim, 2019, accessed September 4, 2020, https://www.pilgrim.es/camino-frances/etapa-17-carrion-de-los-condesterradillo-de-los-templarios/terradillos-de-los-templarios/

xl "Guzmán el Bueno Square," Visit Leon, https://www-visitaleon-com.translate.goog/plaza-guzman-bueno?_x_tr_sl=es&_x_tr_tl=en&_x_tr_hl=en&_x_tr_pto=wapp

xli "Convento de San Marcos, León, Spain," Spotting History, https://www.spottinghistory.com/view/8187/convento-de-san-marcos/

xlii "Church of San Pedro de Rectivia," Astorga Guide, https://astorga-co.translate.goog/es/turismo/monumentos/iglesia-de-san-pedro-de-rectivia/?_x_tr_sl=es&_x_tr_tl=en&_x_tr_hl=en&_x_tr_pto=sc

xliii "Santa Catalina de Somoza, Leon French Way," Sendtur, https://www.senditur.com/en/population/santa-catalina-de-somoza/

xliv "The Cruz de Ferro," Fundación Jacobea, February 8, 2021, https://www.fundacionjacobea.org/en/ways-of-santiago/202/

xlv" Cruz de Ferro: A Spiritual Experience on the Camino Frances," Camino Adventures, accessed August 1, 2020, https://www.caminoadventures.com/blog/cruz-de-ferro/

xlvi "Castillo de San Bias Ponferrada: historia, estilo y cómo legar," Diario de León, August 10, 2021, https://www-diariodeleon-es.translate.goog/articulo/mas-bierzo/castillo-san-blas-ponferrada-historia-como-llegar/202108101038412137039.html?_x_tr_sl=es&_x_tr_tl=en&_x_tr_hl=en&_x_tr_pto=sc

xlvii Curtis Williams, "O Cebreiro: The greatest Eucharistic miracle you've never heard of," Catholic Herald, June 24, 2021, https://catholicherald.co.uk/o-cebreiro-the-greatest-eucharistic-miracle-youve-never-heard-of/

xlviii "The Powerful Woman Known as Maria Solina - The Most Famous Witch of Galicia," Ancient Origins, January 8, 2017, https://www.ancient-origins.net/history-famous-people/powerful-woman-known-maria-solina-most-famous-witch-galicia-007333